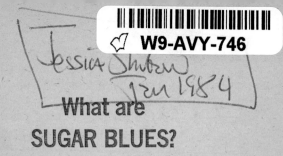

What are
SUGAR BLUES?

Multiple physical and mental miseries caused by the consumption of sugar.

What specific health problems does sugar cause?
Diabetes, obesity, coronary thrombosis, tooth and gum decay, varicose veins and stomach trouble and, indirectly, mental disturbances.

Read William Dufty's **SUGAR BLUES** and learn how you can eliminate the poison of sugar from your life and discover a thinner, healthier you. **SUGAR BLUES** is a memoir, a cookbook and a primer on how to kick the sugar habit.

"Everything you always wanted to know about sugar and weren't able to find out is in **SUGAR BLUES** . . . Incredibly thorough . . . one of the most revealing, instructive and helpful books ever written . . . Dufty rips the facade off the sugar pushers who are going to make their fast bucks over our dead bodies—if we let them. Sounding a warning against establishment cookbooks, Dufty completes his **SUGAR BLUES** with a detailed presentation of a fantastic range of food menus he has created . . . over the years since liberation from the White Plague."

John Shelley in *Let's Live Magazine*

About the Author

After his deliverance from decades of heavy $C_{12}H_{22}O_{11}$ addiction, William Dufty introduced the work of the renowned Japanese Sensei (Guide) with his translation of YOU ARE ALL SANPAKU in 1965. Chief intercontinental cook for Gloria Swanson, a prize-winning New York newspaperman, and a contributing editor to the East-West Journal, Dufty's credits include the international best seller LADY SINGS THE BLUES.

SUGAR
BLUES

William Dufty

WARNER BOOKS

A Warner Communications Company

This Warner Books Edition is published by
arrangement with Chilton Book Company

Warner Books, Inc.,
666 Fifth Avenue,
New York, N.Y. 10103

Ⓦ A Warner Communications Company

Printed in the United States of America

First Warner Books Printing: September, 1976

40   39   38   37   36

For Billie Holiday
Whose death changed my life
and
Gloria Swanson
Whose life changed my death

Sugar Refined sucrose, $C_{12}H_{22}O_{11}$, produced by multiple chemical processing of the juice of the sugar cane or beet and removal of all fiber and protein, which amount to 90 percent of the natural plant.

Blues A state of depression or melancholy overlaid with fear, physical discomfort, and anxiety (often expressed lyrically as an autobiographical chronicle of personal disaster).

Sugar Blues Multiple physical and mental miseries caused by human consumption of refined sucrose—commonly called sugar.

Contents

It Is Necessary
to be Personal

Once upon a time, when I was a hopeless square about sucrose $(C_{12}H_{22}O_{11})$, I triggered an unforgettable encounter between Gloria Swanson and a sugar cube.

I had been summoned to a lunchtime press conference in the Fifth Avenue office of a New York attorney. Things were well along when I tiptoed in. Miss Swanson, more alert and thoughtful than anyone in the room, removed her purse from the chair at her side and made room for me. I had never seen her offscreen before. I was not expecting to see her there. I was not ready for her at all.

A caterer's coolie arrived with the picnic—pastrami on rye, salami on pumpernickel, cardboard jugs of coffee, a tray of monogrammed sugar cubes. My colleagues from several New York daily newspapers kept on wrangling as the rations were scattered around. I unwrapped my sandwich, sprung the lid off of my coffee jug, picked up a sugar cube. I was unpeeling it when I heard her commanding whisper:

"That stuff is poison," she hissed. "I won't have it in my house, let alone my body."

I drew back from the precipice and looked at her. Those immense blue eyes widened, her signature tombstone teeth gleamed in that bite beyond the smile. She was Carrie Nation confronting demon rum, William Jennings Bryan beholding the Cross of Gold, Moses with a pork chop on his plate. Like a child caught with one mitt in the cookie jar, I dropped the sugar cube. I noticed the space in front of Miss Swanson was bare of clutter. She wasn't having any of our picnic. She had brought her own—a piece of tree-ripened, unsprayed something. She offered me some. I had never tasted anything better in my life. I told her so.

Of course, we had all heard the legends about Swanson's exotic health regimen. Poems have been written about her age-defying presence. Seeing her close up, eyeball to eyeball, it was impossible to doubt that she must be doing something right.

"I used to get positively livid when I watched people eating poison," she whispered. "But I've learned that everyone has to find out for themselves—the hard way. They can eat ground glass in front of me now and I don't even twitch. Go ahead," she said, daring me to mix sugar in my coffee. "Eat your white sugar—kill yourself. See if I care."

Again she flashed the bite beyond the smile. It haunted me for days. Whenever I reached for those sugar tongs, I would draw back and think of her injunction. You never know you're hooked until you decide with your noodle that you're not going to do something anymore; then you discover your head is not running things. I discovered I had a sugar habit and a big one. I wanted to kick it but I didn't know how. I'd had it for years.

I must have been hooked very early, because my earliest memory of mealtime at home with the family was a kind of purgatory of meat and potatoes which I suffered through in order to get to heaven: A sweet dessert.

Grandma always kept a hundred-pound bag of good Michigan beet sugar in the pantry off her kitchen with a generous tin scoop on top. When I picked dandelions for her during Prohibition, she washed them and put them in a huge crock to soak, sprinkled sugar and lemon over them—for speedy fermenting—and thus produced bootleg wine. I remember her scattering sugar on the tops of cherry and apple pies, in cookies and fried cakes, and in huge, boiling vats of peaches and plums at canning time in the autumn. Sugar went into tomato relish and all kinds of pickles, sweet and sour. When we came home from school, Mrs. Moulton, our neighbor and full-time cook, would give us fresh-baked bread spread with butter and heaps of brown sugar on top.

It is possible to remember, but hard to believe what it was like to live in a small Midwestern town of fifty years ago that has gone forever. The family controlled what children put into their stomachs, completely and utterly. We had very little to say about it. Our parents were our protectors. Everyone knew what they would permit and what they would not permit. It was no more possible to sneak a hamburger or a Coca-Cola than it was to rob a bank or miss church on Sunday.

The town only had one restaurant. It had once been a saloon. If I walked into a local emporium with a nickel to buy something edible, the owner would have called my father at his office and I would hear about it when he came home. The three grocery stores each had candy counters, and the drugstore on the corner had a soda fountain. Ice cream was something you had on Sunday and you made it yourself. On state occasions, it might be ordered from the drugstore and delivered on the run by a local track star. Dry ice and freezers were something out of the year 2001.

Breakfast, dinner, and supper were eaten at home—with Mrs. Moulton as warden—or not at all. There was no way to open the icebox without her watchful presence. Then we became the first family in town to have a Frigidaire. Homemade ice cubes were an invention more wondrous and mysterious than the radio. The cellar began to fall into disuse. Canning began to give way to store-bought things.

Soda pop, Coca-Cola, and the like of soft drinks

simply did not exist for us. Canada Dry ginger ale was around, but that was part of Daddy's Prohibition stash, something for grownups to drink sometimes with their Canadian hooch. It was years later, when I was eight, that a visitor from the outside world introduced the decadent idea of floating ice cream in a glass of the stuff. We might have known about such things earlier had we been permitted to view those corrupting movies—but they were beyond the pale, across the other side of the railroad tracks. Cotton candy and other confections sold at fairs and bazaars were as *verboten* as films. "It will make you sick," we were told. When we noticed other youngsters eating it without going into convulsions, we would call this to our parents' attention, but such pseudo-scientific evidence never cut any ice.

My first sins occurred during our first summer at Crystal Lake. Compared to the town where we lived, Crystal Lake was Babylon or Las Vegas. It had a casino over the water where strangers danced in the dark to a band that claimed (on the side of their bus and the front of the drums) to be from Hollywood. There was a golf course, tennis courts and speed boats, Indians selling handwoven baskets to weekend tourists, girls who smoked cigarettes, boys who went in swimming at night without any tops, and roadside gas pumps with shanties where bottles of technicolored sugarwater were always on ice: orange, cherry, strawberry, lemon, and something called Green River. I never lost any sleep over those familiar flavors. The deep purple grape started me on the road to perdition. I had never tasted anything like it at home. The grape pop trip got to be something I couldn't control. I began to feel a secret kinship with the town drunk.

I remember the first time I rifled my mother's purse while she was napping. I only took a nickel. One nickel at a time. If she didn't have a nickel in change, I didn't dare take a dime. Two bottles might amount to an overdose for all I knew. My gums might turn a telltale purple or my teeth might start to dissolve. Somehow, I knew how much temptation I could handle; I was careful not to blow the whole thing.

We spent our summers at Crystal Lake until I was

twelve or thirteen. By that time I was making $75 a week in the wintertime season—an undreamed of fortune in those days—as a prodigal jazz pianist on the radio. But I couldn't write out a check at a roadside stand. When my summer grape pop habit got out of control, I had to lie, cheat, and steal to support it.

The day my voice began to change was the beginning of the end of my radio career. If my voice didn't sound childlike anymore, there was nothing remarkable about the way I played piano. Puberty brought other terrors. My face, neck, and back exploded with unsightly pimples. At first I thought it was leprosy and I made a few novenas. I had never noticed anything like this on older boys before. Perhaps I could overlook their flaws, but not my own. I was ashamed to wear the topless swimming trunks that were coming into fashion. The family nurse suggested Noxzema. The family laundress was thrilled when that didn't work.

I know now I was suffering for my sins. If anybody had had the perception to point it out to me at the time, they might have saved me years of agony. But who knew about my secret sugar habit? Who ought to have guessed? Where was the family doctor?

Well, our town had one, but he wasn't Dr. Marcus Welby. He lived across the street from us, and one of the terrors the whole town lived with was the thought of possible emergency when no one was on hand except Dr. Hudson. For Dr. Hudson was a dope fiend. Those words were spoken of others, never of him. The people of the town merely said "Poor Mrs. Hudson." The good doctor sometimes walked about town like a zombie. He had a detached bungalow office behind the house. After dark, the kids used to sneak up to his windows and peep in to see him lying on his black leather chair with the stirrups—completely out of it.

When there was an accident in town, volunteer firemen would break down the door of the doctor's office, douse him with water, and stand over him while he put a tourniquet on a farmer's arm that had been caught in a thresher. Then they would rush the victim to the nearest town. If you could afford it, as we could, you summoned the doctor from the next town by telephone.

So none of us ever saw a doctor until we were good and sick. The appalling significance of things that never happened. I was sent to the dentist twice a year—when that came into fashion. The dentist related cavities to overdoses of sweets. But I never heard a doctor open his mouth about it.

The old-timers like Grandma spoke about eating excesses: It will make you sick, that meant ill to your stomach—in danger of vomiting and such. How could I relate my skin problems to my secret vices. I began noticing that lots of boys my age had similar skin disorders—but not all. Then I heard rumors out behind the barn that my affliction could be caused by excessive masturbation.

I had a friend whose brother was in a Catholic seminary in Chicago, studying to be a priest. He was the big authority on canon law and sex. He spread the word that in the archdiocese of Chicago, masturbating was only a venial sin. If you did it in Michigan, it was mortal. In Illinois, you could have a one-man show at night, wash your pants under the pump in the morning, and trot off to communion.

I took to drowning my sorrows in malted milks, which I discovered in high school. We had moved to a large city by then, and I had to travel several miles downtown to a central high school. I was allowed ten cents a day for streetcar fare—a nickel each way. Lunch out of a box? I refused to carry anything as unchic as homemade sandwiches and fruit. The 1929 crash was behind us, things were tough all over. A cut-rate drugstore downtown was pushing a special king-sized chocolate malted—all you could possibly drink for a dime. For two years, I walked every morning and night in all kinds of weather—just so I could blow that dime and guzzle five malteds every week. My skin problems went from bad to worse. I remember being mortified when I had to take a shower at the school gym. Then I heard rumors that acne could be caused by sexual repression. Free souls, I was told, didn't have that kind of problem. I was more than willing to take the plunge—more out of hope of relief from pimples than pent-up passion. Getting a girl into trouble, contracting VD, these were terrors I would gladly embrace if I could walk shamelessly into juvenile court with that skin you love to touch.

In our high school set nobody smoked. Cigarettes were far too expensive at ten cents a pack and were considered vaguely unmasculine. Many boys lived with a vision of the Ford roadster they would inherit at graduation if they abstained from tobacco. Meanwhile, we smoked untaxed, homegrown things like dried corn silk, dead grape vine—even something the Mexicans called marijuana. All of them made me sick. I could get a better high off a banana split. We never dreamed that Mexican stuff would be merchandised a few decades later like bootleg beer.

In the twenties, I had been so rich I never carried a cent on me. In the thirties—mooching my way through college holding a job or two on the side—I was so poor I put every cent on my back where it would show. I remember starving with great elegance—going without lunch in a chalk-striped British flannel suit with a stiff Duke-of-Kent collar and contrasting shirt. College was a complete and utter drag—a boring kind of mandatory sentence you had been told you had to serve. I took to collegiate journalism as a kind of lark. There I discovered that the cigarette companies virtually subsidized the university paper with their advertising. Some of the best looking girls on campus worked for the tobacco companies as cigarette pushers—giving away free cigarettes and offering free instruction in inhaling the way Constance Bennett and Bette Davis did in the films. I smoked the free ones but I never developed the habit of buying them. I would always reach for a sweet in preference to a Lucky Strike.

One of the boring things we were required to suffer through was a course called physical education. One was required to swim or trot or play volleyball or lift weights for a certain number of hours each week. They watched you do it, your card was punched, and that was that. Once a year you had a quick cursory physical exam. If you asked the young doctor a question about something that was bothering you, he was careful not to tread on the terrain of the local medical society. "See your family doctor about that," he would say. His job was to spot latent hernias and athletes' foot.

On summer vacation, I hitchhiked thousands of miles and lived on Pepsi-Cola in those large, economy-sized nickel bottles. It was not until I visited the South for the first time that a girl turned me onto something called "dope." They served it at soda fountains with lots of crushed ice, vanilla flavoring, syrup, and soda. Up North it was called Coca-Cola. Down there, common usage preserved overtones of its native origins as a headache remedy.

After suffering through two years of college, I finally dropped out. It took daring in those days to dream of facing life without a degree. But I could sniff another war in the offing. I felt my real choice was going to be between Leavenworth Penitentiary and Flanders' fields.

In the summer of 1965, I met a wise man from the East, a Japanese philosopher who had just returned from several weeks in Saigon. "If you really expect to conquer the North Vietnamese," he told me, "you must drop Army PXs on them—sugar, candy, and Coca-Cola. That will destroy them faster than bombs."

I knew what he was talking about. When I was drafted in 1942, something like that happened to me. Army food was decreed from on high somewhere. We were, as every mother was assured, the best fed troops in all human history. But army chow set my teeth on edge from the very start. I wanted no part of it. So morning, noon, and night I haunted the Post Exchange. It was a two-year orgy of malted milks, sugared coffee, pastry, candy, chocolate, and Coca-Cola. After many months of that, I developed a fancy case of bleeding hemorrhoids which scared me to death. I always associated this gruesome malady with advanced age, and here I was in my twenties. Nothing mattered too much anyway, I was headed for Flanders' fields where all was lost.

My first real adult experience with the American medical establishment was with its caricature—U.S. army medicine. In due course, my body was shipped overseas. Bound for Britain, I trotted around the top deck of the blacked out S.S. Mauretania with a carbine on my shoulder and a heavy army greatcoat soaked with Atlantic spray. Two hours on, two off. By the time we docked at Liverpool, I had a lovely case of walking pneumonia. The medic looked at my thermometer and sent me packing back to KP duty. This went on for six days. Finally, on the seventh day, the thermometer hit the lucky number. Bells rang, faces softened into sympathy, they rushed me onto a stretcher and the ambulance careened to the nearest British hospital! Intensive care, an oxygen tent, and huge doses of the wonder drug of the time—sulfanilamide. It was then so new a drug that blood samples were taken every hour on the hour to make sure they weren't killing me. I lapsed into a lovely coma and stayed there for days. Wonderful, sweet-smelling nurses changed the bed regularly, poked me for blood, bathed me lovingly all over. Charming, upper-class British ladies comforted me with lilacs. The chaplain lurked in the outer hall. It began to look as though I'd never make it to Flanders' fields. It didn't seem worth the effort. D-day was just around the corner.

Then I awoke one morning, sweating, conscious. I saw some calf's-foot jelly on my table and I sensed an erection. The army had outwitted me! I'd been foiled, doomed to survive for a while longer at the convenience of the government.

When I toddled down the hall the first time to be weighed, the nurses gasped when they saw the scale. Army regulations said you could not be discharged from the hospital until you weighed as much as when you came in; if you stayed in the hospital more than twenty-eight days, you returned not to your outfit but to a Repple Depple—a replacement depot where bodies were warehoused, waiting for orders in your size, weight, and classification. My outfit was hardly Shangri-la, but the Repple Depple was a fate worse than death. Could I put on twelve pounds in six days? Each day, British newsboys came through the hospital peddling bad news. I bought three papers every day, always paying with a pound note. The heavy coins I received in change were fastened to my midriff and groin with hospital tape. Every day when they weighed me in, I had gained a couple of pounds by magic. On D-day, I climbed the scale triumphantly. My weight was back to the level it had been when I entered the hospital. Within hours I was with my outfit, headed for Flanders' fields. My buddies nursed me and protected me and brought me back to life by carting me goodies from the PX—I was too weak to get there myself.

Eventually, I was packed off by train to Glasgow, by ship to Algiers, then by truck to Oran in the Mediterranean. Three weeks in the desert and I was as good as new. There was no PX for miles. My only diversions were the ocean and Algerian beer. After the landings in southern France, I was packed off to join the First French Army: Arabs, Senegalese, Goums, Sikhs, Vietnamese, with French officers and noncoms. We lived off the land, no fancy rations and luxuries. Some brought along pots and pans, ducks and geese, sheep and goats, wives and mistresses. For months I went unpaid, I had to forage for clothes and shoes, and I never saw the inside of a PX again. Most of the natives we ate with hadn't tasted sugar in years. It was all on the black market. We lived on horsemeat, rabbit, squirrel, dark French peasant bread, and whatever else could be scrounged. Winter in the Vosges mountains was brutal and endless, yet I never had a cold or a sniffle. I was never sick for a day in the eighteen months I spent in France and Germany with them.

Was I bright enough to understand this controlled experiment in nutrition I'd been unwittingly involved in? I might have saved myself years of waste, but I was a total idiot, without half the brain or instinct for survival possessed by the lice in my helmet.

On my return to the States, I went on a glorious bender: Pie à la mode, cake with whipped cream, malted milks by the dozen, chocolate, and Pepsi. Sugar . . . sugar . . . sugar.

Within weeks I was flat on my back with one strange malady after another. My hemorrhoids blossomed. Every day my fever rose and fell. Batteries of tests produced names of diseases: Infectious mononucleosis, atypical malaria, hepatitis, shingles, exotic skin conditions, ear infections, eye diseases. When I ran out of money, I discovered the wonders of socialized medicine at the Veterans Administration. I became a charter member of Blue Cross and Blue Shield. I enrolled in one of the first prepaid group medical plans. For over fifteen years, I subjected myself to an endless whirligig of doctors, hospitals, diagnosis, treatment, tests and more tests, drugs and more drugs. During all that rigamarole, I cannot recall a single doctor (out of the dozens who treated me) who ever displayed the slightest curiosity about what I ate and drank.

Inevitably, the day arrived when the drugs were no longer effective. Migraine headaches would not go away. For ten days I couldn't work, sleep, eat, or move. I checked into the VA Hospital in Manhattan as an emergency case. I simply could not endure the pain any longer. They gave me the works: batteries of tests and a physical as complete as I'd ever had. After all the machines had spoken, the young doctor translated it all for me. No cancer, no brain tumor, no this, no that. In fact, he smiled happily, I was a perfect specimen, normal in every respect for my age.

Incredulous, I stammered: But what do I do about the headaches. If they don't go away in a week or two, he suggested, come back anytime.

A *week* or two? I was ready for the worst and this was it. I couldn't endure another hour. I telephoned a friend whose father had been a famous physician. He had connections with a fancy society physician on Park Avenue. They took out a huge forbidding syringe and sprayed something very cool up my nostrils. After a nap I had my first relief in days. I knew enough about drugs to know it had been cocaine. Well, I thought, this is how junkies begin.

Then my friend put me on a diet. This seemed bizarre but I decided to humor him. I didn't know anywhere else to get cocaine. He took me off cigarettes and coffee, suggested oatmeal in the morning, rice for lunch, and more rice and chicken for dinner. His diagnosis: Postural hypotension—slowing down of circulation. He also prescribed hot baths morning and night and calisthenics at midday. I tried giving up coffee and cigarettes, but it made it almost impossible for me to work. My day began with coffee—huge jugs of it with sugar and cream. I might have four or five before noon. After that destroyed my appetite for lunch, I would taper off on Pepsi-Cola. By dinner time, I was in such a sugar stupor it took Chinese duck or lobster à diablo to rouse my appetite. I tried his diet and got temporary relief. Then I would binge until the headaches returned. Then I would try again. I was learning, but I didn't realize it at the time.

One night, in one sitting, I read a little book that said very simply that if you're sick, it's your own damn fault. Pain is the final warning. You know better than anyone else how you've been abusing your body, so stop it. Sugar is poison, it said, more lethal than opium and more dangerous than atomic fallout. Shades of Gloria Swanson and the sugar cube. Hadn't she told me everyone has to find out for themselves—the hard way? I had nothing to lose but my pains. I began next morning with firm resolve. I threw all the sugar out of my kitchen. Then I threw out everything that had sugar in it, cereals and canned fruit, soups and bread. Since I had never really read any labels carefully, I was shocked to find the shelves were soon empty; so was the refrigerator. I began eating nothing but whole grains and vegetables.

In about forty-eight hours, I was in total agony, overcome with nausea, with a crashing migraine. If pain was a message, this was a long one, very involved, intense but in code. It took hours to break the code. I knew enough about junkies to recognize reluctantly my kinship with them. I was kicking cold turkey, the thing they talked about with such terror. After all, heroin is nothing but a chemical. They take the juice of the poppy and they refine it into opium and then they refine it to morphine and finally to heroin. Sugar is nothing but a chemical. They take the juice of the cane or the beet and they refine it to molasses and then they refine it to brown sugar and finally to strange white crystals. It's no wonder

dope pushers dilute pure heroin with milk sugar—
lactose—in order to make their glassine packages a treat
to the eye. I was kicking all kinds of chemicals cold
turkey—sugar, aspirin, cocaine, caffeine, chlorine, fluo-
rine, sodium, monosodium glutamate, and all those other
multisyllabic horrors listed in fine print on the tins and
boxes I had just thrown into the trash.

I had it very rough for about twenty-four hours, but
the morning after was a revelation. I went to sleep with
exhaustion, sweating and tremors. I woke up feeling
reborn. Grains and vegetables tasted like a gift from the
gods.

The next few days brought a succession of wonders.
My rear stopped bleeding, so did my gums. My skin
began to clear up and had a totally different texture
when I washed. I discovered bones in my hands and feet
that had been buried under bloat. I bounced out of bed
at strange hours in the early morning, raring to go. My
head seemed to be working again. I had no problems anymore. My shirts were too big. So were my shoes. One
morning while shaving I discovered I had a jaw.

To make a long, happy story short, I dropped from
205 pounds to a neat 135 in five months and ended up
with a new body, a new head, a new life.

One day I burned my Blue Cross card. About that
time, I noticed a picture of Gloria Swanson in *The New
York Times.* I sat right down and wrote her a letter.
You were right, I said. Wow, were you ever right. I didn't
get your message then but I've got it now.

That was in the 1960s. Since then I have been sugarfree. I haven't been near a doctor, a hospital, a pill, or
a shot in all that time. I haven't even touched so much as
an aspirin.

Today, when I see someone unpeeling a sugar cube,
I twitch just as I remember Gloria Swanson twitching
at that lunchtime press conference. I yearn to collar them
in some quiet corner and tell them how easy it is to lose
the sugar blues.

Consider yourself collared. What have you got to lose?

SUGAR BLUES.
Ev'rybody's singing the Sugar Blues. . . .
I'm so unhappy, I feel so bad
I could lay me down and die.
You can say what you choose
but I'm all confused.
I've got the sweet, sweet Sugar Blues
More Sugar!!
I've got the sweet, sweet Sugar Blues.

The song "Sugar Blues" was published in 1923, the year the United States rocked with the Teapot Dome scandal and millions of sugar diabetics began shooting up with a newly discovered miracle drug, insulin.

1923 was also the heyday of Prohibition. When booze became illegal here, sugar consumption zoomed. The whole country acted like a gathering of arrested alcoholics spending the evening at AA; they couldn't keep their mitts out of the candy jar. Teetotalers were often the biggest sugar fiends, vowing alcohol would never touch their lips while pouring in the sugar which produces alcohol in tummies instead of bathtubs.

Like other nemeses in the black blues experience—gin, cocaine, morphine, and heroin—sugar happened to be white. The lyric of "Sugar Blues" shrewdly conveys the antagonistic polarity of human experience with sweet and perilous white stuff: attraction, repulsion, the Gimme-Stop-Me, Get-Away-Closer, Pull-It-Out-Deeper feeling at the root of the blues. Natural body wisdom tells you it's no good, and yet you want it baaaaaad.

Sugar Blues began as a song celebrating a completely personal human condition. It deserves, fifty years later, to become the universal name for an addictive planetary plague.

Poets—especially the ones who write the nation's songs—are often years ahead of physicians and politicians at coming up with the proper name for global malaise.

I haven't managed to discover or reveal in the succeeding pages everything I always wanted to know about sugar and was afraid to find out. However, I've learned

enough to conclude that what passes for medical history
needs to be bulldozed and overhauled.

In the eternal order of the universe, man-refined sugar,
like all other things, plays its part. Perhaps the sugar
pushers are our predators, leading us into temptation,
peddling a kind of sweet, sweet, human pesticide which
lures greedy seekers after La Dolce Vita into self-destruc-
tion, weeding the human garden, naturally selecting the
fittest for survival while the rest go down in another
biblical flood—not water this time, but Coke, Pepsi, and
Dr. Pepper—purifying the human race for a new age.

"In general, the practicing scientist hardly concerns
himself with history," says Dr. Francois Jacob, Nobel
prize winner and author of *The Logic of Life: A History
of Heredity? (The New York Times*, April 11, 1974.)
"I was not happy about the way they tell the history of
biology. In each paper, a scientist writes what his predecessors learned, and so forth, and winds up with a linear
history, from error to truth. It's not like that."

It sure ain't.

The Mark Of Cane

Nostalgia is as old as Adam. Whenever earning our bread by the sweat of our brow gets to be too much, we are inclined—like Adam—to long for the good old days. The notion of a heavenly pastoral past crops up in mythology the world around. Like all universal myths, it lurks as something deep in the memory of the human race: Paradise Lost of the Book of Genesis, the Golden Age of Taoism, and Buddhism. Perhaps the Garden of Eden was more than a piece of Middle East real estate; perhaps it once encompassed much of this planet, from the Polynesian Islands to Shangri-la in Tibet.

It is impossible not to dream about what it must have been like. The Bible provides some clues. First of all, no sweat. Man lived naturally off the bounty of nature. Second, no cities. The word civilization means nothing more or less than the art of city living. In the good old days there was none of that. Third, no sickness. Biblical man had a lifespan incredible by modern standards. Ancient Oriental anatomical charts not only record the acupuncture meridians but also what are called beauty marks in the West—the dark spots that appear on the body at birth or later. A mark at four o'clock beneath the right eye of the male or at eight o'clock beneath the left eye of the female indicated the catastrophic probability of "death by sickness." When these charts were compiled, thousands of years ago, "natural death"— just going to sleep without waking up—was the normal way to die. Last, but not least, refined sugar (sucrose) did not form part of the human diet.

People did have almonds and chestnuts and walnuts and pistachio; apples and figs and grapes and olives and mulberries; barley and wheat and rye and millet; cucumbers and melon and carob and mint and onion and anise and garlic and leeks; lentils and mustard and milk and honey and a multitude of natural goodies. All of these were brimming with natural sugars. Even ginseng, but no man-refined sugar. (The rediscovery of ginseng in our time coincides with the rediscovery of China and acupuncture. Newsmagazines sometimes called it "a Red Chinese herb." Few remember that our grandparents learned about its magic properties from the Indians of the North American continent and used it—with squirrel brains—to treat gunshot wounds in the Old West.)

From the Garden of Eden through thousands of years, what we call sugar was unknown to man. He evolved and survived without it. None of the ancient books make mention of it: Mosaic Law, the Code of Manu, the I Ching, the Yellow Emperor's Classic of Internal Medicine, the New Testament, the Koran.

The prophets tell us a few things about the status of sweet cane in ancient times: It was a rare luxury, imported from afar and very expensive. What else they did with it except offer it up as a sacrifice, we can only surmise. The far country the sweet cane came from may have been India. Polynesian myths and legends make much of the sweet cane. There is evidence that China exacted tribute from India in the form of imported sweet cane. It seems to have been native to tropical climes. If countries outside the tropical belt tried to cultivate it, they apparently had little success. A passage in the

Atharva-Veda is a paean to sweetness: "I have crowned thee with a shooting sweet cane so that thou shalt not be averse to me." In ancient India, the sacred cows may have chewed on it. The Indians grew it in their backyards and started chewing on it themselves for its sweetness. The sweet cane "was cultivated with great labor by husbandmen who bruise it when ripe in mortars, set the juice in a vessel until concreted in form like snow or white salt." The scrapings were taken with chapati bread or with pottage. A decade later or so they began pressing the cane and drinking the juice in the same way that the American Indians tapped the maple trees to make syrup. Apple cider or toddy from the date palm have to be drunk while fresh, so did the sweet juice from the sweet cane. It was as fragile as cider and would not keep without fermenting.[1]

The Greeks had no word for it. When Nearchus, admiral in the service of Alexander the Great, sailed down the Indus to explore the East Indies in 325 B.C., he described it as "a kind of honey" growing in canes or reeds. Common soldiers of Alexander the Great found natives of the Indus Valley partaking of sweet cane juice as a fermented drink. It turns up in other Greek and Roman accounts continually compared to the basic staples of the time: honey and salt. Sometimes it was called "Indian salt" or "honey without bees" and imported in small quantities at enormous cost. Herodotus called it "manufactured honey" and Pliny called it "honey from the cane." It was used, like honey, as a medicine. It took a Roman writer of Nero's time to record its Latin name: *saccharum*. Dioscorides described it as a "sort of concreted honey which is called saccharum found in canes in India and Arabia Felix; it is in consistence like salt and brittle between the teeth."[2]

The school of medicine and pharmacology at the University of Djondisapour, the pride of the Persian Empire, is credited with the research and development of a process for solidifying and refining the juice of the cane into solid form that would last without fermenting. Transportation and trade were now possible. This happened sometime after 600 A.D. when the Persians began growing sweet cane on their own. T'ang China imported loaves of "stone honey" from Bokhara where careful skimming of the liquid and the addition of milk contributed to the whiteness of this imperial luxury. A piece of saccharum was considered a rare and precious miracle drug of its time—heavily in demand in time of plague and pestilence.

While the medieval Latin name for a medicinal morsel of the precious substance came to be appropriated later for a sugar substitute in the West, the original Sanskrit word for morsel or piece (of anything) became permanently attached to "Indian salt" and survived transition through the languages of the Muslim empire and the Latin tongues. The Sanskrit *khanda* became the English candy.

The Persian empire rose and fell, as empires always do. When the armies of Islam overran them, one of the trophies of victory was the secret for processing sweet cane into medicine. The Wernher von Braun of Baghdad may have been brought to Mecca. It wasn't long before the Arabs took over the saccharum business.

When Muhammad sickened with fever and died, his kalifa or successor set out, with the faith that moves mountains, to subjugate the whole world with an army of a few thousand Arabs. With military campaigns among the most brilliant in the world's history, he came within an ace of succeeding. Within 125 years, Islam expanded from the Indus River to the Atlantic and Spain, from Kashmir to Upper Egypt. The conquering caliph had ridden to Jerusalem with a bag of barley, a bag of dates, and a water skin. One can read stories about a successor, Omayyad Caliph Walid II, who mocked at the Koran, wore fancy outfits, ate pork, drank wine, neglected his prayers, and developed a taste for sugared drinks. The sauce of the Saracens became the pause that refreshes. Arab armies of occupation took with them the rice grains from Persia and the cuttings of the sweet cane that the Persians had found in India—it was more practical to plant young sugar cane than import the end product.

Islam soon discovered many new diseases and, perforce, divorced science from religion. Great and vital strides were made in medicine and surgery. They used anesthetics; initiated the science of chemistry; discovered the concept of zero; rediscovered algebra; advanced in astronomy; discovered alcohol; produced fantastic work in metal and textiles, glass, pottery, and leatherwork; and manufactured paper after the fashion of the Chinese. Of all their contributions to Western civilization, perhaps those of paper and sugar were eventually to have the greatest impact.

It is tempting to wonder, from eyewitness reports that turn up later, what role sugar played in the decline of the Arab Empire. In the Koran, the sacred book of Prophet Elijah Muhammad, sugar is not mentioned. But the heirs of the Prophet are probably the first conquerors in history to have produced enough sugar to furnish both courts and troops with candy and sugared drinks. An early European observer credits the widespread use of sugar by Arab desert fighters as the reason for their loss of cutting edge. Leonhard Rauwolf is the German botanist who gave his name to the plant *rauwolfia serpentina*. The derivatives of the plant are still in use today as sedatives and tranquilizers. Rauwolf made voyages in the lands of the Sultan through Libya and Tripoli. His journals, published in 1573, contain timeless military intelligence:

"The Turks and Moors cut off one piece [of sugar] after another and so chew and eat them openly everywhere in the street without shame . . . in this way [they] accustom themselves to gluttony and are no longer the intrepid fighters they had formerly been."

Rauwolf viewed sugar addiction among the sultan's armies in much the same way as modern observers discovering American forces in Asia hooked on heroin and marihuana. "The Turks use themselves to gluttony and are no more so free and courageous to go against their enemies to fight as they had been in former ages." This may be the first recorded warning from the scientific community on the subject of sugar abuse and its observed consequences. The word scientist was not to be coined until 1840; the test tube and the laboratory were a good way off; but Rauwolf seems to have had the insight to view human beings as whole men in an environment with a history rather than a litany of labeled symptoms.[3]

After the rise of Islam, sugar became potent political stuff. Men would sell their very souls for it. The same fate that had crippled Arab conquerors was now to afflict their Christian adversaries. En route to wrest the Holy Places from the grip of the Sultan, the Crusaders soon acquired a taste for the sauce of the Saracens. Some of them wanted only to languish in the land of the infidels until they could get their fill of fermented cane juice and sugar candy. European rulers discovered that their ambassadors at the Egyptian court were being corrupted by the sugar habit and won over by bribes of costly spices and sugar. Some had to be withdrawn.

The last major Crusade ended in 1204. A few years later, the Fourth Lateran Council assembled in Rome to plan Crusades against heretics and Jews. Then in 1306, Pope Clement V—in exile at Avignon—received an appeal for a renewal of the Crusades of the good old days. Copies of the appeal went to the kings of France, England, and Sicily. This early diplomatic position paper outlined a southern sugar strategy for bringing the wily Saracens to heel.

"In the land of the Sultan, sugar grows in great quantities and from it the Sultans draw large incomes and taxes. If the Christians could seize these lands, great injury would be inflicted on the Sultan and at the same time Christendom would be wholly supplied from Cyprus. Sugar is also grown in the Morea, Malta, and Sicily, and it would grow in other Christian lands if cultivated there. As regards Christendom no harm would follow."

In the face of serpentine assurances such as this, Christendom took a big bite of the forbidden fruit. What followed was seven centuries in which the seven deadly sins flourished across the seven seas, leaving a trail of slavery, genocide, and organized crime.

British Historian Noel Deerr says flatly: "It will be no exaggeration to put the tale and toll of the Slave Trade at 20 million Africans, of which two-thirds are to be charged against sugar."[4]

In the first round of the European sugar race, the

Portuguese were out in front. The Saracens had introduced cultivation of the sugar cane to the Iberian peninsula during their occupation. Great cane plantations were set up in Valencia and Granada. Henry the Navigator of Portugal explored the West Coast of Africa in searching for fields of sugar cane outside Arab dominion. He didn't find the cane fields he was looking for, but he did discover plenty of black bodies acclimated to slave in the tropical zones where the cane would flourish. In 1444, Henry took 235 Negroes from Lagos to Seville where they were sold into slavery. That was the beginning.

Ten years later, the Pope was induced to extend his blessing to the slave traffic. Papal authority was extended to "attack, subject, and reduce to slavery the Saracens, Pagans, and other enemies of Christ." The ostensible rationale of Christianism abroad was the same one that justified hounding of heretics and Jews at home: to save their souls. The fact that the sweat of black brows could tend the new fields of sugar cane in Madeira and the Canary Isles was a providential fringe benefit for the Portuguese empire. For centuries, the Scriptures were systematically perverted to provide solace for slave-holding Christian sugar pushers. In his prophetic 1923 work "Cane," the black American poet Jean Toomer wrote it on the wall for all time: "The sin what's fixed against the white folks . . . they made the Bible lie."

Sugar and slavery were two sides of the coin of the Portuguese realm. By 1456, Portugal had control of the European sugar trade. However, Spain was not far behind. When the Moors were expelled from Spain, they left behind cane fields in Granada and Andalusia.

On his second voyage to the New World in 1493, Christopher Columbus took along some hunks of sugar cane at the suggestion of Queen Isabella. In his book composed during that voyage, Peter Martyr claims the explorers found sugar cane growing in the islands of Hispaniola. Columbus suggested transporting West Indian natives to work in the Spanish sugar cane plantations. Isabella was against it. When Columbus sent two boat loads of slaves back to Spain, the Queen ordered them returned. After her death, King Ferdinand consented to recruit the first large contingent of African slaves needed in the burgeoning Spanish sugar industry in 1510.

By this time, the Portuguese were growing sugar cane with slave labor in Brazil. One element of their sugar strategy was ingenious. While other European countries were burning Jews and heretics and witches, the Portuguese emptied their jails of condemned criminals and sent them to colonize their possessions in the New World. Convicts were encouraged to interbreed with heathen female slaves to produce a hybrid race that could survive in the tropical sugar cane fields.

Dutch traders got into the act around 1500: Skillful seamanship made it possible for them to engage in cutrate shipping—slaves were sold on credit to make up for a late start. The Dutch soon established a sugar refinery in Antwerp. Raw sugar cane was shipped from Lisbon, the Canary Islands, Brazil, Spain, and the Barbary Coast for processing in the Antwerp refineries. The sugar was then exported to the Baltic states, Germany, and England. By 1560, Charles V of Spain had built the magnificent palaces in Madrid and Toledo out of taxes on the sugar trade. No other product has so profoundly influenced the political history of the Western world as has sugar. It was the nickel under the foot of much of the early history of the New World. The Portuguese and Spanish empires rose swiftly in opulence and power. As the Arabs before them had crumbled, so they too fell rapidly into a decline. To what extent that decline was biological—occasioned by sugar bingeing at the royal level—we can only guess. However, the British empire stood by waiting to pick up the pieces. In the beginning, Queen Elizabeth I shrank from institutionalizing slavery in the British colonies as "detestable," something which might "call down the vengeance of heaven" on her realm. By 1588, her sentimental scruples had been overcome. The Queen granted a royal charter extending recognition to the Company of Royal Adventurers of England into Africa, which gave them a state monopoly on the West African slave trade.

In the West Indies, the Spaniards, following the trail

of Columbus, had exterminated the natives and brought in African slaves to tend their fields of cane. In 1515, Spanish monks offered $500 in gold as loans to anybody who would start a sugar mill. In due time, the British fleet would arrive to drive out the Spaniards. The slaves retreated to the mountains to wage guerilla war. The British annexed the islands by formal treaty and the crown monopoly installed overseers on the sugar plantations and took over the slave trade. Fermented raw sugar cane juice was turned into rum. The first rum runners brought their fire water to New York and New England where it was traded to the North American Indians for precious furs. A penny's worth of rum would buy many pounds' worth of furs, which in turn could be sold in Europe for a small fortune. On the westward journey, the Queen's Company of Royal Adventurers would visit the West African Coast for slaves; these were then transported to the West Indies and sold to the sugar planters to tend more cane to make more sugar and molasses and rum. Sugar and furs for Europe. Rum for the American Indians. Molasses for the American Colonials. (The three-cornered trade would continue until the land in Barbados and other British islands was exhausted, worn out, spent. No further crops would grow.)

Sugar pushing had become so profitable by 1660 that the British were ready to go to war to maintain their control. The Navigation Acts of 1660 had as their object the prevention of the transport of sugar, tobacco, or any product of the American Colonies to any port outside England, Ireland, and British possessions. The Colonies wanted to be free to trade with all European powers. Mother England wanted to protect her revenues and maintain the priceless shipping monopoly. She had the Royal Navy. The Colonies had no firepower, so Britannia ruled the waves . . . and controlled the sugar business. Eventually, by the 1860's, the word sugar had passed into the English language as a synonym for money.

Although some American historians like to argue that it was the British tax on tea that precipitated the War of Independence, others point to the Molasses Act of

1733 which levied a heavy tax on sugar and molasses coming from anywhere except the British sugar islands in the Caribbean. The ship owners of New England had cut themselves in on the lucrative trade in slaves, molasses, and rum. They sailed off with a cargo of rum to the slave coast of Africa to exchange it for blacks, whom they hauled back to the West Indies for sale to the eager British plantation owners. There they took on a load of molasses which they hauled back home to be distilled into rum and then peddled to their heavy drinking local customers. Long before the Boston Tea Party, the annual consumption of rum in the American Colonies was estimated to be almost four gallons for every man, woman, and child. The Molasses Act of 1733 posed a serious threat not only to the American Colonial trade cycle but also to its thirst for demon rum.

"No cask of sugar arrives in Europe to which blood is not sticking. In view of the misery of these slaves anyone with feelings should renounce these wares and refuse the enjoyment of what is only to be bought with tears and death of countless unhappy creatures."

Thus wrote French philosopher Claude Adrien Helvetius in the middle of the eighteenth century when France had moved into the front ranks of the sugar trade. The Sorbonne condemned him; priests persuaded the court he was full of dangerous ideas; he recanted—in part to save his skin—and his book was burned by hangmen. The virulence of his attacks on slavery brought his ideas to the attention of all Europe. He said in public what many people thought in secret.

The stigma of slavery was on sugar everywhere, but most particularly in Britain. Everywhere sugar had become a source of public wealth and national importance. Through taxes and tariffs on sugar, government had remained a partner in organized crime. Fabulous fortunes were being amassed by plantation owners, planters, traders, and shippers; and the sole concern of European royalty was how they were to take their cut.

It only took three centuries for the European consciousness to be raised to the point where the first Anti-Saccharite Society was formed in 1792. The British sugar boycott soon spread throughout Europe. The British East Indian companies—already up to their ears in the opium trade—capitalized on the slavery issue for an advertising campaign, using the sugar boycott to practice moral one-upmanship.

"East India Sugar not made by slaves" was their eighteenth-century slogan. "B. Henderson China Warehouse—Rye Lane Peckham, Respectfully informs the Friends of Africa that she has on sale an Assortment of Sugar Basins [bowls] labelled in Gold Letters: East India Sugar Not Made By Slaves." In finer print they spelled out their pitch: "A family that uses five pounds of sugar per week will, by using East India instead of West India for 21 months, prevent the Slavery or Murder of one Fellow Creature. Eight such families in 19½ years will prevent the slavery or murder of 100."

His majesty's government, with its vested interest in both slavery and sugar, spoke loftily of the empire. Britain was the center of the sugar industry of the entire world. "The pleasure, glory, and grandeur of England has been advanced more by sugar than by any other commodity, wool not excepted," said Sir Dalby Thomas. "The impossibility of doing without slaves in the West Indies will always prevent the traffic being dropped. The necessity, the absolute necessity then, of carrying on must, since there is no other, be its excuse," quoth another eminent political figure of the time.[5]

It had taken no time at all for the British empire to become totally hooked on the issue of sugar. In other empires, the rare medicament had gone as far as becoming a costly luxury. Britain, however, had gone all the way. Want had become need. Gluttony had produced necessity. Sugar and slavery were indivisible. Therefore, they were defended together.

When the British West Indies were plagued with slave revolts, heavily outnumbered colonials living in terror petitioned the Crown for protection. "We cannot allow the colonies to check or discourage in any degree a traffic so beneficial to this nation," it was said in Parliament. "The Negro trade and the natural consequence resulting from (it) may justly be esteemed an inexhaustible source of wealth and naval power to this nation," said another pillar of the British empire.

At the time of its introduction to Britain, sugar was prohibitively expensive, a courtly luxury in a price class with the most expensive drugs on the market today. At $25 a pound, it was the equivalent of a year's salary for a working man. Around 1300, according to surviving accounts, a few servings of sugar accounted for a third of the cost of a magnificent funeral feast. In the mid-sixteenth century, by the reign of Elizabeth I, the price had been cut in half. By 1662, Britain was importing 16 million pounds of sugar a year. The cost had been cut to a shilling a pound, which was equivalent to the cost of three dozen eggs. Two decades later, the price was cut in half again. By 1700, the British Isles were accounting for 20 million pounds a year. By 1800, it was 160 million pounds a year. In a century span, the consumption of sugar had gone up eightfold. In another hundred years, Britons were spending as much on sugar as they spent for bread. Seventy-two pounds per person per year and still going up.

Napoleon Bonaparte left his mark on the sugar story both as producer and consumer. Weary of being robbed by the merchants of Venice in earlier times, the French got into the business of sugar refining in a big way. Around 1700, refined sugar was France's most important export. Their sugar industry prospered until the Napoleonic Wars. When Britain retaliated with a naval blockade, French refineries were cut off from the sources of raw stock. The price of sugar went sky high; bonbons were too expensive for anyone but the royal court. Napoleonic armies—like the battalions of Islam—were starved for sweets during the period they took their turn at conquering much of continental Europe. Then Napoleon struck back. In 1747, German scientist Franz Carl Achard had been experimenting in Berlin with "a kind of parsnip recently arrived from Italy." Its original source was said to be Babylonia. Achard's work continued under the sponsorship of Frederick William III of Prussia. However, French scientists—under pressure from the blockade and the emperor—undertook an intensive research program.

Benjamin Delessert found a way to process the lowly Babylonian beet into a new kind of sugar loaf at Plassy in 1812. Napoleon awarded him the Legion of Honor. Napoleon ordered sugar beets planted everywhere in France, an imperial factory was established for refining; scholarships were granted to schools for starting courses in sugar beet crafts; 500 licenses were created for sugar refineries. By the very next year, Napoleon had achieved the herculean feat of producing eight million pounds of sugar from homegrown beets. When Napoleonic armies set out for Moscow, their sugar rations were ensured. Like the Moors before them, they were turned back while traveling north. The mighty French army, in the unaccustomed climate, had met their match and more, including the armies of a backward people who had not yet accustomed themselves to sugar in their tea.

After Napoleon had beaten Britain's sugar blockade, the Quakers in Britain took up cultivation of the sugar beet as an antislavery gesture. The sugar cane industry construed this as subversive activity and demanded that the Quakers be uprooted. Most of Britain's sugar beets were fed to the cows and it was not until there was a shipping shortage in another world war that the British sugar beet industry got going again.

The French were first to abolish the slave trade by law in 1807. It took another quarter century of agitation before emancipation was proclaimed in the British colonies in 1833. That meant slavery was outlawed except in the cradle of liberty, the United States of America, land of the free. British sugar planters in Barbados and Jamaica were ruined; slaveholders were indemnified by the British government with $75 to $399 a head for their slaves. In 1846, protective tariffs went down, disenchanted blacks rose against their masters, and East Indian immigrants were brought in to man what was left of the once powerful international sugar business. But American technology was waiting in the wings to pick up the pieces. A triad of inventions in the beginning of the nineteenth century set the stage for the big-time entry of the U.S. into the sugar business: James Watt had perfected his steam engine; Figuier had completed a method for making charcoal out of animal bones; and Howard had produced the vacuum pan. However, the slavery of one kind or another never went out of style as far as sugar was concerned. The sugar industry was the model for other agribusiness conglomerates that were to follow decades later. Sugar beets had still to be planted, thinned, and topped by hand. Growing sugar cane required backbreaking labor under the hot sun of those climates where the cane thrived. Tending and cutting of sugar cane could not be mechanized. It had to be done by hand. Most of the hands were black.

The United States had barely freed itself from the colonial domination of Britain before it began practicing wholesale economic colonialism of its own in Cuba. Cuba became the classic example of a poor country economically hooked to a larger country. The best Cuban land—after British islands were exhausted—was used to supply America with raw materials for their giant and complicated refineries. Until the age of the vacuum pan, steam, and charcoal, no such thing existed as the refined white commercial sugar used today. Primitive refining processes produced raw, light brown sugar. It took those animal bones and those giant refineries to turn it into pure white crystals.

In early America, the sugar pushers were on their own. Government interference didn't exist. The Pure Food and Drug Laws were still to be created. The Department of Agriculture had yet to come into existence. Before the Civil War, all agricultural matters were handled by a division of the office of the U.S. Patent Commissioner. Sugar cane was one of the last crops introduced into the continental U.S. An inconsequential amount was grown with slave labor in Louisiana. The founding fathers of America took no more interest in the business of sugar than had their late repressor George III of England. They looked on it merely as a sure source of tax revenues. The tiny federal government budget was raised totally through the imposition of excise taxes (one of which caused the Whiskey Rebellion) and duties on imported goods. Cuba was a back door sugar colony. Approximately 90 percent of America's sugar came from there. Import duties of almost 2¢ a pound on imported raw Cuban sugar bound for American refineries accounted for 20 percent of the total federal revenue from import duties.

Americans soon outdistanced the British and virtually every other nation in sugar bingeing. The U.S. has consumed one-fifth of the world's production of sugar every year but one since the Civil War. By 1893, America was consuming more sugar than the whole world had produced in 1865. By 1920, at the time of the noble experiment in the prohibition of alcohol in the U.S., that figure for sugar consumption had doubled. Through war and peace, depression and prosperity, drought and flood, sugar consumption in America has risen steadily. It is doubtful there has ever been a more drastic challenge to the human body in the entire history of man.

In a strange way, the trail of the opium poppy has kept a parallel historical pace with the mark of cane. The use of both began as medicines; both ended up being used as habit-forming sensory pleasures. The opium traffic, like the sugar trade, seems to have begun in Persia. Both were discovered and introduced far and wide by the Arab empire. It took only a few centuries for both items to pass from medicinal usage to that of a purely pleasurable pursuit. Opium smoking began in China in the seventeenth century. The Portuguese were the first western traders to capitalize on both commodities. Then the British took over.

An early emperor of China foresaw—when alcohol was discovered—that it would raise havoc among his subjects, but he issued no prohibitions on its use. By 1760, however, Chinese imperial authorities felt obliged to prohibit opium smoking and outlaw the opium trade. Prohibition, as usual, made things worse. The British fought the Opium Wars with China rather than allow any interference with their lucrative opium trade. The Royal East India company maintained its monopoly on opium cultivation in East India the same way the Royal West India company maintained its monopoly on the cultivation of sugar cane in the West Indies. Opium running—like sugar pushing—became the basis for some of the great fortunes in Britain and America. In both cases, appalling human slavery and degradation were on the other side of the golden coin. The Opium Wars ended with the treaty of Nanking in 1842, and opium imports into China were opened up again at Britain's insistence in 1858.

By that time, the chemists had gone to work on both sugar and opium and produced refined versions of each. The refinement of opium was called morphine. The same industrial revolution which produced the steam engine and the evaporating pan also brought the invention of the hypodermic needle. Morphine shots became the wonder drug of their time, a cure for all ills, including a new malady that had been discovered in sugar-bingeing nations called sugar diabetes. After the American Civil War, morphine addiction in the U.S. was called the "army disease." The abuse of morphine in the Union armies of the North was so widespread that thousands of veterans went home hooked on the stuff. During the Civil War years, soldiers also developed a yen for cans of condensed milk preserved with great quantities of sugar.

When physicians belatedly discovered the addictive properties of morphine, the chemists went to work again and came up with a further refinement of morphine that was much touted by the medical men as a new non-addictive pain killer. Its multisyllabic chemical name, diacetylmorphine, was soon supplanted by the name of heroin. Heroin was hailed in its turn as the miracle wonder drug of its time. It replaced morphine in the treatment of sugar diabetes.

Shortly after the excise taxes on sugar were repealed in America at the turn of the century, the government undertook to use its tax powers to control the widespread abuse of opium, morphine, and heroin. The government didn't get around to rediscovering *Canabis sativa*—hemp, hashish, or marijuana, the use of which was more ancient than either sugar or opium—until the late 1930s. In some quarters early in the 1900s, there were spokesmen who judged sugar the greatest of all addictive evils, while the attitude toward opiates was relatively benign.

According to Dr. Robert Boesler, a New Jersey dentist, in 1912:

Modern manufacturing of sugar has brought about entirely new diseases. The sugar of commerce is nothing else but concentrated crystallized acid. If, in former times sugar was so costly that only the wealthy could afford to use it, it was, from the national economic standpoint, of no consequence. But today, when, because of its low cost, sugar has caused a degeneration of the people, it is time to insist on a general enlightenment. The loss of energy through the consumption of sugar in the last century and the first decade of this century can never be made good, as it has left its mark on the race. Alcohol has been used for thousands of years and has never caused the degeneration of a whole race. Alcohol does not contain destructive acids. What has been destroyed by sugar is lost and cannot be recovered.

The good doctor's warning about the American nation was as sweeping as Rauwolf's diagnosis of the Moors over three hundred years earlier. In 1911, the eleventh edition of the *Encyclopaedia Britannica* contained a complete, do-it-yourself guide for the acquisition, operation, and care of the opium pipe.

"So far as can be gathered from the conflicting statements published on the subject," said the *Britannica*, drawing on dozens of official pharmacological and International Opium Commission reports:

Opium smoking may be regarded much in the same way as the use of alcoholic stimulants. To the great majority of smokers who use it moderately, it appears to act as a stimulant and to enable them to undergo great fatigue and to go for a considerable time with little or no food. According to the reports on the subject, when the smoker has plenty of active work it appears to be no more injurious than smoking tobacco. When carried to excess, it becomes an inveterate habit; but this happens chiefly in individuals of weak willpower, who would just as easily become the victims of intoxicating drinks, and who are practically moral imbeciles, often addicted to other forms of depravity.

The *Britannica* brushed off Chinese arguments against opium as being economically determined. "There can be no doubt that the use of the drug is opposed by all thinking Chinese who are not pecuniarily interested in the opium trade or cultivation, for several reasons, among which may be mentioned the drain of bullion from the country, the decrease of population, the liability of famine through the cultivation of opium where cereals should grow, and the corruption of state officials."

Any backward glance reminds us that everything changes. And the social acceptability or public alarm over other people's appetites, habits, and addictions has changed more often than it has remained the same. The difference between sugar addiction and narcotic addiction is largely one of degree. Small quantities of narcotics can change body-brain behavior quickly. Sugars take a little longer, from a matter of minutes in the case of a liquid, simple sugar like alcohol to a matter of years in sugars of other kinds.

The enduring American fantasy of the dope pusher—imbedded in law and myth—is a slimy degenerate hanging around school playgrounds passing out free samples of expensive addictive substances to innocent kids. This fantasy devil was created at the turn of the century by and for a country of booze and sugar addicts with an enduring nostalgia for the friendly country store where so many of them got *their* habit.

Mark Twain tells us in his autobiography that in the slave-trading town of Florida, Missouri, around 1840, there were two stores in the village—one belonging to his uncle.

It was a very small establishment . . . a few barrels of salt mackerel, coffee, and New Orleans sugar behind the counter; stacks of brooms, shovels, axes, hoes, rakes, and such; . . . a lot of cheap hats, bonnets, and tinware strung on strings and suspended from the walls, . . . another counter with bags of shot on it, a cheese or two, and a keg of powder; in front of it a row of nail kegs and a few pigs of lead, and behind it a barrel or two of New Orleans molasses and native corn whiskey on tap. If a boy bought five or ten cents' worth of anything, he was entitled to half a handful of sugar from the barrel, . . . if a man bought a trifle, he was at liberty to draw and swallow as big a drink of whiskey as he wanted.

Everything was cheap: apples, peaches, sweet potatoes, Irish potatoes, and corn, ten cents a bushel; chickens ten cents apiece; butter, six cents a pound; eggs, three cents a dozen; coffee and sugar, five cents a pound; whiskey, ten cents a gallon.[6]

Sugar was a lot more expensive than whiskey and other staples. But there they were, pushing free samples, hooking the kiddies good. Mark Twain—like most kids with an uncle who had a sugar barrel—was a "sickly and precarious and tiresome and uncertain child," who lived, he tells us, "mainly on allopathic medicines."

By 1840, the sugar pushers and the diseasestablishment* were solid partners. Washington raked in two cents in federal taxes on every five-cent pound bag of sugar for another fifty years. Addicts supported the government—rather than vice versa—once upon a time.

---

*That part of the establishment—once minor, now major—which profits directly and indirectly, legally and illegally, from human misery and malaise.

How We Got Here
From There

I'll buy a huge piece of meat, cook it up for dinner, and then right before it's done, I'll break down and have what I wanted for dinner in the first place—bread and jam . . . all I ever really want is *sugar*.

Andy Warhol, New York Magazine, *March 31, 1975*

So many of us have such heavy sugar habits today, it's hard for us to imagine the reaction of a sugarfree Crusader languishing in the land of the Infidel, taking his first sweet trip.

In *Beyond the Chindwin*, Bernard Fergusson tells how men too exhausted even to speak were given a kind of sugar fudge to eat. ". . . the immediate result was astonishing, like a modern Pentecost. The string of our tongues loosed, and we spake plain."[1] A substance that could produce this potent reaction on the brains of brawny men would hardly be what one would offer as a Christmas treat to the kiddies. Here was something more intoxicating than beer or wine and more potent than many drugs and potions then known to man. No wonder Arab and Jewish physicians used refined sugar carefully in minuscule amounts, adding it to their prescriptions with great care. It was a brain boggler. It could cause the human body and brain to run the gamut in no time at all from exhaustion to hallucination.

Today, the endocrinologists can tell us how it happens.

The difference between life and death is, in chemical terms, slighter than the difference between distilled water and that stuff from the tap. The brain is probably the most sensitive organ in the body. The difference between feeling up or down, sane or insane, calm or freaked out, inspired or depressed depends in large measure upon what we put in our mouth. For maximum efficiency of the whole body—of which the brain is merely a part— the amount of glucose in the blood must balance with the amount of blood oxygen. As Dr. E. M. Abrahamson and A. W. Pezet note in *Body, Mind, and Sugar*, ". . . a condition in which the blood sugar level is relatively low . . . tends to starve the body's cells, especially the brain cells. It is treated by diet. . . . What happens to us when the cells of our bodies and especially our brains are chronically undernourished? The weakest, most vulnerable cells . . . *suffer first*." (Emphasis added.) When all is working well, this balance is maintained with fine precision under the supervision of our adrenal glands. When we take refined sugar (sucrose), it is the next thing to being glucose so it largely escapes chemical processing in our bodies. The sucrose passes directly to the intestines, where it becomes "predigested" glucose. This in turn is absorbed into the blood *where the glucose level has already been established in precise balance with oxygen.* The glucose level in the blood is thus drastically increased. Balance is destroyed. The body is in crisis.

The brain registers it first. Hormones pour from the adrenal casings and marshal every chemical resource for dealing with sugar: insulin from the endocrine "islets" of the pancreas works specifically to hold down the glucose level in the blood in complementary antagonism to the adrenal hormones concerned with keeping the glucose level up. All this proceeds at emergency pace, with predictable results. Going too fast, it goes too far. The bottom drops out of the blood glucose level and a second crisis comes out of the first. Pancreatic islets have to shut down; so do some departments of the adrenal casings. Other adrenal hormones must be produced to regulate the reversing of the chemical direction and bring the blood glucose level up again.[2]

All this is reflected in how we feel. While the glucose is being absorbed into the blood, we feel "up." A quick pick-up. However, this surge of mortgaged energy is succeeded by the downs, when the bottom drops out of the blood glucose level. We are listless, tired; it requires effort to move or even think until the blood glucose level is brought up again. Our poor brain is vulnerable to suspicion, hallucinations. We can be irritable, all nerves, jumpy. The severity of the crisis on top of crisis depends on the glucose overload. If we continue taking sugar, a new double crisis is always beginning before the old one ends. The accumulative crisis at the end of the day can be a lulu.

After years of such days, the end result is damaged adrenals. They are worn out not from overwork but from continual whiplash. Overall production of hormones is low, amounts don't dovetail. This disturbed function, out of balance, is reflected all around the endocrine circuit. The brain may soon have trouble telling the unreal from the real; we're likely to go off half cocked. When stress comes our way, we go to pieces because we no longer have a healthy endocrine system to cope with it. Day-to-day efficiency lags, we're always tired, never seem to get anything done. We've really got the sugar blues.

Members of the medical profession who have studied this note that "since the cells of the brain are those that depend wholly upon the moment-to-moment blood sugar level for nourishment, they are perhaps the most susceptible to damage. The disturbingly large and ever-increasing number of neurotics in our population makes this clearly evident."[3] Not everyone goes all the way. Some people start out with strong adrenals; others, like the late President Kennedy, don't.[4] Degrees of sugar abuse and sugar blues vary. However, the body does not lie. If you take sugar, you feel the consequences.

The late endocrinologist John W. Tintera was quite emphatic: "It is quite possible to improve your disposition, increase your efficiency, and change your personality for the better. The way to do it is to avoid cane and beet sugar in all forms and guises.[5]

What the avant garde of endocrinology tells us today, the sorceress in what we call the Dark Ages knew by instinct or learned by experiment. Generation after generation, century by century, the people turned to the natural healers. Emperors, kings, popes, and the richest barons had sundry "doctors of Salerno," or Moorish and Jewish physicians; but the common people of every state, the whole world, consulted no one but the natural healers, the *Saga*, the *Sage Femme*, the Good Woman, the Beautiful Lady or *Belladonna*—the name of one of her potions still used by physicians today. Anatomy, alchemy, and pharmacology flourished with these people long before such studies became general practice. Natural healers believed the universe was governed by law and order of which every petal of every plant was a part. They were physician and minister, friend and good neighbor. When physicians were few, practicing savage male rituals like bloodletting and lopping off extremities, the natural healers were able to cure people by combining the healing power of plants with the laying on of hands and common sense advice about diet, fasting, and prayer. Often, the sorceress was the midwife and nurse who officiated at birth and death. If a child was born deformed, the sorceress might mercifully snuff out its life with the sleeping pillow. If an old soul was dying slowly and painfully, the sorceress might do the same, use the pillow to hasten the end.

Philippus Aureolus Paracelsus (a.k.a. Theophrastus Bombastus von Hohenheim), a great physician of his time, who taught Goethe who taught Darwin, burned the pharmacopoeia of 1527, and declared that he had learned from sorceresses all he knew.[6]

The natural healers understood the power of many plants and foods. In order to distinguish between healthful edible food and poisonous substances, they often used an instrument common among ancient civilizations: A forked twig, a pendulum—a divining rod—dangling from a piece of string. The forked rod is believed to divine the presence of water or minerals by dipping downward when held over a vein. This art of dowsing has survived in many places. My Irish grandfather employed a dowser to scout the best possible location when he wanted to drill a well.

Today, this ancient art has been rediscovered by engineers and scientists throughout the world and reapplied to the measurement of the vitality of foods. Where fresh juice of a sugar beet registers 8,500 units of healthful radiant energy, a refined sugar cube registers zero, though the inert calorie count of both may remain more or less constant.[7]

In the eyes of the sorceress, refined sugar failed another very simple test. It was not a whole food. The words holy, whole, healthy, and hale all stemmed from the same root. A whole food was holy, blessed by the nature spirits, and intended to protect the health of man. Sugar was obviously not a whole food like a green plant or an amber grain. Sugar cane grew in tropical and warm regions. The average peasant, certainly those in Europe, would not refine sugar cane at home like bread, cheese, wine, and beer. Sugar was a foreign substance, imported from afar, made by unseen hands from a tropical plant that the sorceress had never studied with the dowser. If it had any history, it was an alien history. Judgment was therefore suspended unless and until a sorceress from Cheltenham could consult with a sorceress from Barbados. Meanwhile, it was brought from afar by lackeys of church and state who—in the eyes of the natural healers—had an unblemished record for having brought nothing but death and taxes, toil and trouble, wars and pestilence.

The attitude of thoughtful men of this time is typified by the legend of the fools of Gotham. When the king announced his intention to honor their village by erecting something on the order of Nixon's San Clemente Western White House in their midst, the elders of Gotham officially proclaimed their joy and satisfaction. However, knowing it meant disruption of their life and confiscation of their eggs and chickens, the local sorceress was consulted on how to prevent this calamity. Thereupon, everyone in the town was soon afflicted with temporary insanity, which persisted until their beloved monarch called off his plans. The only dissent possible was to play the fool.

The natural healers commanded loyalty far and wide. Everywhere, people lived with the greatest respect for their practical, down-to-earth wisdom. As such, they constituted a menace to a corrupt church and corrupt states. It would not be long before such authorities set out in systematic alliance to collaborate in the destruction of all practitioners of natural healing.

It began when the Crusaders came marching home, with tall tales to tell. They also brought back a few tricks that they had picked up in the land of the Infidels. One of them was the windmill, which soon meant that grain could be ground into meal on the top of a hill, as well as down by the old mill stream. Another was the trick of using sugar as a fermenting agent in making beer and wine. This sneaky process was called *sophistication*. To sophisticate beer meant to corrupt it or spoil it by adding some foreign or inferior substance. Sugar was foreign and inferior to natural malt and hops.

The word sophisticate eventually went out of fashion; it was replaced by adulterate; this gave way to the bland quantitative description of foreign inferior substances as additives. Today, we're so sophisticated, and our food is so corrupt, that our sophisticators have us believing doubletalk. Does our food need to be "fortified" or "enriched"? Why refine flour and then enrich it? The refinement process strips many vital elements from the grain. So much for progress.

In the good old days when beer was beer, sophistication was a fighting word. Serious lovers of the brews took stern measures to ensure that they were drinking nothing but pure beer made with grains, malt, and hops. Tasters would spill a suspected brew out onto a wooden seat and test it by sitting square in the puddle in their leather breeches. After due deliberation and evaporation, the taster would rise from the wooden bench. If his leather-bound *derrière* adhered to the wood, the brewer was in trouble for adding sugar to his beer. Pure malt beer was not considered to yield an adhesive extract.

Consumerism was wild and woolly way back then. Retribution was swift and severe. The brewer caught adding sugar to his beer could be hauled into the pillory or ridden out of town. In the reign of England's Edward the Confessor, the eleventh-century record shows that "a knavish brewer of the City of Chester was taken round the town in the cart in which the refuse of the privies had been collected." Betty Crocker, look out!

Today one hears about Good King John and his Magna Charta, the first bill of human rights proclaimed in 1215. It is not so widely known that in those days the pillory and the tumbril were trotted out as deterrents to the "sophistication" of bread, meat, beer, and wine. In 1482, a wine sophisticator in Germany was condemned to drink six quarts of his own wine. He died in the middle of the commercial.

People hewed to tested, traditional ways; they were suspicious of newfangled foreign tricks. "When people lost sight of the way to live," wrote Lao Tsu, "came codes of love and honesty."

That point arrived in Britain in 1816; an act was passed which outlawed brewers even possessing sugar or molasses. In the twentieth century, possession of drugs is sufficient grounds for criminal charges. In the nineteenth century, possession of sugar by a brewer was considered evidence of intent to sophisticate his brew. By that time, however, the pillory and the tumbril had given way to imprisonment and fines—knavish brewers could afford to take more chances.

In olden days, beer was more than the color, bubble, and fake foam of today's plastic age. It was a staple food—liquid bread. Nursing mothers drank it for breakfast. A brewer who added sugar to his beer was threatening the survival of the race. When he was carted around town in a *merde* wagon, the message was clear: The human body and brain cannot handle sugar. They knew.

People learned from the sorceress or knew in their own veins that sugar was much too sweet not to be bad for them. But, like Eve in the Garden, they were tempted. They hoped to get away with it. Some people seemed to. Or thought they did. Or thought they did right up until the point—months or years later—when they found out differently. Especially the high and mighty. Sooner or later there were signs. Occurrences. Warnings. Their bodies were telling them something.

Soldiers and sailors, freighting precious cargoes of expensive sugar across thousands of miles, found that the stuff had a way of sticking to their fingers. They began to have more trouble with their teeth. Servants in the homes of the rich, where precious sugar was kept under lock and key, began to notice that the urine in the slop jars of the high and mighty started smelling exceptionally sweet. It was not something that could be talked about with anyone but the sorceress. Sailors shipwrecked at sea on sugar cargo ships tried to survive on a diet of sugar and rum. They went bonkers and often died. There was some talk about that. Men who worked in the new cities in sugar depots and refineries seemed to develop galloping consumption in great numbers. Sometimes they talked about it. Other times, when they'd been pinching bits of sugar here and there, it was not something one could talk about.

Ancient civilizations such as those of the Orientals believed that all disorders of body and mind proceed from what we eat. As the Oriental sages phrased it, the mind and the body are not two. The sorceress . . . wise woman . . . natural healer believed this too. However, by the time sugar was introduced widely in Europe, the natural healers were uncovered—practically overnight—as a declared enemy of church and state. Ailing people consulted them at very real peril. One literally risked life and limb having any truck with them. In turn, they risked life and limb to aid you.

The church declared, in the fourteenth century, that "if a woman dare to cure without having studied, she is a witch and must die." Catholics and Protestant churchmen forbade the exercising of healing arts or the dispensing of common sense wisdom under pain of death.[8] Never mind that such people had spent their entire lives in practical study. They had studied the order of the universe, the seeds and stars, the animals, birds, and bees in their native habitat. Nature and tradition were their teachers, not the scriptures as interpreted by the priests. The printing press did not exist. All knowledge and history not in the hands of all-powerful priests was passed on from natural healer to natural healer.

If you sought out a sorceress complaining of an upset stomach, she would question you on what you'd been eating, give you sound advice and perhaps a herbal infusion to settle your stomach. If you went to a natural healer complaining of melancholy, migraine, or madness, he would also know it must have been something you ate. Sugar, perhaps. So you were given stern advice and perhaps a potion or an infusion to settle your brain.

Suddenly, those days were gone. Natural healing had become witchcraft. If your hallucinations were attributed to sugar and word of it got around, the whole encounter could be turned on its head. You had been bewitched. The sorceress was spreading evil tidings against sugar to harm a new national enterprise blessed by the church and profitable to the state. Bewitchment was the province of the exorcist and the priest. The cure prescribed was for the bewitched person to denounce the natural healer as a witch or a wizard, the source of the unholy spell! The punishment? Burning at the stake.

Inquisitors complained bitterly that bewitched persons consulted the sorceress and were cured by natural means. "The common method of taking off bewitchment," they wrote, "is for the bewitched person to resort to wise women, by whom they are very frequently cured, and not by priests or exorcists. . . . Such cures are affected by the help of devils, which it is unlawful to seek; therefore it cannot be lawful thus to cure bewitchment, but it must be patiently borne."[9]

In the age of witch hunts, the disorders, occurrences, and signs were divided into two categories: Those thought to be your own fault (physical) and those thought to be the work of the devil (mental). The milksick, a stomach-ache, galloping consumption, and other obvious signs and warnings were clearly physical. Invisible symptoms, however, from melancholy to migraine to madness were bewitchment.

With the support of kings and princes, the medieval church asserted complete control over medical education and practice. The infamous 1486 manual for witch hunters, *Malleus Maleficarum (The Hammer of Witches)*, defined witches as "those who try to induce others to perform evil wonders." Healing was one of the wonders they had in mind. Heresy was sweepingly defined as "infidelity in a person who has been baptized." Midwives were singled out as "surpassing all others in wickedness." There may never have been male chauvinist pigs to surpass the Inquisitors who declared that "all witch-craft comes from carnal lust, which is in women in-satiable."[10] When male physicians were barred from attending births, a curious German physician in drag as a midwife crashed a delivery. He was found out and burned at the stake. Now the pendulum had swung all the way.[11]

Any sudden drastic onset of illness—or what looked like illness—pointed to witchcraft. To diagnose witch-craft, Inquisitors relied on physicians to distinguish between those disorders due to natural causes and those stemming from witchcraft. Yet another way of distin-guishing between natural (physical) disorders and super-natural (mental) disorders was a medieval Rorschach test: Molten lead was held over the patient's body and then poured into water. If the lead formed a recognizable image, punishment was swift. Whatever the shape of the lead, the Inquisitors could always find a reason that proved, indubitably, that the patient was suffering from exactly the problem originally diagnosed.

Latin was the language of the physicians and the priest. So physicians came to use the Latin word *symptoma* from the Greek word *symptoma*, for sign. What the sorceress had called a sign, warning from nature, the physician began to call a symptom. Few physicians could tell you something you didn't know in your own bones. They could only examine you, listen to your complaints, then give your signs, warnings, or symptoms a fancy new name in Latin or Greek. That way the priest had no corner on mystery.

If a doctor said, "Aha, it may be a stomachache," he was only telling you something you'd just told him. If he said, "It must have been something you ate," you wouldn't be exactly overwhelmed with his wisdom either. When he exclaimed, "Aha, this looks like a very interesting case of dyspepsia," he's done something for you. You're the first in your block to have a new disease. A new disorder found in a new object, a book whose pages were written in Latin.

Johann Weyer, court physician to Duke William of Cleves, one of the few medical men of his age to speak out against witch hunts, was very rough on his sixteenth-century colleagues who collaborated with the Inquisition. He attacked "uninformed and unskilled physicians [who] relegate . . . all the diseases, the remedy for which they overlook, to witchcraft. They, the physicians themselves," he declared, "are thus the real malefactors."[12]

His book was promptly put on the Index.

For centuries, uninformed and unskilled physicians would continue to relegate signs of sugar blues—the simple remedy for which they overlooked—to bewitchment. Three centuries of medical mischief would produce a veritable babel of Greek and Latin symptoma: Schizophrenia, paranoia, catatonia, dementia praecox, neuroses, psychoses, psychoneuroses, chronic urticaria, neurodermatitis, cephalaigia, hermicrania, paroxysmal tachycardia—all as scarifying as the devil himself.

The wise people who understood what sugar blues were all about had been driven underground. Their litany of signs and warnings that the human body and brain cannot handle sugar was driven underground with them. It would take centuries for these signs and warnings to be rediscovered. Eventually, those zealous missionaries of Christianity would take the cross and the flag and the sugar cube and the Coke machine around the world. The church blessed slavery abroad in the sugar business as salvation for the heathens' black souls. Physicians and priests condemned natural healers at home as witches and consigned them to damnation.

Now that the competition had been wiped out, physician and priest did what conquerors in cahoots always do: The spoils were divided. The priest and exorcist took custody of the psyche, leaving the soma to the physician and surgeon. Body and brain were partitioned into north and south, like Korea and Viet Nam. Finally, the priests were phased out in favor of the psychiatrists. Dualism has endured, however: Mayo Brothers treat the body; Menningers, the brain. The National Institute of Health is separate from the National Institute of Mental Health.

When Roman Emperor Constantine embraced Christianity and began coercing his subjects to join the official Roman state church, it was the people in the rural areas who resisted; city priests scornfully denounced the *pagi* or country people. The Inquisitors never ventured down the dark pagan roads to knock on any doors because they were outnumbered in such areas; the natural healers were defended and protected as keepers of the flame; their wisdom and traditions were preserved intact . . . underground. Witches were not for burning.

Much of that deep historical antagonism is buried in language and symbols. Christians called natural healers sorcerers, from the Latin word which meant someone who drew lots, or Tarot cards, or yarrow sticks to foretell the future. Christians began to call all unbelievers pagans. Pagans called their natural healer the good woman. The natural healer dealt with herbs and potions. These were mysteries to the priests, who felt it necessary to maintain a total monopoly on all mysteries. Centuries of horror are buried in the saga of the transformation of the natural healer into the Halloween witch.

In the summer of 1973, I walked through a primeval forest in a remote area of southwestern France with a natural herbal healer and watched him perpetuate what his ancestors had done without interruption for more than four hundred years. It was like going back on the time track all the way. This remote forest resembles our images of the Garden of Eden. We walked gingerly, taking care not to trample or disturb the sacred order of the universe underfoot. He knelt to taste the early morning dew. He passed by dozens of growing things to pause before one, then picked it as carefully as one might lift a baby from its mother's lap. He pressed it to his face and his inhalation became a kind of prayer. We retreated to an ancient wooden shed where plants were arranged on racks to dry. Each had been picked at the proper time, according to the moon and the stars as well as to the time of maturity. They are stacked to dry for days, hours, weeks. Each has its own timetable. Everything in its own season. The wood is preserved intact, inviolate, an inexhaustible source of natural healing remedies, some to be used singly, others in combination. Some are for infusions, to be drunk before meals. Others are for fomentations in which ailing people soak their hands and feet.

The healer learned all this from his father, who used to lie in the fields—studying the insects, the birds, the bees, and the animals, learning their secrets by observation—like Darwin and Goethe and Paracelsus—then checking his conclusions against ancestral documents maintained for centuries and verified constantly by trial and error, practice, and more practice . . . the *practice* of herbal healing. His father had taken him on herb-collecting trips all over the countryside, by the dawn's early light as well as by the dark of the moon. People came from miles around to consult with his father about their miseries. Sometimes they would be given potions to take home. Perhaps a hot tub might be prepared with a selection of dried branches; the patient would soak away his pain in the tub in the kitchen. No one with the miseries ever left the healer without being questioned on eating and drinking habits. One would be cautioned about the quality of the bread being eaten, the wine being drunk. Always a stern injunction was given against sugar.

Ailing people usually came in the morning or afternoon for consultation. Once, a special patient arrived in the dead of night. The healer treated him in strictest confidence; the door was locked to other visitors, and the curtains were drawn. Under such circumstances, Papa prepared the hot water and the herbs himself; he would never embarrass the visitor by questioning him on his eating and drinking in the presence of others. For this patient was the physician from the next village. Unable—

with all his "scientific" learning from the church and state-approved medical colleges—to heal himself. The doctor had to repair, as had his father and grandfather before him, to the lowly and disreputable herbal healer, the sorcerer, whose ancestor might have been burned as a wizard.

A modern psychiatrist, Dr. Thomas S. Szasz, has scathingly summarized the price of hypocrisy in *The Manufacture of Madness:*

. . . The modern physician, and especially the psychiatrist, systematically repudiates his real medieval ancestor, the lowly and disreputable sorcerer and witch. Instead, he prefers to trace his descent directly from the Hippocratic physicians of ancient Greece, skipping over the embarrassment of the Middle Ages in silence . . . the medical profession has paid the heavy price that such a bargain with falsehood invariably entails. By denying his origins—indeed by identifying with those who have aggressed against his predecessors—the modern physician forfeits his identity as a modest but independent healer skeptical of the dogma of established social authority, and becomes instead a servile vassal of the State. . . . In the official histories of contemporary medicine, the denial of the sorceress and witch as healer forms an important link in this fateful transformation of the physician's role from individual entrepreneur to bureaucratic employee.[13]

In the remote corner of Gascony where I visited herbal healer Maurice Mességué, the Inquisition had passed them by. However, the disasters of World War II—the fall of France, the Nazi occupation—had finally reached the village. The young apprentice healer left his village and journeyed to the outside world. When the son repeated elsewhere the simple natural cures that his father, grandfather, and great-grandfather had accomplished every day, they were taken either as miracles or as quackery, according to which modern superstition viewed them. Mességué successfully treated personages such as Admiral Darlan, Mistinguette, and Jean Cocteau, as well as the then president of the French Republic, Edouard Herriot. Monsieur Mességué's simple cures were sometimes so spectacular that his famous patients talked too much. He came to represent a threat to orthodox medical authorities which they could not ignore. He was hauled into courts throughout the French Republic on more than forty occasions for practicing medicine without a medical degree—for daring, like the witches, to cure without having studied in official institutions.

The trials were spectacular advertisements for herbal medicine. The orthodox diseasestablishment in France made Maurice Mességué famous. Judge after judge duly found him guilty, sentenced him to a fine of one or two francs, then sought his professional services for the ailing wife or mistress waiting in the chambers. Eventually, the healer wrote three books—all bestsellers in Europe—about his adventures and his natural cures. In each he repeats the simple prescription learned from his forefathers: Whole natural food, naturally grown. What the avant garde of modern medicine has just now begun to tell us, his ancestors have been preaching for over four hundred years: stay away from all refined cane and beet sugar in all forms and guises. He returned in triumph to Gascony, where he was duly elected mayor of the beautiful city of Fleurance. He lives in a magnificent chateau where his mother had toiled as a maid. He became the owner of a huge primeval forest, where he walks in the morning. This vast tract of land is held in trust as an inexhaustible source of natural herbs and plants with which to minister to a polluted and chemicalized world outside.

In 1964, I prepared a translation of the first of some fifty books written by a Japanese natural healer. My introduction to Sakurazawa's *You Are All Sanpaku* detailed the experiences I had had healing myself according to his simple teachings.

The book contained a chapter on sugar which said, among other things:

Western medicine and science has only just begun to sound alarm signals over the fantastic increase in its per capita sugar consumption, in the United States especially. Their researches and warnings are, I fear, many decades too late . . . I am confident that Western medicine will one day admit what has been known in the Orient for years: sugar is without question the number one murderer in the history of humanity—much more lethal than opium or radioactive fallout—especially those people who eat rice as their principal food. Sugar is the greatest evil that modern industrial civilization has visited upon countries of the Far East and Africa. . . . Foolish people who give or sell candy to babies will one day discover, to their horror, that they have much to answer for.

Natural healers today may differ on many points, but on one thing they agree: The human body cannot handle man-refined sugar . . . sucrose.

In Sugar We Trust

In the Dark Ages, troubled souls were rarely locked up for going off their rocker. Such confinement began in the Age of Enlightenment, after sugar made the transition from apothecary's prescription to candy maker's confection. "The great confinement of the insane," as one historian calls it,[1] began in the late seventeenth century, after sugar consumption in Britain had zoomed in two hundred years from a pinch or two in a barrel of beer here and there to more than two million pounds per year. By that time, physicians in London had begun to observe and record terminal physical signs and symptoms of the sugar blues.

Meanwhile, when sugar eaters did not manifest obvious terminal physical symptoms and the physicians were professionally bewildered, patients were no longer pronounced bewitched, but mad, insane, emotionally disturbed. Laziness, fatigue, debauchery, parental displeasure—any one problem was sufficient cause for people under twenty-five to be locked up in the first Parisian mental hospitals. All it took to be incarcerated was a complaint from parents, relatives, or the omnipotent parish priest. Wet nurses with their babies, pregnant youngsters, retarded or defective children, senior citizens, paralytics, epileptics, prostitutes, or raving lunatics— anyone wanted off the streets and out of sight was put away. The mental hospital succeeded witch hunting and heresy hounding as a more enlightened and humane method of social control. The physician and priest handled the dirty work of street sweeping in return for royal favors. Initially, when the General Hospital was established in Paris by royal decree, one percent of the city's population was locked up. From that time until the twentieth century as the consumption of sugar went up and up— especially in the cities—so did the number of people who were put away in the General Hospital. Three hundred years later, the "emotionally disturbed" can be turned into walking automatons, their brains are controlled with psychoactive drugs.

Today, pioneers of orthomolecular psychiatry such as Dr. A. Hoffer, Dr. Allan Cott, and Dr. A. Cherkin, as well as Dr. Linus Pauling have confirmed that mental illness is a myth and that emotional disturbances can be merely the first symptom of the obvious inability of the human system to handle the stress of sugar dependency.

In "Orthomolecular Psychiatry," Dr. Pauling writes:

The functioning of the brain and nervous tissue is more sensitively dependent on the rate of chemical reactions than the functioning of other organs and tissues. I believe that mental disease is for the most part caused by abnormal reaction rates, as determined by genetic constitution and diet, and by abnormal molecular concentrations of essential substances. . . . Selection of food (and drugs) in a world that is undergoing rapid scientific and technological change may often be far from the best.

A deficiency of [vitamin B_{12}] whatever its cause . . . leads to mental illness, often even more pronounced than the physical consequences. The mental illness associated with pernicious anemia . . . often is observed for several years . . . before any of the physical manifestations of the disease appear. . . . Other investigators have also reported a higher incidence of low B_{12} concentrations in the serums of mental patients than in the population as a whole and have suggested that B_{12} deficiency, whatever its origin, may lead to mental illness.

Nicotinic acid (niacin), when its use was introduced, cured hundreds of thousands of pellagra patients of their psychoses, as well as of the physical manifestations of the disease. . . . More recently, many other investigators have reported on the use of nicotinic acid and nicotinamide for the treatment of mental disease. . . . Another vitamin that has been used to some extent in the treatment of mental disease is ascorbic acid, vitamin C. . . .

Mental symptoms (depression) accompany the physical symptoms of vitamin-C deficiency disease (scurvy). . . . It is my opinion, from the study of the literature, that many schizophrenics have an increased metabolism of ascorbic acid, presumably genetic in origin, and that the ingestion of massive amounts of ascorbic acid has some value in treating mental disease.

There is the possibility that some human beings have a sort of cerebral scurvy, without any of the other manifestations, or a sort of cerebral pellagra, or cerebral pernicious anemia . . . every vitamin, every essential amino acid, every other essential nutrilite represents a molecular disease which our distant ancestors learned to control when it began to afflict them, by selecting a therapeutic diet, and which has continued to be kept under control in this way.[2]

In "Megavitamin B_3 Therapy for Schizophrenia," Dr. A. Hoffer noted that: "Patients are also advised to follow a good nutritional program with restriction of sucrose and sucrose-rich foods."[3]

Clinical research with hyperactive and psychotic children, as well as those with brain injuries and learning disabilities, has shown:

An abnormally high family history of diabetes—that is, parents and grandparents who cannot handle sugar; an abnormally high incidence of low blood glucose, or functional hypoglycemia in the children themselves, which indicates that their systems cannot handle sugar; dependence on a high level of sugar in the diets of the very children who cannot handle it.

Inquiry into the dietary history of patients diagnosed as schizophrenic reveals the diet of their choice is rich in sweets, candy, cakes, coffee, caffeinated beverages, and foods prepared with sugar. These foods, which stimulate the adrenals, should be eliminated or severely restricted.[4]

The avant garde of modern medicine has rediscovered what the lowly sorceress learned long ago through painstaking study of nature.

"In more than twenty years of psychiatric work," writes Dr. Thomas Szasz, "I have never known a clinical psychologist to report, on the basis of a projective test, that the subject is a normal, mentally healthy person. While some witches may have survived dunking, no 'madman' survives psychological testing . . . there is no behavior or person that a modern psychiatrist cannot plausibly diagnose as abnormal or ill."[5]

So it was in the seventeeth century. Once the doctor or the exorcist had been called in, he was under pressure to do something. When he tried and failed, the poor patient had to be put away. It is often said that the surgeons bury their mistakes. Physicians and psychiatrists put them away. Lock 'em up.

The excesses of the Inquisitors and witch hunters eventually produced a predictable backlash, a wave of revulsion and horror. Physicians and priests who had starred in these dramas were now in an uneasy partnership that reminded everyone of the blood on their hands. Yesterday's heresies became institutionalized as the multiple new Protestant orthodoxies. People left the church in droves, and the royal partners had to rush into the breach and impose heavy fines on the dropouts for missing church on Sunday. Things went from bad to worse. The orgies of witch burning and exorcism had failed to stem the tide of bewitchment, possession, and madness—now physicians and clergymen were under pressure to come up with a new explanation for the symptoms and signs of the sugar blues that boggled men's brains and disturbed their emotions.

In 1710, an anonymous clergyman-physician came up with the answer. Had they been giving Nobel prizes in those days, he surely would have rated one. His simple, sure-fire explanation for madness would satisfy physicians and priests for three centuries. It would keep them happy, busy, and rich. Although children had been doing it since the dawn of time, neither the Greeks, Romans, Egyptians, Orientals, nor Persians had a proper word for it. The anonymous clergyman-physician raided his Bible and perverted the legend of Onan into a new sin called *onanism*. He wrote a book, *Onania, or the Heinous Sin of Self-Pollution*. The physicians raided their Latin dictionaries and corrupted the closest Latin word: *manustupration*, to defile by hand. This was smoothed into the word masturbation, which finally made the Oxford English Dictionary in 1766. *Onania* was a best seller. The scientists who knew a good thing when they saw it, got into the act, dropping some of the hellfire religious crudities in favor of pseudoscientific buttressing. Besides, who could say that masturbation did not produce insanity? For a successful case against the theory, you would have to admit to having masturbated for years; then prove your sanity. Nobody dared to try it.

How about the sweet land of liberty? The Father of American Psychiatry was also one of the Founders of the American Revolution, a signer of the Declaration of Independence, Benjamin Rush, M.D. He got on the Oh, No, Onan bandwagon early to insist that solo sex play was the pursuit of madness and produces: ". . . impotence, [painful urination, locomotor incoordination, tuberculosis], dyspepsia, dimness of sight, vertigo, epilepsy, hypochondriasis, loss of memory, manalgia [whatever that is], fatuity, and death."[6]

The great French psychiatrist Esquirol joined the chorus, declaring that masturbation "is recognized in all countries as a common cause of insanity . . . unless it is stopped at once; it is an insurmountable obstacle to cure . . . reduces a patient to a state of stupidity, [tuberculosis], marasmus [gradual wasting of tissue], and death

. . . may be a forerunner of mania, dementia . . . leads to melancholy and suicide." The notion that masturbation caused insanity was accepted by the civilized world.[7]

Masturbation supplied a perfect safety valve for medical brains. We can cure you *unless* you masturbate and keep on masturbating, they declared. Therefore, if you were incurable you were put in an asylum, which had a sure cure for masturbation: the strait jacket. Those on probation wore chastity belts by day and spiked rings for sleeping.

It was only a matter of time until the surgeons joined in. Their contribution? The Old Testament ritual of circumcision. Eventually, an operation for removal of the female clitoris was devised.

In the 1850s, Dr. Isaac Baker Brown, prominent London surgeon (later president of the Medical Society of London), created a surgical procedure called the clitoridectomy, on the ground that masturbation was a form of "moral leprosy" which caused hysteria, epilepsy, and convulsive diseases.

No less a dignitary than the president of the Royal College of Surgeons published a paper recommending circumcision for the treatment and prevention of this "shameful habit" and proposed going even further: Surgery for severing the dorsal nerves of the males' penis and ovariectomy for females. The ultimate answer to masturbation and insanity, of course, was castration and hysterectomies. In the twentieth century, another giant step forward: lobotomies—incision into the brain.

"By about 1880," writes historian A. Comfort, "the individual who might wish for unconscious reasons to tie, chain, or infibulate sexually active children or mental patients—the two most readily available captive audiences—to adorn them with grotesque appliances, encase them with plaster casts, leather or rubber, to beat, frighten or castrate them, to cauterize or denervate the genitalia, could find humane and respectable medical authority for doing so in good conscience. Masturbatory insanity was now real enough—it was affecting the medical profession."[8]

The first medical union in this country, years before

the AMA, was the Association of Medical Superintendents of American Institutions for the Insane. It was founded in 1844, at a time when general stores on the American frontier were giving away a half pound of sugar free to every youngster who came into the store to make a purchase of a nickel or more. The first pronouncement of the first union of headshrinkers in the sweet land of liberty was a resolution in defense of the straitjacket: "Resolved, that it is the unanimous sense of this convention that the attempt to abandon entirely the use of all means of personal restraint is not sanctioned by the true interest of the insane."[9]

In 1855, an editorial in the *New Orleans Medical and Surgical Journal* declared that "neither the plague, nor war, nor smallpox, nor a crowd of similar evils have resulted more disastrously for humanity than the habit of masturbation; it is the destroying element of civilized society."[10]

While official U.S. medicine was railing against masturbation, they were also denouncing as quackery the ideas of I. P. Semmelweis, who discovered in the mid-1800s that the cause of child-bed fever was the failure of doctors to take the simple precaution of thoroughly washing their hands before going from the autopsy table to the delivery room. Despite the defense of such stalwarts as Oliver Wendell Holmes, Semmelweis was hounded as a charlatan and a quack; he eventually died in an insane asylum in 1865.

If physicians a hundred years ago had trouble accepting the radical notion that their own dirty hands spread unnecessary disease and suffering, it was a bit much to expect them to connect the whopping rise in sugar consumption with new diseases.

At the end of the Victorian era, the masturbation theory of madness had begun to run out of gas. Then Sigmund Freud arrived on the scene. Freud decided that masturbation didn't necessarily drive you insane or drive you to suicide; it was a sign of a new disease, neuroses. The remedy was no longer the chastity belt or surgeon's knife but the psychiatrist's couch. A chastity belt might set you back ten bucks or so; psychiatrists expected to be paid by the hour and the treatment took weeks, months, years.

In 1897, Freud wrote, ". . . It has dawned on me that masturbation is the one major habit, the 'primal addiction,' and that it is only as a substitute and replacement for it that the other addictions—for alcohol, morphine, tobacco, etc.—come into existence." He didn't mention cocaine or sugar, he was hooked on both himself.[11]

In one of his books, Dr. Freud noted that he was summoned to the home of an anxious Viennese mama to examine her son. The hawkeyed Freud noticed a telltale spot on the lad's trousers and made discreet inquiries. The boy claimed it was raw eggwhite. Of course, the good doctor wasn't fooled for a minute, he leaped to the conclusion that his patient was "suffering from the troubles arising from masturbation."[12] Dr. Szasz comments acidly in *The Manufacture of Madness,* "The young man did not send for Freud and there is no reason to believe *he* was suffering from anything at all; the person who was suffering was the *mother,* presumably from the son's maturing sexuality."

Centuries of comic book horrors practiced by the medical and psychiatric fraternity in the treatment of "madness caused by masturbation" are strangely missing from our medical history books. Among millions of words devoted to self-glorification, not one is devoted to masturbatory insanity, according to Dr. Szasz. Like the involvement of the physician in the horror of the witch hunt, this sorry story is sunk without a trace. Dr. Szasz compares this most aptly to the Constitution of the United States, which manages not to mention the subject of Negro slavery. In the same way, official psychiatry remains among the most retarded sectors of the medical fraternity in recognizing that the inability of the human system to handle sugar is reflected in a whole range of symptoms of what they insist on calling "mental illness."

It was as late as 1911 that Eugen Bleuler coined the fearsome word "schizophrenia" which supplanted dementia praecox—the latter merely means precocious madness (the symptoms appear among the young). The only thing new was the name. The symptoms were as old as sugar. In earlier times, physicians bewildered by the same symptoms had pronounced their patients bewitched; now they were pronounced schizophrenic. Where once such people had been turned over to the exorcist, now they were abandoned to the psychiatrist. Masturbation did not drive anyone mad anymore. What did? The efforts of Mama trying to stop masturbation. Or insanity could have been caused by toilet training that was too much too soon . . . breakfast quarrels with Papa . . . inconsistent discipline . . . lack of love or too much of it—anything in the family history that could be recalled: poverty, riches, stress, or ease.

When psychiatry proved no better than exorcism, some shrinks turned to more drastic methods, like shock treatments of all kinds, from drugs to electricity to insulin. In 1935, Egas Moniz of Lisbon introduced the ultimate answer to schizophrenia: The prefrontal lobotomy, surgical incision into the brain. In 1949, Moniz was awarded a Nobel prize for having pioneered the ultimate horror.

Traditional Oriental medicine had always insisted that the mind and the body are not two. What we call diseases and illnesses are merely symptoms that the entire body is out of kilter. To make a man whole again, he has only to eat whole food. Communist China's foremost neuropsychiatrist insists ". . . neuroses and psychoses do not exist here, not even paranoia."[13]

Sagen Isiduka, fabled Japanese doctor/anti-doctor (he was so called for his insistence on hewing to traditional ways despite Japan's adoption of many of the practices of Western science and medicine since the 1800s), taught his disciples that what the West called mental illness could be cured by diet.

"As cancer is the extreme Yin illness of people with strong constitutions, schizophrenia is the most extreme Yin illness of people with weak constitutions," wrote Nyoiti Sakurazawa (Isiduka's successor) who lectured, wrote, and taught in Europe and America from the 1920s until his death in 1966.[14]

As with acupuncture, in Oriental medicine everything stems from the unifying principle of Yin/Yang. Sugar is the extreme Yin food as red meat is the extreme Yang food. Excess Yin sugar produces excess Yin diseases like cancer and what we call schizophrenia.

A "weak constitution," as defined by traditional Oriental medical practice, is determined by genetic heredity, which is modified by the mother's food intake during the foetus's first months of life in the womb. To the Orientals, the outward sign of a weak constitution is a small earlobe attached to the cheek without a natural division. Large, detached earlobes are a sign of a strong constitution and a sound genetic inheritance. Western diagnosticians confirm this ancient Oriental diagnosis by telling us that large detached earlobes are a sign of strong adrenal glands.[15]

Long before the explosion of interest in Oriental medicine as a result of the U.S. rapprochement with China in the 1970s, while acupuncturists like Sakurazawa were being denounced prematurely as quacks, an endocrinologist in New York was at work rediscovering the validity of some of the basic tenets of the ancient Oriental medical arts.

In the 1940s, Dr. John Tintera rediscovered the vital importance of the endocrine system (especially the adrenal glands) in "pathological mentation"—or brain boggling.

In two hundred cases under treatment for hypoadrenocorticism (the lack of adequate adrenal cortical hormone production or imbalance among these hormones), he discovered that the chief complaints of his patients were often similar to those found in persons whose systems were unable to handle sugar: Fatigue, nervousness, depression, apprehension, craving for sweets, inability to handle alcohol, inability to concentrate, allergies, low blood pressure. Sugar blues! ! !

He finally insisted that all his patients submit to a four-hour glucose tolerance test (GTT) to find out whether or not they could handle sugar.

The results were so startling that the laboratories double-checked their techniques then apologized for what they believed to be incorrect readings.

What mystified them was the low flat curves derived from

disturbed early adolescents. This laboratory procedure had been previously carried out only for patients with physical findings presumptive of diabetes.

Dorland's definition of schizophrenia (Bleuler's dementia praecox) includes the phrase, "often recognized during or shortly after adolescence," and further, in reference to hebephrenia and catatonia, "coming on soon after the onset of puberty."

These conditions might seem to arise or become aggravated at puberty, but probing into the patient's past will frequently reveal indications which were present at birth, and during the first year of life, and through the preschool and grammar school years. Each of these periods has its own characteristic clinical picture. This picture becomes more marked at pubescence and often causes school officials to complain of juvenile delinquency or underachievement. *A glucose tolerance test at any of these periods could alert parents and physicians and could save innumerable hours and small fortunes spent in looking into the child's psyche and home environment for maladjustments of questionable significance in the emotional development of the average child.* [Emphasis added.] The negativism, hyperactivity, and obstinate resentment of discipline are absolute indications for at least the minimum laboratory tests: urinalysis, complete blood count, P.B.I. determination, and the 5-hour glucose tolerance test. A glucose tolerance test can be performed in a young child by the micro-method without undue trauma to the patient. As a matter of fact, I have been urging that these four tests be routine for all patients, even before a history or physical examination is undertaken.

In almost all discussions on drug addiction, alcoholism, and schizophrenia, it is claimed that there is no definite constitutional type that falls prey to these afflictions. Almost universally the statement is made that all of these individuals are emotionally immature. It has long been our goal to persuade every physician whether he is oriented toward psychiatry, genetics, or physiology to recognize that one type of endocrine individual *is* involved in the majority of these cases—the hypoadrenocortic.[16]

Tintera published several epochal medical papers. Over and over, he emphasized that improvement, alleviation, palliation, or cure was "dependent upon the restoration of the normal function of the total organism." His first prescribed item of treatment was diet. Over and over again he said: "the importance of diet cannot be over-emphasized." He laid out a sweeping permanent injunction against sugar in all forms and guises.

While Egas Moniz of Portugal was receiving a Nobel prize for devising the lobotomy operation for the treatment of schizophrenia, Tintera's reward was to be harassment and hounding by the pundits of organized medicine. While Tintera's sweeping implication of sugar as a cause of what was called schizophrenia could be confined to medical journals, he was let alone, ignored. He could be tolerated—if he stayed in his assigned territory, endocrinology. Even when he suggested that alcoholism was related to adrenals that had been whipped by sugar abuse, they let him alone; because the medicos had decided there was nothing in alcoholism for them except aggravation—they were satisfied to abandon it to Alcoholics Anonymous. However, when Tintera dared to suggest in a magazine of general circulation that "it is ridiculous to talk of kinds of allergies when there is only one kind, which is adrenal glands impaired . . . by sugar," he could no longer be ignored.

The allergists had a great racket going for themselves. Allergic souls had been entertaining each other for years with tall tales of exotic allergies—everything from horsefeathers to lobster tails. Along comes someone who says none of this matters, take them off sugar, and keep them off it.

Perhaps Tintera's untimely death in 1969 at the age of fifty-seven made it easier for the medical profession to accept discoveries that had once seemed as far-out as the simple Oriental medical thesis of genetics and diet, Yin and Yang. Today, doctors all over the world are repeating what Tintera announced years ago: Nobody but nobody should ever be allowed to begin what is called psychiatric treatment anyplace, anywhere unless and until they have had a glucose tolerance test to discover if they can handle sugar.

So-called preventive medicine goes further and suggests that since we only think we can handle sugar because we initially have strong adrenals, why wait until they give us signs and signals that they're worn out? Take the load off now by eliminating sugar in all forms and guises, starting with that soda pop you have in your hand.

The mind truly boggles when one glances over what passes for medical history. Through the centuries, troubled souls have been barbecued for bewitchment, exorcised for possession, locked up for insanity, tortured for masturbatory madness, psychiatrized for psychoses, lobotomized for schizophrenia.

How many patients would have listened if the local healer had told them that the only thing ailing them was sugar blues?

Blame It On the Bees

By 1662, sugar consumption in England had zoomed from zero to some 16 million pounds a year, this in little over two centuries. Then, in 1665, London was swept by a plague. More than 30,000 people died that September. Since only one pest house, or hospital, existed for the entire city, sick people were locked up in their homes, under guard, behind doors painted with huge red crosses. Others fled the city; everything ground to a halt. While swarms of quacks sold worthless potions and pills, learned physicians used knives and burning caustic to lance the underarms and groin swellings. When their surgery did more harm than good, and the doctors themselves became infected, they stopped that treatment. In a year, the epidemic ran its course. The plague was named after its most obvious symptom, the swelling (or buboes), and became known as the bubonic plague. The swelling plague. The plague of boils.

People who lived in the country virtually without sugar seemed to escape the plague. Had anyone called it the city sugar plague, they might have been denounced as menaces to commerce and crown and strung to a gibbet.

Shortly after the plague, Thomas Willis (anatomist and physician, one of the first members of the Royal Society, and an honorary fellow of the Royal College of Physicians) took a house in London's St. Martin's Lane, where he began a medical practice which was to mark him as one of the finest physicians of his time. His first anatomical writings in 1664 (he was known for the elegance and purity of his Latin style) described part of the brain as the circle of Willis—as it is still known today in anatomy. He also wrote, in English, *A Plain and Easy Method for Preserving Those that are Well from the Infection of the Plague, and for Curing such as are Infected.*

Willis was the first to describe in writing—if not the first to discover—a new and extraordinary sweetness in the urine of his rich and famous patients. In a second medical treatise, *Pharmaceutice Rationalis* (in Latin, published in 1674), he described this symptom as *diabetes mellitus.*

The Greek *diabetes* simply described inordinate passage of urine. In Latin, the same symptom would be described as *polyuria.* The Latin *mellitus,* which Willis combined with the Greek *diabetes,* means honey-sweet. *Mel* is Latin for honey, *itis,* for inflammation.

We now have the discovery, in London after the plague, of a new symptom: The passage of inordinate amounts of extraordinarily sweet-smelling urine.

After two hundred years of sugar eating, especially by the rich and famous patients who could afford Dr. Willis, why not call the new disease *polyuria saccharitis,* Latin for sugar inflammation? Well, plain speaking was not exactly the vogue in medical circles at that time. The British had just beheaded one king and restored his son to the throne. Willis was an ardent Royalist who fought against the roundheads; he eventually became private physician to King Charles II. The king, like all royal personages since Good Queen Bess, was up to his neck in the lucrative sugar trade.

What would you do if you had the king for a patient,

as well as numerous other high-titled personages who made money hand over fist in the sugar trade? Since one does not want to offend one's clientele unnecessarily—or risk the loss of your trade or your head—by suggesting that the sugar racket might be the cause of a new malady, you name the problem in Greek. Even better, one blames it on the bees. Honey has been around since the beginning of time and nobody has ever figured out a way of making a fortune from bee-keeping. Blame it on the bees and use hermetic Latin words for honey inflammation, and you can boost your medical reputation, as well as ensure your place in medical history without any risk.

Anyway, Willis made his enduring contribution to the science of nosology—the branch of medical science that deals with the classification of diseases—and rates a footnote in what passes for medical history. He played it safe. Galileo had run afoul of the Inquisition the year before. Men of science were playing it safe, especially those with royal connections. Scientific kowtowing to industry is very much with us still. After an entire Japanese village was decimated by eating fish poisoned with mercury-laden industrial waste, the myriad resultant symptoms were christened Minamata disease—the name of the village, not the mercury.

Willis intuitively spotted the connection between sugar and scurvy centuries before the discovery of vitamin C. When sugar cane or sugar beet is refined, all the vitamins including vitamin C are lost, discarded. Natural sugar, such as that in raw fruits and vegetables, supplies the body with vitamin C. In the seventeenth and eighteenth centuries, the difference between a classic French dessert, raw fruit, and a British dessert of the same time, sugared pudding, added up to scurvy.

(In relation to consumption, now called tuberculosis and blamed on a bacillus, evidence suggests that a sugar-rich diet may create the necessary conditions in our bodies for the bacteria. Three hundred years ago, in the 1700s, deaths from tuberculosis—especially in Britain—increased dramatically. The highest incidence occurred among workers in sugar factories and refineries, according to Naboru Muramoto. In 1910, when Japan acquired a source of cheap and abundant sugar in Formosa, the incidence of tuberculosis rose dramatically.)

James Hurt, Doctor in Physicke, wrote "The *Family Companion for Health* or *Plain, Easy,* and *Certain Rules* which being *Punctually Observed* and *Followed* will infallibly keep *Families* from *Disease* and *Procure* them a Long *Life*," which was published in 1633 as "Klinike or the Diet of Disease." Dr. Hurt was not a member of the Royal Society, the AMA of his time. He was a natural healer who believed that the doctor should be a teacher who concerned himself with diet and health rather than the kind of fame attainable from affixing one's name to a new disease. He wrote in English, for the common folk, rather than in Latin for the members of the Royal Society. His seventeenth-century ideas about sugar are so old-fashioned that they are right on the button:

Sugar in itself be opening and cleansing, yet being much used produceth dangerous effect in the body: as namely, immoderate use thereof, as also of sweet confections, and Sugar-plummes, heateth the blood, ingendreth obstructions, cachexias, consumptions, rotteth the teeth, making them look blacke; and withal causeth many times a loathsome stinking breath. And therefore let young people especially beware how they meddle too much with it.[1]

Cachexias—a medical term that has gone out of style— is derived from the Greek, *kakos,* for bad, and *hexis,* for condition, which originally meant a state of ill health produced by malnutrition. Medical dictionaries today note that cachexias may occur in chronic diseases such as advanced malignancies, advanced pulmonary tuberculosis, and so forth. It has taken three hundred tortuous years for medical science to rediscover the obvious and proclaim that the myriad symptoms of multiple diseases with multisyllable names are caused by sugar.

It is mind boggling today to read through medical histories and other tomes and find again and again that the basic cause of diabetes mellitus is still unknown, that it is chronic and incurable, or that it is due to the failure of the pancreas to secrete an adequate amount of insulin. It's still Greek to the best of them. Language and history are tortured and twisted in order to prove that diabetes has been around for thousands of years.

When the Ebers papyrus—"one of the most venerable of medical documents" was discovered in 1872 at Luxor, Egypt, we are told that a number of prescriptions were provided for "medicines to drive away the passing of too much urine."[2] Although this is only one symptom of diabetes, medical historians leap to the conclusion that what they call diabetes has been around for well over three thousand years. That seems very conveniently to acquit the man-refined sugar of today. Or does it? The Egyptians did not have refined sucrose. However, they did have plenty of honey, as well as the natural sugar from the date palm. Candy was made by sweetening dough with honey and dates. The mixture was cut into triangles and was akin to the baklava eaten today. Gluttons in the upper classes who could afford it might overdo it on date sugar and honey. Date sugar and honey are complete foods; one can eat just so much of them without getting sick. For thousands of years, nobody outside the tropical belt had access to date sugar.

"I find it hard to explain why Hippocrates never described a case of diabetes," noted Dr. G. D. Campbell, the South African expert on the disease. "Such a careful clinical observer could hardly have failed to recognize its florid manifestations, either alone or complicating one of the many cases that he meticulously described. Certainly it must have been an uncommon disorder, probably of the order of frequency or sporadicity seen only today in peasant communities."[3] Modern medical history leans heavily on the Greeks when supporting a prejudice. When they don't, they can be skipped over.

"During the nineteenth century," medical history tells us, "the incidence of diabetes seemed to increase over that of ancient times." Figures on the incidence of diabetes in ancient times do not exist. Figures relating the consumption of sugar in early America to the number of deaths from diabetes have not been compiled. However, Danish authorities do have such statistics, but the medical histories in the U.S. rarely mention them or make any connection between sugar and diabetes.

In 1880, the average Danish citizen consumed over 29 pounds of refined sugar annually; at that time, the recorded death rate from diabetes was 1.8 per 100,000. In 1911, consumption had more than doubled: some 82 pounds of sugar per Dane annually; the recorded death rate from diabetes was 8 per 100,000. In 1934, Danish consumption of refined sugar was approximately 113 pounds per person annually; the recorded death rate from diabetes was 18.9 per 100,000.

Before World War II, Denmark had a higher consumption of sugar than any other European country. (The word Danish also means a pastry sugarbomb.) In Denmark, every fifth person suffers from cancer. In half a century, the annual Swedish consumption of refined sugar increased from 12 pounds per head in 1880 to over 120 pounds per head in 1929. Every sixth person suffers from cancer.[4] In the Scandinavian countries, statistics date from the days when sugar consumption was relatively low. Nothing comparable exists in the U.S. While the rest of the world lags behind the Scandinavian countries in compiling and publishing such statistics, the point is inescapable: As sugar consumption escalates wildly, fatal diseases increase remorselessly.

The scenario for the saga of the progress of medical science is always onward and upward, one epochal discovery after another. In the fight against sugar disease, such discoveries were few and far between. Nothing turned up until a dispute between the Russian Oskar Minkowski and his associate J. Von Mering was settled in 1889 by removal of a dog's pancreas to see if the animal could live without it. The dog died: many more died in successive experiments. Before they did, they passed excessive urine which contained from 5 to 10 percent sugar.[5]

Now they were getting somewhere! The cause must lie in the pancreas.

In 1923, Canadian physician Frederick Banting received a Nobel prize for having discovered a way to extract the hormone insulin (which the average human pancreas excretes in adequate supply) and "proving that it could control the abnormal amounts of blood sugar that made diabetes mellitus a slow killer."[6]

In the intervening decades since the 1880s, patients with diabetes have endured the tortures of the damned. They have been alternately starved, glutted with fats, injected with baking soda, and taken off all cereals, because the latter were classified (incorrectly) as carbohydrates by the chemists. Toes, feet, and limbs were amputated. However, sadly enough, despite such efforts on the part of the medical profession, death eventually resulted.

The following summary of pre-insulin insight and therapy was published in the *Encyclopaedia Britannica* in 1911:

Diabetes mellitus is one of the diseases due to altered metabolism. It is markedly hereditary, much more prevalent in towns and especially modern city life than in more primitive rustic communities and most common among the Jews. The excessive use of sugar as a food is usually considered one of the causes of the disease, and obesity is supposed to favor its occurrence, but many observers consider that the obesity so often met with among diabetics is due to the same cause as the disease itself. No age is exempt, but it occurs most commonly in the fifth decade of life. It attacks males twice as frequently as females, the fair more frequently than dark people. . . . Diabetes is a very fatal form of disease, recovery being exceedingly rare . . . there are two distinct lines of treatment, that of diet and that of drugs; diet is of primary importance inasmuch as it has been proved beyond question that certain kinds of foods have a powerful influence in aggravating the disease, more particularly those consisting largely of saccharine and starchy matter . . . various treatment methods aim at the elimination as far as possible of these constituents from the diet . . . the best diet can only be worked out experimentally for each individual patient. . . . Numerous medicinal substances have been employed in diabetes, but few of them are worthy of mention as possessed of any efficacy. Opium is often found of great service, its administration being followed by marked amelioration in all of the symptoms. Morphia and codeia have a similar action. . . . Heroin hydrochloride has been tried in their place, but this seems to have more power over slight than over severe cases. . . .

The discovery of insulin was the kind of modern medical miracle which the diseasestablishment knew how to exploit. Production of insulin was and is a boon to the pharmaceutical industry. Patients with diabetes presented a captive market, a million people in the early 1900s. The surge of sugar addiction in the 1920s ensured that this profitable market would increase annually. Insulin injections were expensive but manageable palliatives, not quick or cheap cures in any sense. Millions of diabetics would become dependent on insulin for the rest of their lives. Insulin was something that could be packaged and sold over the counter in drugstores—together with the attendant hardware, such as needles. It captured the imagination of a vaccination-happy, drug-oriented society. So diabetics were kept alive by the injection of insulin extracted from the pancreatic glands of animals from abattoirs. Many people who might have died survived—if they could afford insulin—to breed diabetic-prone descendants of their own. The classification of varieties of diabetes multiplied. Diabetes mellitus—honey inflammation causing copious passage of urine—was superseded by modern, symptomatic terminology: hypoinsulinism (underproduction of insulin).

Then, in 1924, a year after the discoverer of insulin was awarded a Nobel prize, a professor of medicine discovered the complementary antagonist of hypoinsulinism. Inevitably, doctors and patients experimenting with insulin in its early years took too little or too much. An overdose produced symptoms of what came to be called insulin shock. Dr. Seale Harris of the University of Alabama began to notice symptoms of insulin shock in many people who were neither diabetic nor taking any insulin. These people were diagnosed as having low levels of glucose in their blood; diabetics have high levels of glucose.

Dr. Harris officially reported his discovery that year: Low levels of glucose in the blood were declared to be a symptom of hyperinsulinism: excessive insulin. Up to that time, patients with symptoms of hyperinsulinism had been treated for coronary thrombosis and other heart ailments, brain tumors, epilepsy, gall bladder disease, appendicitis, hysteria, asthma, allergies, ulcers, alcoholism, and a variety of mental disorders.[7]

A Nobel prize was not awarded, however, to Dr. Harris. His discovery was an embarrassment to the diseaseestablishment, not a boon. The remedy he suggested for hyperinsulinism or low blood glucose was not a glamorous new miracle drug that could be packaged and sold across the drug counter in a bottle or licensed to the pharmaceutical industry as a billion-dollar business.

Dr. Harris pointed out that the cure for low blood glucose or hyperinsulinism (also commonly and misleadingly called low blood sugar) was something so simple that nobody—not even the medical practitioners—could make any money out of it. The remedy was self-government of the body. The patient with low blood glucose must be prepared to give up refined sugar, candy, coffee, and soft drinks—these items had caused the troubles. Patients with hyperinsulinism could never be made dependent for a lifetime on anybody else. They had to fend for themselves. A doctor could merely teach them what not to do. Hyperinsulinism or low blood glucose therapy was a do-it-yourself proposition.

Predictably, the medical profession landed on Dr. Harris like a ton of bricks. When his findings were not attacked, they were ignored. His discoveries, if allowed to leak out, might make trouble for surgeons, psychoanalysts, and other medical specialists. To this day, hyperinsulinism or low blood glucose is a stepchild of the diseaseestablishment. It took the AMA twenty-five years to get around to awarding Harris a medal.

In 1929, Dr. Frederick Banting, the discoverer of insulin, tried to tell us that his discovery was merely a palliative, not a cure and that the way to prevent diabetes was to cut down on "dangerous" sugar bingeing.

"In the U.S. the incidence of diabetes has increased proportionately with the per capita consumption of sugar," he warned. "In the heating and recrystallization of the natural sugar cane, something is altered which leaves the refined product a dangerous foodstuff."[8]

Figures from England indicated that insulin may delay deaths from diabetes, that is all.[9]

Before the introduction of insulin in Britain, deaths from diabetes were:

110 per million	in 1920
119 per million	in 1922
112 per million	in 1925

After the introduction of insulin, deaths from diabetes were:

115 per million	in 1926
131 per million	in 1928
142 per million	in 1929
145 per million	in 1931

In the 1930s, brilliant researchers in the U.S. discovered that the Chinese and Japanese who take rice as their principal food had very little diabetes. They also noted that Jews and Italians were among those ethnic groups with a high incidence of diabetes. From this, ignoring the vastly different intake of refined sugar between East and West, they were able to conclude that, since Jews consume a great deal of animal fat and Italians are lavish users of olive oil, diabetics were apt to be those who use excessive amounts of fat.[10]

Other statistics in the U.S. showed that the outbreak of diabetes dropped sharply during World War I (when sugar was rationed). Figures also showed that the incidence of diabetes among young men in the armed forces (where soldiers were supplied with the sugar that civilians had to do without) rose steadily from World War I to World War II.

When a man's knowledge is not in order, said Herbert Spencer, the more of it he has, the greater will be his confusion. Western medicine's answer to the sugar disease was confusion compounded.

Man-refined sugar (sucrose) was introduced to Japan when the Christian missionaries arrived after the U.S. Civil War. At first, the Japanese used refined sugar in the way the Arabs and Persians had used it centuries before: as a medicine. Sugar was taxed as severely as imported patented medicines. By 1906, 45,000 acres of sugar cane were cultivated in Japan, compared with 7 million acres devoted to the cultivation of rice. Interestingly enough, in its war with Russia in 1905, the Japanese armed forces carried their own food in much the same way as the Viet Cong in the 1970s: Each man had enough dried rice to keep him going for three days. This was supplemented with salt fish, dried seaweed, and pickled umeboshi plums.

In the years following victory over the Russians, many Japanese gradually began to abandon ancient traditions in favor of Western ideas of medicine, nourishment, technology, and religion. The gradual introduction of sugar into the Japanese diet brought in its wake the beginning of Western diseases. A Japanese midwife, trained in the techniques of Western medicine as a nurse, fell ill and was abandoned as incurable by the Western doctors she had espoused. Three of her children died the same way. The fourth, Nyoiti Sakurazawa, rebelled at the notion of dying of tuberculosis and ulcers in his teens. He took up the study of ancient Oriental medicine which had been officially outlawed in Japan under the impact of modernization. Sakurazawa was attracted to the unorthodox career of a famous Japanese practitioner, Dr. Sagen Isiduka. Thousands of patients had been cured by Isiduka (through the traditional use of food) after they had been abandoned as incurable by the new medicine of the West.

Dr. Isiduka had discovered the biochemical validity of the ancient, unique principle of Yin/Yang when he uncovered the complementary antagonism between sodium (Yang) and potassium (Yin). Young Sakurazawa studied with Isiduka. When the latter died, Sakurazawa went beyond him; he studied ancient Indian and Chinese medicine, acupuncture, and the sacred books of these civilizations. After World War I, Sakurazawa journeyed to Paris to study at the Sorbonne and the Pasteur Institute. He opened a private acupuncture practice (then virtually unknown) in Paris in the 1920s to support himself. Later, he collaborated with the French physician de Morant—who had become interested in acupuncture during a stint with the French army in Indochina—on the first book on acupuncture in a Western European language (French). This feat rates Sakurazawa a footnote in the German and English translations of the *Yellow Emperor's Classic of Internal Medicine*, which is used as an historical text in medical schools in America.

Eventually, Sakurazawa published many books in Japanese and French on Oriental philosophy and preventive medicine. He translated Alexis Carrel's classic *Man the Unknown* and introduced it to Japan. From personal experiences in East and West, Sakurazawa concluded that Western medicine was many decades late in sounding warnings on the relation between sugar consumption and disease. "Western medicine will one day admit what has been known in the Orient for years," he wrote in *You Are All Sanpaku*. "Sugar is the greatest evil that modern industrial civilization has visited upon the countries of the Far East and Africa."

Sakurazawa prescribed self-government of the body for the healing and prevention of all symptoms, not hyperinsulinism alone, as Dr. Seale Harris had stressed. Naturally, here and abroad, the diseasestablishment laughed and laughed. Where he was not ignored, he was ridiculed. His analysis of sugar disease is simplicity itself:

When we eat, the process of digestion converts food into glucose (a simple sugar which is yin). This glucose is carried in the blood to the pancreas, where the increased blood glucose level stimulates the production of insulin (yang). The insulin is carried in the blood to the liver, where excess glucose is converted to glycogen (a complex sugar which is yang), which is then stored in the liver.

A decrease in blood glucose, on the other hand, stimulates secretion of the cortical hormones in the adrenal gland and the hormones of the pituitary gland (these hormones—ACTH—are yin) which raise the blood glucose level by converting some of the stored glycogen in the liver to glucose. In a healthy body, the blood glucose level is maintained by the interplay of insulin (yang), cortical hormones, and ACTH (yin).

In a poorly functioning organism, however, the swings in the blood glucose level are much greater. If the insulin supplied by the pancreas is excessive, too much glucose will be converted to glycogen; the blood glucose level will fall and remain low. This condition is called hyperinsulinism, or hypoglycemia, the first stage of the sugar blues. This overstimulation of the pancreas is caused by the ingestion of excessive quantities of simple sugars such as refined sucrose, honey, fruits, and indirectly by drugs (including marijuana).

On the other hand, if the insulin supply is inadequate, the liver cannot effectively convert excess glucose to glycogen. This is diabetes. As the pancreas tires of producing insulin to neutralize highly yin foods such as simple sugars, honey, fruits, or drugs, or eventually becomes completely exhausted from the effort, excess sugar begins building up in the blood. The blood glucose level rises and remains high. Excess stimulation by excess sugar, honey, and fruits will lead to hyperinsulinism or hypoglycemia or low blood glucose and then to diabetes or high blood glucose, the next stage of sugar blues.

High blood glucose, what Dr. Thomas Willis called diabetes in 1674, was discovered first because only a urine sample and a sense of smell were needed to detect it. The medical technology for detecting low levels of glucose in the blood, the first stage of sugar blues, was not available until the turn of the twentieth century.

Since the disease is yin, says Sakurazawa, treatment must be yang—a well-balanced diet, neither too yin nor too yang. Sakurazawa suggested whole, unpolished rice, Japanese azuki beans, and Hokkaido pumpkin (any pumpkin or squash is suitable). Sakurazawa had introduced the cultivation of whole natural carbohydrates like rice, Hokkaido pumpkin, and azuki beans in Belgium and France where they had never been grown before, just as the soya bean (the cow of the Orient) had been first introduced in America as a source of cheap vegetable protein in the 1920s. The soya bean caught on like wildfire in the U.S. because it could be fed to cattle, which could in turn be eaten. The pumpkin, the azuki bean, the whole rice, and the other traditional soya bean products like miso, tofu, and tamari didn't catch on as readily. That too will change, Sakurazawa predicted. It has changed. As the food and energy crises of the 1970s mount, it will change even more.

Naturally, the pundits of Western medicine denounced Sakurazawa as a charlatan and a quack. The fact that he practiced something as far out as acupuncture without a Harvard degree—and before the U.S. rapprochement with Red China—was enough to discredit him totally in some quarters. However, his practice of prescribing what Western medicine had mistakenly labeled a high carbohydrate diet for people with high blood glucose or diabetes was, according to some, demonstrably insane. Everybody knew that carbohydrates, which tend to break down into simple sugars during digestion, tend to raise blood glucose levels to dangerous highs.

Sakurazawa was a threat to the sugar business and its stepchild, the insulin industry. He took that as a tribute. He noted in the 1960s:

No Western doctor can cure diabetes, even thirty years after the discovery of insulin. Physicians have continued to recommend insulin, condemning diabetics to walk with an insulin crutch for life. Yet on the twenty-fifth anniversary of the discovery of insulin, the inefficiency of insulin as a treatment or cure for diabetes was publicly admitted. In the meantime, millions of diabetics have paid millions of dollars for this ineffective remedy, not only in the U.S. but all over the world. And the diabetics are increasing every day. Once they begin taking insulin, they can expect to feed the pockets of the doctors and pharmaceutical corporations as long as they live.

Sakurazawa stuck to his guns, insisting that any nutritional regime for diabetics which excluded what the West called carbohydrates was dangerous. He pleaded with Western nutritionists to make the distinction in the *quality* of food which they mechanically labeled carbohydrates: He begged them to make the distinction between whole, unrefined grains as a source of carbohydrates and not lump them indiscriminately with potatoes, white bread, processed grains, and refined table sugar, which are the average sources of carbohydrates in the typical American diet.

One measure of the confusion in the U.S. medical profession over the symptoms of sugar diseases has been the number of suffering doctors—and their wives—who couldn't even help themselves, let alone their patients. The story of Dr. Stephen Gyland from Tampa, Florida, is classic.[11] Dr. Gyland fell ill with a myriad of mental and physical symptoms. His concentration and memory were failing; he was weak, dizzy with rapid, unprovoked beating of the heart; and he suffered from unprovoked anxieties and tremors. Dr. Gyland went to one of the most eminent specialists he knew, only to be told he was neurotic and ought to retire for the good of the profession. He sought another opinion and then another. Before he was through, he had consulted fourteen physicians and three of the most famous diagnostic clinics in America.

Physicians feel they have accomplished a great deal for a patient when they give his disease a name, Immanuel Kant said. Dr. Gyland had more than one name for his disease, he had a multiple choice: neurosis, brain tumor, diabetes, cerebral arteriosclerosis (hardening of the arteries of the brain). It cost him a fortune to end up where he started: sick, unable to work, and baffled by the conflicting jargon. He was near the end of his rope when he happened upon Dr. Harris's original medical paper published in the *Journal of the American Medical Association* in 1924.

Gyland took the five-hour glucose tolerance test (GTT) and learned he had low blood glucose . . . hypoglycemia . . . sugar blues. Following Dr. Harris's prescription, he went on a simple diet that eliminated all refined sugar and white flour. Gyland's symptoms, anxieties, tremors, dizziness, neuroses, and cerebral arteriosclerosis faded. After he recovered, he recalled that one diagnostician had diagnosed the malady correctly but prescribed the wrong remedy! The trouble was compounded by labeling his ailment "low blood sugar" and recommending candy bars to increase it. Naturally, this action could only add fuel to the flame and worsen Gyland's symptoms.

If you've ever gone through this kind of medical rigmarole, as I and millions of others have, one ends up a little bitter, with a sense of mission. Dr. Gyland was properly bitter and blasted off with a letter to the AMA *Journal* (Vol. 152, July 18, 1953), reproaching his colleagues for neglecting and overlooking the pioneering work of Dr. Seale Harris. He vowed to use his hard earned lesson to help diagnose and treat the legions of people suffering from sugar blues, including many who were being told—as he had been—that refined sugar was the cure for their miseries when it was actually the cause.

Dr. Gyland went on to prove it takes one to tell one. More than six hundred patients were treated by him for the same symptoms he had discovered in his own body. He wrote an exhaustive study of his patients, detailing how he diagnosed them, the symptoms presented, and how they responded to his treatment, which always began with the complete restriction of refined carbohydrates— primarily sugar and white flour. A gadfly to the AMA, he was finally permitted to read his paper before one of the medical societies. He waited anxiously for it to appear in one of the AMA journals. Nothing happened. That's how anxious the AMA was to alert its members to the importance of glucose tolerance tests in routine physical examinations. (Three such tests, each of a different length of time, do exist.) The report of Dr. Gyland's important work was finally published (in Portuguese) in a Brazilian medical journal.

While Dr. Gyland was trekking from one specialist to another depressed and dizzy with the sugar blues, a science writer trained at Harvard and MIT was making the same discouraging pilgrimage. He wandered through countless consultation rooms, survived misdiagnoses and mistreatment for more than ten years before he found a doctor who spotted the trouble, confirmed it with a GTT test, and took him off sugar. Writer A. W. Pezet saw his symptoms fade. He asked some hard questions of his physician, Dr. E. M. Abrahamson. "Why do so many doctors know little or nothing about a constellation of symptoms which afflicts millions of people? If the diagnosis is so simple, and the removal of the cause of the symptoms is simpler still, what's happened to medical education?"

Pezet's sense of mission deepened when he discovered that his wife suffered from the same symptoms he had had and quitting sugar gave her the same relief. The result was the Abrahamson-Pezet collaboration, a landmark volume: *Body, Mind, and Sugar*, first published in 1951. Its sale of over 200,000 copies in hardcover was evidence of the intense public interest in the subject. The book, which is dedicated to Dr. Seale Harris, didn't have to await publication in medical journals, as had the material by Harris and Gyland. It went over the heads of the AMA hierarchy direct to the long-suffering, misdiagnosed public. Patients began asking their doctors for GTT tests, and the word hypoglycemia passed into common currency. Unfortunately, use of the terms like low blood sugar and "sugar starved" on the paperback edition, published later, created some confusion. Many people were led to believe misinformed doctors who said that the answer to "sugar starvation" was to eat candy bars between meals.

In 1969, nutritionist Carlton Fredericks collaborated with Dr. Herman Goodman on the invaluable popular book, *Low Blood Sugar and You*.

Despite such medical and general books and articles, the AMA continues to assure America that they know best about what's not supposed to be ailing us. The *Journal of the American Medical Association* pronounced in 1973:

Recent publicity in the popular press has led the public to believe that the occurrence of hypoglycemia is widespread in this country and that many of the symptoms that affect the American population are not recognized as being caused by this condition. These claims are not supported by medical evidence. . . .

Hypoglycemia means a low level of blood sugar. When it

occurs, it is often attended by symptoms of sweating, shaki-
ness, trembling, anxiety, fast heart action, headache, hunger
sensations, brief feelings of weakness, and, occasionally,
seizures and coma. However, *the majority of people with
these kinds of symptoms do not have hypoglycemia.*
(Emphasis added.)

How in the name of Allah can they claim to know?

What are they telling us? Only a *minority*, maybe 49.2
percent, of the U.S. population has hypoglycemia?

Among the people who wondered about that point
was Marilyn Hamilton Light, Executive Director of the
Adrenal Metabolic Research Society of the Hypoglycemia
Foundation. (She had suffered through the same night-
mare as Dr. Gyland.) According to foundation files,
their *average* undiagnosed or misdiagnosed victim of the
sugar blues had visited *twenty physicians and four psychiatrists* before discovering (by word of mouth, pure chance,
or reading) the possibility of their having hypoglycemia—
later confirmed by a GTT test.

Marilyn Light wrote the Department of Health, Education and Welfare and asked for their figures on
the prevalence of hypoglycemia in the U.S.[12] Here's the
answer she received: ". . . *unpublished* data from the
Health Interview show that an estimated 66,000 cases
were reported in household interviews of the civilian,
noninstitutional population during fiscal year 1966-67.
(Emphasis added.)

"Out of 134,000 people interviewed, 66,000 cases of
hypoglycemia were reported. This represents 49.2 percent of those interviewed."

Not a majority, only 49.2 percent!

Further inquiry to the Agency established the following points:

1. The same interview sample is used by the U.S.
government to establish data and trends on all sorts of
health problems.

2. People interviewed were not prompted in any way.
Neither the word hypoglycemia nor the term low blood
sugar appeared on the checklist of chronic conditions
people were asked about.

3. Interviewers had to depend on a catch-all question—"Do you have any other condition?" to get their answers.

4. The respondents had to be aware of their condition, they had to know what to call it, and they had to be willing to volunteer it to the interviewer before they were counted.

5. Despite the fact that the 49.2 figure is already ten years old, and should represent a major alert on the widespread prevalence of the sugar blues (comparative epidemic basis), the HEW never subsequently added hypoglycemia to their survey checklist and "has no plans in the near future to include it."

Are you ready for that?

Can you imagine the HEW and the AMA calling off a drive against cancer or heart disease because it does not yet afflict a *majority* of the population, only a paltry 49.2 percent?

The difference between the expensive diseases like cancer and the cheap ones like sugar blues is crucial. Present-day orthodox treatment for cancer is fiendishly expensive. Your financial ruin is your doctor's yacht. The treatment for sugar blues or hypoglycemia is a do-it-yourself proposition. Kick man-refined sugar and say goodbye to doctor and hospital bills. Mink coats for the wives and sunshine seminars in Bermuda can hardly be squeezed from that.

By the 1970s, the slogan was preventive medicine. What the diseasestablishment means by preventive medicine, however, is regular and costly visits to an MD or clinic for expensive tests and, maybe, a free sermon on smoking or cholesterol if Doc can hide his paunch under his white coat and abstain from tobacco long enough to deliver it. Plenty of money can be made from this kind of preventive medicine, from people terrified of cancer and heart disease. Medicine has only one valid answer for preventing the sugar blues, or hypoglycemia, or prediabetes: preventive nutrition. Stop eating sugar. Stop—before you ruin your adrenals—*before* you end up with symptoms of the sugar blues, hypoglycemia, prediabetic condition, or whatever you want to call it.

How much money can anybody charge you for simple advice like that?

The 1967 HEW data on sugar blues goes unpublished. Because it goes unpublished, the AMA can claim not to know about it. So in 1973, they can notify America with a straight face that claims of hypoglycemia being widespread in this country "are not supported by *medical* evidence." After all, the evidence is only HEW statistical epidemiological evidence. The former patients—misdiagnosed and mistreated—reported the evidence, not the doctors. Therefore, it is not *medical* evidence. That, surely, is quite clear.

Medical evidence as such does not exist because those 66,000 people in the statistical survey did not have medical records to back up their opinions. They didn't have medical records because most doctors and hospitals still refuse to give the patients copies of their diagnoses and test results.

The AMA's credibility is based on our ignorance.

In case the difference between evidence and medical evidence or the difference between facts and scientific facts eludes you, let me explain. If I have a headache or a fever, that's not a fact except to me. If I tell a doctor about it, that's what doctors call anecdotal evidence or testimonial. If the doctor takes my temperature and writes it down, the headache becomes medical evidence. If another doctor copies it, it becomes a scientific fact. Should I need proof that my fever was 101 last Tuesday and ask my doctor for my chart, it will not be given to me. That plain garden variety fact has now become a scientific fact. It's only available to another doctor. If I complain the doctor won't give me the scientific facts about my past condition, that's anecdotal evidence again. This is where I came in.

After practically making a religion of the low carbohydrate diet for diabetics for thirty years, modern medicine was undone by another discovery. Early in 1971, a team of scientists headed by Dr. Edwin L. Bireman reported in the *New England Journal of Medicine* that high carbohydrate diets actually *lower* blood glucose levels in mild diabetics and normal humans. "Diets high in carbohydrates do not raise the blood sugar," said Dr. Bireman. "That's the misconception that most physicians have had during the last thirty years."

The American Diabetes Association then urged the U.S. medical profession to make a complete turnabout and recommend that sufferers from diabetes be put on diets with carbohydrate levels equal to or surpassing those in the diet of healthy people. The ADA action reflected the fact that, since the widespread use of insulin and other symptomatic treatment, many diabetics are eventually afflicted with hardening of the arteries, arteriosclerosis, heart attacks, and strokes. Such conditions are thought to arise from the disproportionately high consumption of fats physicians recommend for diabetics.

Fifty years after the epochal discovery of insulin, the number of diabetics has increased relentlessly. From World War I to Viet Nam, physical examinations of eighteen-year-old draftees tell a story of steadily increasing rejections for diabetes. Figures for 1970s place the current rejection rate up to 12 percent. Diabetes is the leading cause of blindness, as well as a major contributor to disability and death from heart and kidney diseases. Estimates of the number of diabetics in America range from 4 to 12 million. The number of prediabetics, people suffering from hypoglycemia, hyperinsulinism, or low blood glucose—the complementary antagonist and sometimes precursor of diabetes—is estimated to be even higher.

Appeals for self-regulation to control sugar diseases are drowned out by the clamor for more millions of federal funds to find a potion, a pill, a shot, perhaps a magical Medicare atomic pancreas pacemaker—which can one day magically conquer disease.

We want to have our health and eat our sugarcake too.

From the Nipple
to the Needle

It's high noon on a hot July day in Manhattan. A man reels dizzily down the stairs to the subway, clutching the handrail, lunging for the candy vending machines. No candy. No Pepsi-Cola. Only gum. He's sweating. His speech is slurred. He looks like a sloppy drunk, bracing himself against a steel column until the BMT express pulls in. He lunges into the train, gripping the center pole with one hand. Sweat pours through his shirt. Clumsily he removes his jacket, one hand, then the other, clutching the pole. When his jacket slips to the floor he can't pick it up. The train screeches to a halt. He hangs onto the center rail, trying to keep from slumping to the floor. Two passengers grab him, a well-dressed matron and a burly laborer. Two seated passengers arise so he can sprawl on the seats. They loosen his tie.

Do you have heart trouble? the matron asks. Do you have nitroglycerin or something you should swallow? The desperately ill man sighs but cannot speak. The laborer smacks him twice in the face, once on each side.

The shock forces his eye open. In thick-tongued fashion, he stammers he is a diabetic about to pass out unless someone feeds him sweets. The word spreads through the car. Two kids open their picnic lunches, extracting cans of orange soda pop. The motorman radios for an ambulance. A fat woman across the aisle gives him a gooey cupcake. Gradually, he recovers his metabolic balance and gets off the train at Times Square. He is a top political reporter from *The New York Times,* a diabetic for 23 years, who forgot his regular packet of "melt in your mouth, not in your hand" candies. He suffered from insulin shock. Too much insulin. Hypoglycemic reaction. Low level of glucose in the blood. Sugar blues.

A few months later on March 6, 1974, he died of "diabetic complications." The March 25 issue of *New York Magazine* published his story of the subway incident posthumously. "Contrary to all the stories about unfeeling New Yorkers," said the magazine, "[he] was well treated by the people around him. This episode is an example of one more urban myth exploded."

One myth down and another to go. And on and on.

When a junkie dies, known or unknown, is it ever from "metabolic complications?" Of course not. Heroin is a killer. Junkies die of junk. Even when a drunk dies, he dies of his sins. But when a person dies of sugar blues, the mourners often serve sugar at the wake. Sugar-poisoning is a word wedding that rarely appears in print.

The same double standard is evident in the world of art and entertainment. Junkies die like flies every hour of every day on television. Many of these consoling sagas are brought to you by those wonderful people who push sugar and other products laced with sugar at every commercial break.

Camille suffers from TB. Audiences weep when the heroine of "Love Story" drifts into leukemia. Psychos clutter our stages and screens. Heart attacks abound when plots need unthickening. The snake pits, the prisons, and the psychiatric couches have been heard from. Autobiographical confessions and television dramas galore flow from alcoholics and opium eaters. But where are the Lost Weekends of the sugar addicts?

In modern literature, the significant thing may be what's missing. Have you ever read a book or seen a play, movie, or TV program which took into account the sugar plague of the twentieth century? Who has spoken to us from the depths of sugar blues and been publicly heard or produced?

Two exceptions prove the rule. The first occurred on Merv Griffin's syndicated talk show in late 1973. Griffin disclosed his own belated discovery that he was a victim of low blood glucose or hypoglycemia. He had wrestled with an overweight problem and gone through alcoholic binges. His exemplary reaction to the discovery that he had hypoglycemia was to devote several of his shows to enlightened panel discussions on the problems of refined sugar in our diets—how it poisons people and how simple it is to follow a curative diet. The second exception can be found in *The Philosophy of Andy Warhol* (which was published in 1975). Warhol frankly admits that all he ever really wants is sugar. "You can't take a princess to dinner and order a cookie for starters, no matter how much you crave one. People expect you to eat protein and you do so they won't talk." He goes on to explain that "after being alive, the next hardest work is having sex . . I have found that it's too much work." When he was a child, his mother used to give him a Hershey bar "every time I finished a page in my coloring book."

When insulin was new, Sidney Kingsley wrote the Broadway hit *Men In White;* it became a Clark Gable movie. In this story, two doctors have conflict at the bedside of a young girl who is desperately ill. The young doctor diagnoses (correctly) that the patient is in insulin shock (needing glucose), while the senior doctor insists that it is a diabetic coma (needing insulin).

Fortunately, the doctor making the right diagnosis prevails: The child recovers and smiles up at him. Cut.

That stage portrayal of the medical profession's division and confusion was forty years ago. Today, there are millions of autobiographies of personal catastrophes caused by sugar. The patients are fumbling and stumbling around us every day and this drama happens in real life not in books and magazines. Backstage at the theater, not out in front. On the movie and TV sets, never on the screen.

Bottle babies often end up loving the bottle and hating their Mamas, according to Elijah Muhammed, the Black Muslim prophet. He could have been talking about George who's tall, white, and handsome. He was a bottle baby. He got his first sugar through a rubber nipple. After his teeth appeared, he had sugar with his Cheerios and orange juice, and ketchup with his morning eggs. Probably his parents, and millions like them, didn't even realize ketchup contained sugar. (Even in the 1970s, few consumers realize that ingredients are listed on labels in order of decreasing predominance by weight. Different names for man-refined sugar also confuse the issue— ketchup that is labeled tomatoes, sugar, dextrose, vinegar, salt, onions, and spices has two varieties of man-refined sugar—dextrose is the hidden sugar.) Meat and potatoes were served for dinner every night with frozen peas; then came home-made pie, heavy with sugar, or canned peaches in a sugared syrup. When he was a good boy, he was rewarded with a Hershey bar or a bottle of 7-Up and chocolate fudge before bed. His teeth had cavities the first time anybody looked. He had strep throats continually, so his tonsils were yanked out when he was five. He went through all the typical childhood diseases like measles and mumps, plus exotic attacks of allergies that kept him in bed with hot compresses for half the summer of '54.

Grandmother's house (she was Polish) always had an aroma of sauerkraut and hamhocks, carbolic laundry soap, lilacs, and bay rum. Grandma talked a lot about her special diet, but she seemed to have her hand in the chocolate donuts as often as anyone else. George remembers Grandma hiking up the skirt of her flowered frock to stick a needle in her thigh. He didn't think too much about it. Maybe all old women of fifty-two have this thing they call diabetes. When the little boy found a hypodermic needle in the alley one day, he brought it in to Grandma so she'd have a spare. When George was thirteen and Grandma was fifty-nine, she died. She couldn't handle sugar and died trying. None of the family seemed to learn anything from her suffering. When George went to church later with his aunt, they sat in the choir loft and ate rock candy. His mother had inherited Grandma's compulsion for sweets. He could always count on her for candy—so long as he was a "good" boy.

Three years after Grandma died, the family had another diabetic—little George. He had just won his high school varsity letter in tennis. On that first day out in his deep blue sweater, tradition entitled any senior letterman to grab him and twist the orange letter on his chest. Social status in high school was determined by this ritual. He got into a few fights. By lunchtime, he was so knotted up inside that he could hardly eat his hamburger and Boston cream pie. After class, he ran for the water fountain to drink his fill. Within an hour he was in the lavatory letting go.

His weight dropped from 165 to 140 pounds in a very short period of time. His mother knew what it meant. She and Dad drove him to the doctor. Two minutes after George had supplied the urine sample, they had the news: he could lead a "normal" life by shooting insulin in his leg every day like Grandma. Nervous, breathing heavy, swooning from the alcohol fumes, he wondered: How long? Sweet, sickening Jesus, how long? From sweet sixteen until when? That night, the condemned boy's mother let him have a last Hershey almond bar. "Why couldn't it have happened to me?" she sobbed.

George spent a week in the hospital learning to shoot up, practicing first on an orange before he began sticking himself in the leg. He was taught to watch his diet. No more sugar. Everything else was rationed. A whopping 4,000 calories a day to be balanced off with 45 units of Eli Lilly NPH U-80 insulin. Calories were emphasized. Every food had a number, even beer. Quality didn't count. Nobody mentioned it. Only calories. Natural whole carbohydrates like stone ground, whole grain bread counted the same as spongy, supermarket foam made of refined flour and sugar. He was supposed to avoid sugar but nobody told his mother how to avoid the sugar added to supermarket food. Nobody told Mom how to get around that one. "Maybe the Doctor's wife did the shopping," says George. "There was no sign he'd ever looked at a label or knew what was going on. But neither did I."

George was equipped with certain baggage: Syringes, needles, alcohol, pads, Clinistix, insulin, and sugar cubes. Any junkie traveled lighter than that. Each time he urinated, he waved the Clinistix through the stream. If it turned red, he had too much glucose in his blood. Quick, more insulin. The Clinistix was no help at all when he had *too little* glucose in his blood. That meant he had taken too much insulin, overworked, or missed a meal; he could go into shock. An overdose of insulin can be as dangerous as an overdose of heroin. George depended on his glucose-starved brain to send him that message. Quick, the sugar cubes. Teeter-totter all the way. The Medicalert pendant around his neck had a telephone number in case he was discovered passed out. The card in his wallet read: *I am a diabetic. I am not intoxicated. If I am unconscious or my behavior is peculiar, please refer to emergency instructions on reverse side of this card.* The flip side said: *Emergency treatment: If unable to swallow, give sugar in some form—orange juice, Coca-Cola or other sweet beverages, candy, syrup, etc.— and call a doctor.*

He would prepare for a basketball game by taking less insulin. Sometimes, after exertion, he would feel his nose become wet and cold, his arms and legs tingle, the back of his brain go empty and light. That meant the onset of insulin shock. More sugar cubes and he'd be OK.

When working in a supermarket one day, his plastic box of sugar cubes tumbled out on the floor. As he picked them up an old man passed by and said: "Diabetic, huh?" It takes one to tell one. The secret brotherhood. George felt like a derelict soul imprisoned in the body of a youth.

One day after a game, his buddies stopped off to have ice cream—a no-no for him. He knew he needed something else to eat but didn't want to call attention to his affliction, so he braved it out. The rest of the afternoon was a blank. He remembers the car stopping in front of his house and someone handing him his basketball. He took one step into the yard and woke up in the hospital with glucose pouring into his arm from a tube. At the age of 16, he had started with 45 units of insulin daily. By the time he graduated from high school, this was up to 55.

In his second year of college, marijuana or grass was a big deal. Grass and Viet Nam. If you got busted for one, you missed out on the other. George was marked 4F as a diabetic. He missed the army anguish but checked out the grass. As a college junior in 1967, he took his first LSD trip. As a college senior, he had taken a dozen LSD trips and smoked grass every day; he maintained passing grades by writing mystical term papers. Richard Alpert visited the campus to lecture on hallucinogenic drugs and announced that grass lowers the body's glucose level while LSD raised it. This was a blinding revelation to George. His brain might not have acknowledged it but he knew in his veins it was true.

Whenever he got stoned on grass, gnawing hunger drove him to gorge on sweets, apples smeared with peanut butter, bread with saccharin jelly. LSD had the opposite effect. During an acid trip, he would urinate furiously and needed extra insulin when it was over. He prepared for new eventualities with more baggage. When the acid heads began to discover Eastern religions, George tagged along. A classmate found a Japanese book which claimed that diabetes could be controlled and prevented by eating natural whole carbohydrates such as brown rice, azuki beans, and pumpkin. This was totally incomprehensible to George. Doctors had convinced him that a carbohydrate was a carbohydrate was a carbohydrate. According to Western medical religion, rice was a carbohydrate and totally tabu for him. Now his mind was being opened on the subject of food. It began to penetrate that what you put in your face has something to do with what goes on in your head, whether it's smoking grass, tripping on LSD, or eating rice. George began dabbling with chopsticks and natural foods. He switched from hamburger to fish and from Rice-à-Roni to whole brown rice, adding a little Japanese seaweed and some green salad. But he kept on taking 55 units of insulin—45 in the morning and 10 more at night.

Some time later, he woke up in the night thrashing like a dying fish. His roommate called the ambulance which rushed him off to the college infirmary. The doctor there told him 55 units was too much insulin, he was cut back to 45. Maybe the Oriental guru was onto something! A few weeks of rice and seaweed had changed his direction. To celebrate, he threw away his Medic-alert pendant.

After graduation he headed for San Francisco to join a hippie commune. One afternoon, while sitting on the floor smoking grass, he fell asleep and woke up in the hospital with glucose pouring into his veins. Hospitals always pumped him so full of glucose he had to take more insulin as soon as they let him go. Glucose balance is a tricky thing, as George was learning. The next day, when it happened again, a psychiatrist dropped by to ask if George was attempting suicide.

George loathed being dependent on insulin and being obliged to count the hours exactly between meals. He loathed being a diabetic. If he wasn't a diabetic, what the hell was he? He had no better identity at the moment. Invalidism was a tempting way out, a built-in excuse for failure. With insulin, grass, LSD, you choose your dependency. But what if Eli Lilly went out of business?

Late that summer at a rock concert, George was desperately hungry for something sweet. He had his sugar lumps with him, but he wanted something mild like orange juice. He headed for the refreshment stand. The long line moved like molasses. George began to stagger a bit; eventually, he wove an unsteady path to the shelter of a hedge that bordered the sidewalk; he lay on the ground there, fumbling with the rubber band around his box of sugar. Magazines of the early 1970s would have one believe that every other sugar cube in California was soaked with LSD. Here was George acting like an addict. However, he wasn't trying to evade the police, on the contrary, he was seeking aid. Help! ! ! he cackled to a passing stranger. The stranger was hip enough to know an acid freak when he spotted one. He ran the other way. George collapsed. A friend heard him screaming, found him, and started feeding him sugar. Killing him softly, pulling him out deeper.

Next, George got a job on a California ranch where Mokelume Indians came over with a peace pipe full of hashish the first day. But that was the only dope he had during his entire stay there except that Lilly white insulin. He ate whole wheat bread, oatmeal, cheese, apples from the trees, watercress from a stream, and raspberries from a patch. He rode a horse, killed a snake, chopped wood. On hard working days, he reduced his insulin to 25 units. When that was still too much and he felt the gathering storm of insulin shock, he'd eat some honey and go back to work. Too much glucose in the blood was worse in the long run. In the short run, one always remained *conscious*, in control. Too *little* glucose in the blood, or what they call hypoglycemia, can leave you an inert mass out there somewhere on the forest floor. A diabetic learns the hard way about the ultimate terrors of the sugar blues.

Mornings after he had eaten too much, he would wake up with a swollen bladder, wave a Clinistix through his urine and angrily watch it turn red. He would stand there looking out at that beautiful dawn, hating his mother for having made him a cripple. We can't forgive others sometimes because we know we ourselves are in the wrong. George knew it was his own fault for eating too much. Why blame himself for being fearful of hypoglycemia, or insulin shock? When he needed someone to blame, George absolved himself and screamed at his mother two thousand miles away. Blaming her for putting him on the rubber nipple which connected with the steel needle. From nipple to needle, the story of his life!

Next he returned to Berkeley and LSD. He had learned that careful eating could help, and he knew he would have to kick grass as well as insulin. Although living on whole grains and vegetables as the Japanese prophet suggested was great, George wasn't a good cook and didn't want to learn. He wanted Mama to cook for him; she had got him into this, now let her cook his way out.

He stayed off meat but grass forced him to gorge on sticky, sweet food. Even with occasional bingeing, he cut his insulin down to 25 units. He managed to avoid severe shocks to his system but suffered little ones.

He remembers the ultimate last tango in Sacramento. He attempted a seduction and found the female ready and willing . . . and himself disabled. At the first sign of stress, his penis began to shrink—another telltale sign of approaching insulin shock. His young companion watched in amazement as George pulled a honey candy bar out of its wrapper and chomped it down.

That episode clinched matters. It drove him to drastic, foolish things in search of manhood. He tried kicking insulin cold turkey in favor of whole rice, azuki beans, and pumpkin. This was where he came in. He was back to sweet sixteen, drinking quarts of water and passing quarts of colorless urine. So he gave in and took a shot. Then he tried eating nothing at all. Another failure. He went from one extreme to another. He wanted an instant cure. He couldn't find the patience to continue weaning himself slowly and gradually off insulin onto a steady regime of whole grains and vegetables. "Maybe because I was never weaned from my mother's breast?" he asks. "I don't know."

In the summer of 1969, he took about 40 LSD trips. "Trying to kill myself," he admits. His old self, that is. He wandered through the student riots in Berkeley smoking grass and more grass until one day he walked into a bathroom.

"I saw a tall rather pretty girl standing there. I thought I'd seen her somewhere before." Then he noticed he was gazing into a mirror, staring at himself. He got off the psychedelic bus and went for a haircut. He stopped taking LSD and grass. Then he found out what kind of a monster his metabolism had made of him. All he wanted was sugar. He craved sugar like a wino craves muscatel. He ran from one store to another buying candy bars. He discovered he was not alone. This usually happens when one withdraws from LSD. But no doctor ever told him. They don't teach them about LSD in medical schools.

Not yet. Or about hypoglycemia either. Although Seale Harris broke the news in 1924.

"I was a nymphomaniac for fudge," George recalls. "Rewarding myself with suicide." After the binges, he had to crank up his insulin dose to a new high of 60 units a day. Between raids on the candy counter, he decided to head back East and study Oriental medicine whose teachings he had been flirting with for so long. He felt this was the end of the line for him. "I was hopeless, medically and spiritually."

He moved into a commune near Boston where good cooks prepared traditional Oriental food—whole rice, vegetables, a little fish, salads, beans, sea vegetables, traditional soy sauce, tofu (white soy bean cheese), miso (a paste of soy beans, wheat, and salt), and occasional seasonal fruit. Slowly, gradually, his balance returned. He reached that point where sugarfree food tasted sweet to him. His crazy longing for sugar fell away. He lost his craving for milk, yogurt, cheese, even ice cream.

In two years, George was able to reduce his insulin dosage from 60 to 15 units a day. His weight stabilized at 150 pounds. He doesn't carry around sugar cubes anymore. If he feels a small insulin shock coming on, he doesn't even need the honey anymore. He takes a piece of whole grain bread or a mouthful of whole rice. When he chews it well, by the numbers, sometimes up to fifty times, it breaks down into glucose right in his mouth. It's just as effective at balancing his metabolism as the sugar cubes—without what he calls "that runaway Drano impact on my digestive system."

Every week he gets needled by a Hasidic acupuncturist, a fellow he has known since college. "Acupuncture has taught me patience," he says. "My friend tells me my liver was overloaded—maybe from repressed anger and tons of sugar when I was a kid. According to acupuncture theory, if the liver is overactive, it has a destructive effect on the pancreas, where insulin comes from."

On a plane one day, George was seated next to a youngster. He could tell the way the kid's mother was hovering over his airline dinner, counting out the calories, that the lad was diabetic, hooked on insulin.

It had taken George ten tortuous years to find his way. Today the Lilly company is getting them younger and younger. He couldn't resist asking the boy's age, the lad was only nine years old. How long had this boy been hooked already? George was scared to ask.

Of Cabbages and Kings

During the building of the great wall of China, coolies were fed salted cabbage with their rice to keep them strong and healthy. Salting preserved the cabbage in season and out, and it was the only vegetable they had to supplement their complete, unrefined rice. When the Mongols overran China, knowing a good thing when they tried it, they adopted salted cabbage as a very practical traveling ration. The Mongol armies got as far as Hungary in the thirteenth century, where they introduced salted cabbage to Europe. As sauerkraut, it became one of the principal foods of Germany and Eastern Europe.

Julius Caesar's legions, the most efficient fighting machine the world had ever known, ranged far from Rome. The sole provisions were sacks of grain—one for each man. Like the Viet Cong, Caesar's men did not have sugar or kitchens, nor did they have a medical corps, only surgeons for repairing wounds. They ate whole grains plain, on the march, or ground into Roman meal and supplemented with cabbage and any other vegetables they could scrounge. Pliny has said that cabbage kept

Rome out of the hands of physicians for many centuries.

It was the European armies traveling in the other direction that ran into trouble. In his history of the invasion of sugar-rich Egypt by the Crusaders of St. Louis in 1260, Sire Jean de Joinville described the fungous putrid bleeding gums, the hemorrhagic skin spots, and the swollen legs that plagued Christian armies and led to the ultimate defeat and capture of the holy knights and their commander.[1]

The Chinese, the Mongols, and the Romans knew that salted cabbage aided scorbitus, as the Romans called it— the Latin word described the skin symptoms. In English it became scurfy, then scurvy. European peasants seemed to know what to do about it; wise women, midwives, and herbalists prescribed all sorts of wild green plants as "scurvy grass."[2]

The Christian armies and navies were ravaged by scurvy. While church and state were burning natural healers as witches, sorcerers, poisoners, and dealers in black magic, churchmen and royalty were victims of their own official magic: The notion that scurvy could be cured by the touch of a royal personage, an emperor or king. If one emperor claimed to be able to cure scurvy with his divine touch, what other king could admit to being less divine? Voltaire has recorded an encounter between a Christian saint suffering from scurvy and a sick king who hoped that the saint's touch could relieve his ailment. Nothing happened.[3]

What is the story of cabbages and kings? From the Arabs in Persia to the Crusaders in Islam to the explorers of the Elizabethan Age, soldiers and sailors were often the first ones on their block to get hooked on sugar. Caliphs, sultans, kings, and queens could issue orders and commands; they had the means and divine right to first claim on things in short supply, but you can be sure that plenty of sugar stuck to the fingers of common soldiers and sailors who freighted the precious stuff across thousands of miles.

One major difference exists between armies and navies. Armies can always live to some extent off the land. The rations of the naval and merchant seamen are established by royal decree; they tend to reflect the greed, corruption, and official prejudice in high places. Armies confiscate good peasant food. Navies eat at the king's whim. Peasants on the land with the animals ate whole food and remained whole. Men who lived away from the land in new cities or on board ships discovering new worlds ate food that was increasingly refined; eventually they sickened.

During one of Christopher Columbus's early voyages to the New World, a group of his sailors fell desperately ill. Columbus was about to jettison the sick men to the fish when a green island came in view. When the sick men begged to be left on land to die, Columbus assented. Unloaded in this island paradise and left to expire, the sailors were tempted by unknown fruits and plants. They partook of these strange tropical things. Gradually, to their amazement, all began to recover. When Columbus passed by the island months later on the return journey to Europe, he was amazed when bearded white men hailed the ship. Even more astonishing was the discovery that the sailors were alive and healthy. In honor of the event, the island was named Curaçao—the Portuguese for cure.

Vasco da Gama, searching for passage to the Indies by way of the Cape of Good Hope, lost 100 of his 160-man crew to scurvy. Magellan set sail in 1519 on his way round the world with a fleet of five ships. Three years later, having discovered islands like Guam and Curaçao, he returned to Spain with one ship and only eighteen members of his original crew.[4]

In Elizabethan times, British sailors began dying of scurvy by the hundreds. Scorbutical sailors were suspected of malingering; flogging was prescribed as an appropriate remedy. The Royal Navy was often virtually out of commission because half the sailors were ill.

The history of scurvy is classic by now. When it is retold, it is usually suggested that no way existed at that time for carrying fresh vegetables aboard ship on long sea voyages. It is as if there had never been any explorers out there ahead of Queen Bess's men. How about the Vikings, the Phoenicians, and the sailors of the Far

East? How did they escape the scourge of scurvy? Some carried their version of Julius Caesar's cabbage as sauerkraut, or else they had pressed or pickled vegetables in brine. Others carried beans, lentils, and other seeds which they sprouted to supply what we like to call ascorbic acid or vitamin C. The village druidess might have been able to advise the queen's Navy had she not been so busy hiding out to avoid being burned at the stake. That, too, was a strenuous time for practitioners of unorthodox medicine. After all, it wasn't until 1684 that the last sorceress was executed for witchcraft in merry England.

When the expedition of French explorer Jacques Cartier was ravaged by scurvy in Newfoundland in 1535, the friendly American Indian medicine men prescribed a local green plant—an infusion of spruce needles saved the day. In 1593, Admiral Sir Richard Hawkins protected the crew of the H.M.S. *Dainty* with oranges and lemons. Each time the scurvy story is recounted, however, one element is rarely mentioned. Something new had been added to the diet of the Elizabethan sailors that the Vikings, the Roman legions, the Phoenicians, and the navigators of the Far East managed without; the same item that began to play havoc with the Crusaders, the treasure they had brought back from their Arab conquests: Raw sugar and rum. In the beginning, soldiers and sailors got hold of rum and sugar anyway they could. Before long, both had become part of the official rations of Britain's Royal Navy.

One of the earliest recorded medical warnings about a possible relation between scurvy and sugar came from Dr. Thomas Willis. The warning appeared after his death in a book written in Latin and published in Switzerland, *Diatriba de Medicamentorum Operationibus in Humano Corpore (Diatribe on the Operation of Medicine in the Human Body).*

"I do much disapprove things preserved or very much seasoned with sugar," Dr. Willis wrote. "I judge the invention of it and its immoderate use to have very much contributed to the vast increase of scurvy in this last age. . . ."

No evidence is available to show that anyone else paid

much attention to the warning of the eminent Dr. Willis. Certainly not the British admiralty. Scurvy continued to afflict the British Navy and the toll mounted to the thousands. All this while, the British dominated and controlled the sugar trade. In 1740, Commodore Anson left England with six vessels and 1,500 seamen. Four years later, he returned with one ship and 335 men.

In the 1750s, James Lind, a surgeon's mate on H.M.S. *Salisbury*, fired by the hardships of the Anson fiasco and the multiple cases of scurvy he had observed on his own ship, undertook one of the earliest recorded controlled experiments in human nutrition.[5] At sea on the *Salisbury*, Lind isolated twelve well-matched scurvy victims, dividing them into six groups of two each. All received the regular Royal Navy ration:

Water gruel sweetened with sugar in the morning;
Fresh mutton broth often times for dinner;
At other times, puddings, boiled biscuits with sugar, and etc.;
[The etc. probably means sugared jellies or jams.]
For supper, barley, rice and currants, sago, raisins, and wine.

Contrast this with a typical upper-class breakfast in Britain in 1516, before sugar addiction became the fashion:

On fish days Milord and Lady split a loaf of bread—unrefined, wholemeal, staff-of-life bread.
Then they had two manchets (loaves of bread or rolls made with refined bolted white flour).
A quart of beer and some wine.
Two pieces of salted fish, six baked herrings, and a dish of sprats.
On flesh days: mutton or boiled beef instead of fish.

(In the 1500s, precious little sugar was to be had unless you were invited to court and somebody gave you a pinch —like someone turning you onto cocaine today.)

Each of Lind's six teams received a different supplementary remedy. Four had liquid additives: cider, vinegar, a dilute sulfuric acid mixture, and ordinary seawater. The fifth received a remedy "recommended by a hospital surgeon, a paste of garlic, mustard seed, horseradish, balsam of Peru, and gum myrrh." The last pair were given two oranges and a lemon every day.

"These they ate with greediness," Lind noted, with "sudden and visible good effects." One member of the citrus-eating team was fit for duty in six days; the other was soon well enough to nurse the other subjects.

Whether or not Lind had ever heard of Dr. Willis of the Royal Society and his warning about sugar, he didn't follow through. It does not seem to have occurred to anyone except Dr. Willis to experiment by subtracting something from the rations, especially something as new and potent and untried as sugar. Doctors, then and now, elevated themselves by prescribing something new. They often lost face *and* patients by prescribing something pleasant to the taste. By the sixteenth century, the British population at home had begun to lose their hair and teeth. Until then, only the privileged had been affected. Even the man in the street had become a sugar addict. The connection between sugar and scurvy was deemed practical but "unscientific." Vegetables, fruits, berries, and nuts—these natural sources of what we now call vitamin C—had been sweets until concentrated, refined sugar (sucrose) was marketed. Sugar was an unnatural sweet that had been robbed of its vitamin C in the refining process, which was when 90 percent of the natural cane was removed. The replacement of natural sweets by artificial concentrated sweets forms an existential cause of scurvy.

The discovery James Lind had made was duly reported to the British admiralty. Of course, the British diseasestablishment knew better than to admit that scurvy could have been caused by an inadequacy in the Royal Navy rations. Everybody knew that the British empire had the best fed sailors in all human history and that its Navy was superior to anything afloat. So they continued to flog scorbutical sailors for almost fifty years.

Lind left the Royal Navy a year after making his discovery. After taking his degree at Edinburgh University, he entered private practice and eventually became private physician to George III at Windsor. However, he continued his research and, in 1753, published his treatise on scurvy. Meanwhile, the delay in changing the Royal Navy's rations took an estimated 100,000 lives in less than fifty years. Lind died in 1794. A year later, when the good doctor was no longer around to say he told them so, the pendulum was finally reversed. What had up till then been declared "poppycock" was issued as a formal order: Every British seaman would henceforth have a dose of citrus juice with his daily rum allotment. With the arrogance typical of administration in any age, word circulated that this was a secret weapon for maintaining British mastery of the seas. "A new scientific truth does not triumph by convincing its opponents and making them see the light," said Max Planck. "But, rather, because its opponents eventually die and a new generation grows up that is familiar with it."

The British called lemons limes at the time; British sailors were known the world around as Limeys. If Lind had taken his sailors off sugar or given them infusions of pine needle tea or bancha tea or fed them cabbage, sprouts, scurvy grass, seaweed, or raw fish—all of which abound in ascorbic acid—the British might have had an entirely different monicker.

Britain's confusion between lemons and limes played havoc with Sir George Nare's polar expedition in 1875. West Indian limes instead of Mediterranean lemons were packed for the voyage: Scurvy broke out and the expedition was ruined. An inquest failed to agree on the cause of the debacle. Very soon, Pasteur's germ theory of disease became the fashion. Dr. Lind's simple discovery was as out of style as the ancient sorceress with her effective scurvy grass. Eminent physicians proclaimed that scurvy was due to acid intoxication. In 1916, a discovery credited scurvy to a constellation of devil germs. Then constipation got all the credit. Finally, during World War II, two German doctors assigned to care for Russian POW's came up with the notion that scurvy was transmitted by vermin. The notion that disease is caused by an external devil placates an atavistic need in man. We will fight to the death to avoid accepting responsibility for making ourselves sick.

If it took the Royal Navy forever to accept an idea

that any country healer could have told them, their forty-
two years of foot-dragging began to look like a speed
record compared to the action taken by other arms of
the British empire. For instance, the board of trade which
controlled the merchant marine resisted the cure for
scurvy for over a century. Records show that merchant
seamen afflicted with scurvy (which usually proved fatal)
had the task of delivering lemons to the ships of the
Royal Navy.

Across the seas, in an America racked with civil war,
the record is no better. The Union Army—whose soldiers
were bingeing on sugared condensed milk—reported
30,000 cases of scurvy. It took the U.S. Army another
thirty years to learn what any Indian medicine man could
have told them, let alone follow the dietary example of
the British.

At the turn of the nineteenth century, after sugared
condensed milk had become a national addiction, nursing
babies began to go out of style—mothers fed condensed
milk to their children. Lo and behold, another variety of
scurvy began to appear. The symptoms were called Bar-
low's disease, after the doctor who put two and two
together.

In the summer of 1933, an intrepid American dentist
ventured into the outermost reaches of the Canadian
Rockies, Yukon territory. Dr. W. Price found Indian
tribes whose health and teeth were uncorrupted by contact with the culture and commerce of the white invaders.
Winters in the Yukon go as far as 70° below zero. Obviously, lemons or oranges are not grown there. Most of
the Western sources of vitamin C are nonexistent. The
Indians were living almost entirely by hunting wild animals. The American traveler wondered why the Indians
weren't plagued with scurvy. He questioned an old Indian
through an interpreter:

"How do your people escape scurvy?"

"That is a white man's disease," was the Indian's
reply.

"Isn't it possible for an Indian to contact scurvy?"
was the next question.

"It is possible," said the Indian. "But the Indians know

how to prevent scurvy. The white man does not."

"Why don't you tell the white man how to prevent it?"

"The white man knows too much to ask the Indian anything."

"Would you tell me if I asked?"

The ancient Indian said he was willing but would first have to consult with the tribal chief. When he returned, he said his chief was willing to share the secret with the visitor because he was a friend of the Indian who had advised them not to eat the flour and sugar sold in the white man's store.

The Indian then described in detail the way the hunters kill a moose, then open up the carcass at the back, just above the kidneys. Here are found what the Indian described as two small balls of fat. The adrenal glands! These two small balls of fat were cut into as many pieces as there were people in the family. Each would eat his appointed share. The walls of the moose's second stomach were also eaten. Primitive people, whose scientists had studied wild animals on the loose had learned to eat internal organs of animals; often the muscle meat and filet mignon were thrown to the dogs. Modern civilized man, eating for pleasure and not for survival, does the reverse. The Indians in the Yukon were able to obtain ascorbic acid, vitamin C, from the adrenal glands of the moose and the grizzly bear for centuries.[6]

In 1937, two scientists, Dr. Albert Szent-Gyorgyi of Hungary and the British chemist Sir Walter Haworth were each awarded a Nobel prize—for rediscovering the secret of ascorbic acid, vitamin C. (Dr. Szent-Gyorgyi's Nobel was in Physiology and Medicine; that of Dr. Haworth—which was shared with Paul Karrer—was in Chemistry.) Szent-Gyorgyi had happened on his first important clue when he isolated a substance in the adrenal glands of an ox which contained very unusual chemical properties. For five centuries the white man had known too much to ask the Indian anything.

In 1855, Chief Sealth of the Duwamish Tribe, which inhabited what is now the state of Washington, wrote to President Franklin Pierce protesting the president's proposal to buy the tribal lands. The city of Seattle, a corruption of the great chief's noble name, is now built in the heart of Duwamish land. His letter warned of the white man's corruptive, destructive habits:

How can you buy or sell the sky—the warmth of the land? The idea is strange to us. We do not own the freshness of the air or the sparkle of the water. How can you buy them from us?

We know that the white man does not understand our ways. One portion of the land is the same to him as the next for he is a stranger who comes in the night and takes from the land whatever he needs. The earth is not his brother, but his enemy, and when he has conquered it, he moves on. He leaves his father's graves, and his children's birthright is forgotten.

The air is precious to the red man. For all things share the same breath—the beasts, the trees, the man. The white man does not seem to notice the air he breathes. Like a man dying for many days, he is numb to the stench. . . .

The white man must treat the beasts of this land as his brother. I am a savage and I do not understand the other way. I have seen a thousand rotting buffaloes on the prairies left by the white man who shot them from a passing train. . . . What is man without the beasts? If all the beasts were gone, men would die from great loneliness of spirit, for whatever happens to the beast also happens to man. All things are connected. Whatever befalls the earth befalls the sons of the earth.

One thing we know which the white man will one day discover. Our God is the same God. You may think now that you own him as you wish to own our land. But you cannot. He is the Body of man. And his compassion is equal for the red man and the white man. This earth is precious to him. And to harm the earth is to heap contempt on its creator. . . . Continue to contaminate your bed and you will one night suffocate in your own waste.

We might understand if we knew what it was that the white man dreams, what hopes he describes to his children on long winter nights, what visions he burns into their minds. . . .

Our warriors have felt shame. And after defeat, they turn their days in idleness and contaminate their bodies with sweet food and strong drink.[7]

How to Complicate Simplicity

. . . . The sugar boom also penetrated the civilization of the *bohio* and the very depths of the jungle. Everything bowed before the royal decree. "Clear more land to plant cane." And the magnificent primeval forests, bowing beneath the dread command, assumed a prominent but sorrowful role in the Cuban pageant. No country on earth is more rich in the blessings of its woods than the pearl of the Antilles. Forty excellent cabinet and building woods are grown in the Cuban forests: mahogany, rosewood, logweed, ebony, the fragrant Spanish elm. In clearing up land to make way for sugar, Cubans felled and burned phalanxes of century old royal palms, which yielded food, milk, rope, and numerous necessities of peasant life were sacrificed to the Great God Sugar.

And with more subtle significance, the coming of the sugar industry on a large scale changed the world of the peasant. Formerly the rural Cuban had squatted so contentedly on his square land which produced about everything he wanted, that a German peddler coined the immortal phrase: The "damned wantlessness" of the Cuban countryman.

Now with his land sold to the sugar corporations, he found himself a part of a great industrial enterprise, which provided him with a house and wages on its own terms. Temperamentally he was unsuited to this stream of modern industrial progress in which he found himself. . . ."He has no part in directing this industrial giant; he has no voice in its management. Yet to it he must look for education, recreation, and bread. He has, willy, nilly, exchanged a simple life for a vassalage to a foreign colossus. His future is not his own. It is determined for him in a director's room in New York."[1]

America is a country that has elevated waste to an industry. Wasting "inexhaustible" resources and buying up those of other lands has been basic policy. Halfway through the twentieth century, the U.S. is up to its ears in an energy crisis and a food crisis. The two have always been intertwined. One major difference between America and Europe—and most of the founding forefathers of America came from Europe, after all—is that new resources existed in the U.S. to squander and plunder. The natural geographic chasm between East and West was widened with the invention and use of a single tool: the mill. One could now select from wheat meals, oat meals, rye, barley, and Indian corn meals.

In the beginning, grain was ground between stones. Man's own energy was expended to change grain to meal. Porridge, cakes, or bread were made from the meal. The instant the whole grain is ground into meal, its natural energy or its life force—whether one calls this nutrients, vitamins, or enzymes—is reduced. Once the grain is pulverized, it will not sprout, it cannot reproduce itself. Mills driven by human energy were replaced by water mills. Then the Crusaders introduced the windmills from Arab lands. Eventually, stones were replaced by steel rollers; water became steam, and then electricity.

Power increased and meals became more and more refined. That which is termed civilization—separation from the land—advanced. More and more energy was used to remove more and more life force from the grains by milling, crushing, and sifting initially through woolen cloths, which were replaced by those of linen, and finally, seines of silk. People ate refined meals and they became refined. The grain is a fruit with the seed or germ in it. More and more of this was removed, starting with the germ and the seed. If the grains of wheat that fell between rollers were planted in the earth, one grain would sprout many, many grains. The end product of the processing of grain, however, the meal, was dead. It would rot if put into the soil. The vital energy had been extracted, lost, killed, spent.

Thus, all man's energy was harnessed to crushing the natural energy of grain. Bleaching, gassing, and all the other refinements were perfected one by one. At first, blood was used to clarify the juice of the sugar cane. Eventually, that method was replaced and charred animal bones were used to bleach the sugar.

The germ and bran of the wheat caught in the bolting cloth was called offal—a word which means waste or byproduct of a process. The waste of the sugar cane, bagasse, was fed to cows and other animals. As people became more and more refined from eating refined wheat and refined sugar, consumption of the animals that had eaten the rejected part of grain and cane also increased. The mill had taken over man's chewing; now the animals were used in the same way. Whole grains must be chewed and chewed or they cannot be digested. Whole wheat bread has to be well chewed, also. However, refined bread can be bolted. As usual, humans choose the easiest way, the quickest way.

Since World War II, the food industry in the U.S. has gone a long way toward ensuring that their customers (just about all of America's children, as well as a good proportion of the adults) do not have to chew breakfast. The bleached, gassed, and colored remnants of the life-giving grains are roasted, toasted, frosted with sugar, embalmed with chemical preservatives, and stuffed into a box much larger than its contents. Fantastic amounts of energy are wasted by sales and advertising departments to sell these half-empty boxes of dead food—money-back coupons, whistles, and toy guns are needed to induce refined women to lift these half-empty boxes off supermarket shelves.

One of the reasons East was East and West was West

and the twain were considered unbridgeable was that the
mill did not exist in the East for centuries after its invention and incorporation into the West's way of life.
Man and soil were considered one, whole, healthy, and
holy—all derived from the same root. Whole grain meant
holy, healthy grain. The Japanese ideogram for peace
was a mouth with a whole grain of rice in it. Waste
was considered an offense against nature and the order
of the universe. The Chinese child whose bowl contained
leftover rice was told that any future spouse would have
one pockmark for every grain wasted. In the East, grain
was harvested in the fields. Stalks of rice were beaten
in wooden pans to remove the outer hull. Then the
rice and chaff were bounced from a cloth into the air.
The wind carried off the chaff and it fell back to the soil.
The grain of rice—whole and complete, the fruit with
the seed—was harvested and kept and eaten whole. The
rest of the plant—everything that was not eaten or used—
was returned to the soil. Grains of rice were eaten whole,
chewed in the mouth, instead of between stones in a
mill. Little or nothing was left for the animals. Even
now, few domestic animals are maintained in the East.
Human wastes, like residues of all kinds, were not wastes
at all. The excess man did not use in his own body was
returned to the soil from whence it had come.

During the flowering of the industrial age in Europe
and America, millers in every land competed with one
another in perfecting more complicated devices for tor-
turing wheat berries into fine white flour. As the refinement of sugar reached the ultimate state where it was
bare of anything save calories, extensive court litigation
ensued patented milling and refining devices. Shortly after
the perfection of machines for the ultimate refinement
of sugar and flour, a German invention, the Engelberg
machine, was patented. It went well beyond the hand
threshing of rice that had been previously accomplished
in the fields. Each grain was stripped of its intermediate
and inner shells. As with wheat grain and sugar cane,
precious nutrients and minerals were removed; little was
left but the pure white hydrate of carbon core. Suddenly,
the lowly coolie food from the East had been made fit

for the delicate palates and refined appetites of the West. Polished rice was introduced to the West as rice. The entire word was appropriated to describe what actually were the leavings. In French, white rice is *riz*. Unpolished, complete rice is *riz complêt*. Following that rationale, someone could sell you an apple core when you asked for an apple. When you complained, they might say: Why didn't you say you wanted a complete apple?

The Engelberg polishing machines were introduced to the rice-eating countries in the Orient. Rice may have been an exotic delicacy in the West; in the East, it had been the principal food for centuries.

The process of moving from whole grains through the various stages of ground meals had taken several centuries in the West, thus biological deterioration of the people was gradual. However, such deterioration was visited upon the Orient very rapidly. Polished white rice was new, modern, refined, and civilized. It was accepted wherever modernization was vogue. In its wake, it brought sudden outbreaks of new symptoms. Eventually, these new symptoms were labeled *beriberi*, after the Senegalese word for weakness.

When outbreaks of beriberi followed the introduction of white rice into Japan, the common people frequently realized what the solution was. Traditional habits, fortunately still fresh in their memory, told them to go back to eating old-fashioned, complete rice. When they did, all was well. Eating whole rice, they became whole and healthy again. To this day, if you visit a Japanese restaurant in America or Europe and ask for unrefined, brown rice, the waitress is apt to ask you with some concern if you are not feeling well.

As with the British admiralty coping with scurvy a century before, the Western-educated medical officers of the Japanese navy were unable to understand such a simple tack. After the introduction of refined white sugar and white polished rice on Japanese battleships, beriberi began plaguing the sailors the way scurvy had the British. Instead of going back to eating unpolished rice like the peasants, the Japanese navy went the whole way and adopted western rations like those of the British and German navies. Meat and condensed milk, among other things, were added to the diet of the Japanese sailors.

It was only imperialist colonizers, supersalesmen for European technology, and the great scientific geniuses of the West who thought of beriberi as a mysterious plague to be conquered by modern science. At first it was classified as a tropical disease. It was studied as a parisitic infection. Among the suggested therapies for beriberi were quinine, arsenic, bloodletting, cold douches, steambaths, sunbaths, strychnine, and massage. In Java in the 1890s, the Dutch army, Dutch missionaries, and colonial administrators were afflicted with a veritable epidemic of beriberi. They slept under mosquito netting and sprayed each other with carbolic acid and were careful not to let the dirty natives touch them on the way to church, but nothing seemed to protect them from beriberi.

The top German-trained physicians and scientists were ordered to Java to conduct scientific experiments to find a cure. Many of the scientists died or went home on stretchers. One who returned for a second round of duty was young Dr. Christian Eijkman.[2] He worked alone in a jungle laboratory, near Batavia, which was attached to a small hospital for beriberi victims, inoculating chickens with the blood of beriberi patients. The chickens seemed to be immune. Then one day he noticed a chicken staggering around with all the apparent symptoms of the disease. Eureka, he was onto something. Soon, however, all the chickens—those he had inoculated and those he had not—seemed to have the same symptoms. His hopes were dashed. Then, as mysteriously as they had fallen ill, the chickens recovered, without any help from Western medicine.

Eijkman turned detective. A single clue existed. Ordinarily, the chickens were fed with brown, unpolished rice—the cheap kind the Javanese natives ate. A shortage of the unpolished rice had arisen, so the chickens had been fed white, refined rice—the kind the refined European patients in the hospital were fed, together with pure refined white sugar, pure white bread, butter, jam, and all the sweet goodies the missionaries and colonials imported. As soon as this shocking waste of good white rice was discovered, the chickens had been put back on the unrefined rice. Eijkman began experimenting with the chicken feed. Soon he discovered the secret that the Javanese natives refused to share with their sugar-eating army of occupation. If you eat white rice and sugar, you get beriberi. Eat brown, whole, unpolished rice and recover.

This was no news among the simple people of the Orient. One of the natural laws they still observed was that everything is perfectly balanced in nature. Natural law decrees that man should eat whole food, the entire fish, the root of the leek, the top of the carrot, vegetables that grow wild in the sea as well as those man cultivates on land. The emperors of Japan tried to teach this by example—always eating whole rice.

The good doctor then surveyed the modern, hygienic Dutch prisons where natives were interned for transgressions against the army of occupation. The prisoners were being fed white rice just like the patients in the colonial hospital. Out of 3,900, beriberi was contracted by 270. Outside prison, among the natives living in grass shacks (under conditions considered appallingly unhygienic by the antiseptic-minded Dutch colonials), the principal food was unpolished rice, which the natives thrashed themselves. Eijkman was unable to find a single case of certified beriberi among a population of 10,000.

Timidly, Eijkman made his first report in 1893, "On a Polyneuritis Similar to Beriberi Observed in Chickens." Nobody paid any attention. Eventually, he was shipped back to Europe. A colleague who replaced him, Dr. C. Grinjs published findings in 1901 based on experiments suggesting that beriberi in birds, as well as men, is caused by the lack of some vital substance in polished rice that is present in rice bran.[3]

In 1907, two Norwegian workers, Holst and Froelich, induced beriberi in chickens and pigeons. The guinea pig chosen as the experimental mammal was fed polished rice; the animal came down with something which was diagnosed as scurvy.[4] Suddenly, this was big news in scientific quarters in the West. The lesson would seem to have been very simple: Western man could learn a thing or two from the simple folk of the Orient. They had been eating whole, unpolished rice for centuries as their principal food. That, however, was far too simple for the Western scientific community, which just then was in the throes of an explosion of interest in the new science of chemistry which seemed to be getting to the root of all the secrets of life.

In 1911, at the Lister Institute in London, a Polish chemist, Dr. Casimir Funk, took Eijkman's experiment with the chickens and the rice and set about to complicate it. He spent four months grinding and polishing 836 pounds of unpolished rice. From it, he extracted 170 grams of rice bran, which was made into a solution. An infinitesimal amount was fed to a pigeon paralyzed with beriberi—it recovered within a few hours. In 1912, Funk published his daring, radical theory that a vital substance in natural unpolished rice is removed in refining.[5]

"When there is a failure of human understanding," said Goethe, "men make up new words." So Casimir Funk, victim of the mania for nomenclature—preferably from the Latin or Greek—undertook to christen this mysterious natural life force which he "discovered" in unpolished, whole brown rice. He took the Latin word for life, *vita*, and combined it with the word *amine*—amino acids are components of protoplasm—and came up with the word *vitamine*. The anti-beriberi vitamine. Had he stuck to the Anglo-Saxon fashion of naming his discovery after himself—as doctors name symptoms—he might have christened this mysterious life force the funky funkies and spared this crazy world a lot of confusion.

The next step occurred at the University of Wisconsin in 1912. German chemists had discovered the balanced diet: proteins, carbohydrates, fats, salts, and water. This was the scientific age Mary Shelley had portrayed when she created the character of Dr. Frankenstein. The original Dr. Frankenstein was the real flesh and blood brother of Baron Liebig, the superman of the new science of chemistry. Liebig announced that he was on the brink of brewing an artificial milk in his laboratory which would be an improvement over anything that ever dripped from mothers or cows. Source and quality of food were not important in that period, the focus was on chemical formulae.

Stephen Babcock, who studied with Liebig in Germany, later became a pioneer scientist with the U.S. Department of Agriculture in the latter half of the nineteenth century. He analyzed the food given to a test group of cows, and then analyzed the manure they deposited. To his amazement, he found that more minerals came out than had gone in. He presented both chemical formulae to the laboratory head, asking—with a straight face— which would be best as food for the cows. Chemically, virtually no difference existed between the food and the manure. Food and manure were chemically the same. It couldn't matter to anyone but the cows. And cows had nothing to say about it, being captives of the new science. (A hundred years later, another scientist has come up with a process for recycling manure into food for cattle.) [6]

At the University of Wisconsin in 1912, Professor E. V. McCollum conducted nutritional experiments on rats. Various combinations of proteins, carbohydrates, and fats were fed to the rodents. On some combinations, the rats thrived. On other combinations, the rats withered. However, both the sustaining and the insufficient diets had exactly similar chemical compositions. Obviously, chemistry was not the whole answer. The captive rats were on diets of milk, sugar, and other lethal combinations eaten by civilized Westerners. Had the rats been given the freedom of their natural instincts to select their food, McCollum might have learned a valuable lesson. However, through trial and error, he concluded that all proteins do not have the same nutritive value; that all carbohydrates are not the same; and that some fats are different from others. Once again, only a scientific community spellbound by German chemistry could have found this news at all. McCollum isolated a nutrient present in certain fats, as well as alfalfa leaves, and in the livers and kidneys of animals. He took it out of butter and put it in margarine. When fed to rats which up to then were on diets containing sugar and milk, the rodents thrived. Eureka, this was absolute proof of the existence of some "new" substance which McCollum called fat-soluble A. Here entered the scientific genius for labels. The letter A was added to the word vitamine coined by Casimir Funk—vitamin A. Another billion dollar business was born.[7]

In 1906, Frederick Hopkins of Cambridge University had called for more research on vitamins: ". . . This much is certain: every food contains trifling amounts of substances from which the body benefits. . . ." If that statement is accepted as accurate, it then follows that sugar is not a food.

In 1920, Hopkins joined with Dr. W. H. Wilson of St. Mary's Hospital in London in making this statement: "The proof that deficiency diseases, when occurring amongst men on a ration scale deficient in necessary vitamins, can be prevented by the addition of articles containing these vitamins must be regarded as definitely established. The history of epidemics of scurvy and beriberi during the war affords conclusive evidence."[8]

Now if these discoveries meant anything, they meant that there was something present in the whole, unpolished rice—whether you call it vitamins or funky funkies—which is vital to health and life—whether it be that of Javanese chickens or Western man. It meant that stripping rice and sugar—through the refining process—removed the nutrients. It thus follows that eating these substances is not good for you. (In 1973, a U.S. senate committee used the word antinutrient to describe sugar.) Thus such substances are actually harmful, since they upset the existing balance in the body, bloodstream, and vital organs. Did the leaders of science share this great discovery with the man in the street? Did the AMA launch an educational crusade to tell the people of America, of the world, that a diet of white rice and sugar could give you beriberi or neuritis or whatever you want to call it? Were we told that a diet containing whole rice and omitting sugar would cure one—or keep one healthy?

Pellagra and beriberi were both named for symptoms of the individual disease. Pellagra progressed into general disability, then death—after death a general tissue degeneration was observed. For years, pellagra was thought to be an infectious tropical germ related to sleeping sickness and the tsetse fly. After yellow fever had been conquered by military experiments with vaccine, vaccine cures were expected for every disease that occurred in the tropical zone. Arsenic and other poisons were tried, but pellagra baffled the great medical minds of Europe for two centuries.

All the time, the peasants of Italy and Spain—where the disease had become epidemic—kept saying, "Feed a pellagrin well, and he'll do well." That was too simple for the medical brains searching for vaccines, tsetse flies, and Nobel prizes. The poor peasants seemed to survive. It was apt to be the rich folks—with money enough to call a doctor—who were dying.

By 1914, pellagra had reached epidemic proportions in the American South. The Surgeon General and the U.S. Public Health Service were under tremendous pressure from Congress and the public to find a quick cure for this Italian plague. Leading American Medical scientists, with unlimited research funds, had experimented fruitlessly for five years.

Doctors in the South were sure it was contagious. Whole villages in South Carolina, Georgia, and Mississippi were suddenly swept by the strange flame-red skin rash. Finally, the Public Health Service found someone willing to go where other doctors feared to tread (reports had it that the plague was contagious). Joe Goldberger, a Hungarian-born Jew from New York's Lower East Side, was an excellent bacteriologist and an expert on tropical diseases. Remember, this was an age of microbe hunting.

Goldberger, rather than studying cultures and biopsies of dead people in a laboratory, went to the hospitals and insane asylums to examine pellagra victims who were still living. "How many of your doctors and nurses catch pellagra?" He asked the head of a Georgia insane asylum. "Well, none of us ever do. Only the patients die of it," replied the doctor. Thus the scientific theory that pellagra was contagious was laid to rest.

Told that pellagra afflicts the poor rather than the

rich, Goldberger theorized that it might have something to do with the fact that poor folks don't always get the right stuff to eat.

"Couldn't be," the asylum doctors reported. "Here doctors and patients eat the same food." Goldberger insisted on checking. So he visited the dining halls and saw the meals: corn meal mush, hominy grits, cane sugar syrup. Refined corn and sugar! Attendants and nurses were helping themselves to all of this, of course, as well as good cuts of meat and glasses of milk.

Goldberger found the same thing when he visited orphanages. Corn bread, hominy grits, biscuits, and molasses comprised the diet of youngsters between six and twelve years of age. Refined grains and sugar again. What meat and milk there was went to infants and teenagers. The disease was concentrated in that middle group, the six to twelve-year-olds whose diet was heavy in refined foods, those "antinutrients."

Within a few months, Goldberger was convinced. He obtained U.S. government funds for a nutritional experiment at two parochial orphanages in the same town. Within a few weeks, no new cases of pellagra appeared, and there was marked improvement among the children who had been sick.

Before publishing results of his experiments, Goldberger had to reverse his field: he had to induce pellagra in healthy people by restricting their diet. Only one place existed where that could be done, without a public hue and cry should events backfire. Not even a Georgia chain gang would do. A prison with walls was necessary. The governor of Mississippi went along with Goldberger's scheme when assured the experiment could not be fatal.

Goldberger isolated eleven adult male volunteers on a Mississippi prison farm for six months. The convicts were fed all they could eat of best white bread, corn pone, hominy grits, sweet potatoes, salt pork, cane syrup, cabbage, and coffee. The experiment began in April 1915. The men—among them lifers and murderers —were promised freedom at the end of the experiment. Breakfast was biscuits, cornmeal mush, polished rice, cane syrup, coffee, and sugar; at noon, cornbread, collard greens, sweet potatoes, cane syrup, and hominy grits. Supper was grits, biscuits, mush, gravy, cane syrup, sugar, and coffee. For variety, supper was sometimes served at noon. It was a diet of refined grains, refined flour, cane syrup, and sugar. A little meat was added occasionally. What started out as a lark for the convicts swiftly turned into unpleasantness. Within a few weeks, all were complaining of backaches, stomachaches, and dizziness— early symptoms of pellagra. But because the red skin lesions had not appeared, the ultimate symptom for which the disease had been named, the experiment dragged on. After five months, the men were weak and haggard, but there were no red marks. Time was running out, the warden, the prisoners, and the medical detective were all worried.

The telltale rash was supposed to appear first on the knuckles and on the back of the neck. One morning at roll call, Goldberger's assistant warden undertook an all-over inspection of one subject. There, underneath the scrotum, was the telltale red butterfly rash. He examined others. Seven showed the telltale rash in the same place. Goldberger sent out a rush call for a pellagra expert from Memphis and a skin specialist from St. Louis. They came. They examined. They reported conclusively that six of the convicts undoubtedly had pellagra.

Goldberger published his findings, as medical protocol decrees, in a scientific journal. The plague of the dreaded pellagra—which had Congress, the Surgeon General, and the scientific community in an uproar for years—was simply what the Italian peasants had said. Diet causes it and diet cures it. A diet of refined cereals and sugar causes it. Feed a pellagra well and he'll do well.[9]

Was Goldberger awarded a Nobel prize that year or any year? Did he receive a Congressional Medal of Honor, or a medal from the AMA? A few of the best minds in medicine accepted his findings. The vocal majority landed on Goldberger like a ton of bricks. They challenged his findings, they vilified him. They relied on epidemiological evidence that pellagra was a plague like typhoid fever, that it was infectious, it had to be caused by a germ. The diehards wouldn't give in. "Blind, selfish, jealous prejudiced asses," Goldberger called them. He sought to convince the skeptics by injecting himself with blood from pellagra victims, he swallowed intestinal discharge from pellagra victims, he gulped down powdered, scaled-off skin from people ill from the dread sickness. He didn't die, but he didn't make the medical hall of fame either.

Walter Reed became a national hero, and the subject of a play and a movie. All this after Reed's experiments in Cuba with yellow fever resulted in a vaccine which temporarily made the Cuban sugar plantations safe for U.S. exploitation. Maybe that explains why the hospital where America's presidents are treated is named after Walter Reed and not Joe Goldberger.

Science and medicine marched on. The next step was protracted and complicated enough to make Casimir Funk's discovery look primitive. Rather than teaching giddy, sugar-eating Westerners to quit polishing the life out of rice, the scientists slaved away in their laboratories trying to prepare magic vitamin crystals out of massive quantities of life-giving rice polishings. How were the polishings obtained? By stripping whole rice. These crystals were worked on by chemists around the world in an effort to break them down to a chemical formula.

Dr. Robert R. Williams and his colleagues spent twenty-six years isolating five grams of pure crystals from a whole ton of rice polishings. With these crystals, the molecular structure of this mysterious life-giving element was at last determined. It took two more years to rebuild the molecule synthetically, step-by-step, in their laboratory. When that stupendous task was finally accomplished in 1936, another world war was around the corner. The announcement of the substance, which was called thiamine or vitamin B_1, was big news in *The New York Times* of August 23, 1936:

Twenty-six years ago, Dr. Robert R. Williams, who has since become chemical director of the Bell Telephone Laboratories, began to devote his spare time to the study and investigation of vitamin B_1.

. . . Three years ago he announced, in association with collaborators, the development of the first successful large-scale method of extracting the substance from its natural plant sources in pure crystalline state, which at once made it available in its most potent form for use by the medical profession in the treatment and relief of neuritis. There remained only one further step—to imitate nature by creating the vitamin artificially in the laboratory.

. . . Shuffling and re-shuffling in endless combinations as many as fifty different chemical compounds, the scientists have succeeded in duplicating nature's secret combination.

Williams and Cline give credit to many collaborators in the important chemical achievement which not only will make the vitamin available to the medical profession in unlimited quantities but also will materially reduce its market price and bring it within the means of the lower income groups. At present the market price of the natural product is $400 a gram.

The publication of this article was an accolade. Further recognition and validation appeared several weeks later in an article in *The New York Times* by William L. Laurence: "September 15, 1936—The etiologic (causal) relationship of defective nutrition to polyneuritic beriberi (a nervous disorder due to a deficiency in vitamin B_1) has been appreciated for many years," Dr. Maurice Strauss stated today. "Only recently, however, has it become known that many other disorders of the nervous system may be the result of nutritional deficiency.

"It has been demonstrated that the polyneuritis associated with chronic alcoholism, pregnancy, and certain gastrointestinal abnormalities are identical clinically and pathologically to polyneuritic beriberi."

Read that August story in *The New York Times* carefully. Does it mention that whole brown rice has vitamin B_1 in it and white rice doesn't?

Of course not. Brown, unpolished rice was retailing for about ten cents a pound at the time. Did the newspaper article tell you to rush to your nearest grocery and buy some? Hell, no. Drop in at the Bell Telephone Lab and buy some vitamin B_1 for $400 a gram. After vitamins had been turned into another billion dollar religion, Dr. Casimir Funk tried valiantly, like Pasteur, to undo what he had begun.

"Vitamins are not any magical possessions," he said. "They exist in milk because the mother or the cow assemble them from the food she had eaten. . . .

"What would be the use of preparing all our foods artificially as long as nature is producing her own foods in sufficient abundance. . . . It would be folly even to think of turning ourselves into domestic manufacturers and consumers of self-made food as long as nature gives us enough. . . ."

By then it was too late. The vitamin game was big business; there was no stopping it. The mills of the great gods of grain were soon grinding the life out of whole grain rice. We were sold the white rice which—added to the antinutrient sugar in our diet—began establishing imbalances in our bodies. Then commerce busily, proudly "created" vitamin B_1 pills from the rice polishings. These were then sold to us; after all, we were now in sore need of them.

At the beginning of World War II, the British crown colony of Singapore was threatened with a food crisis— the kind that faces many lands today. Malaya and Singapore did not grow all the rice they needed; imports were about to be sharply reduced. The British medical officer of Singapore, Dr. Scharff, made the same kind of hard decision that had saved Denmark in World War I during the German blockade. Polished white rice was forbidden by military decree. Only unpolished brown rice could be sold. British military authorities were influenced by one factor only: Inadequate supplies. They were worried about quantity: Quality was of no concern. They simply didn't want any food riots on their hands. A hundred tons of brown rice represented a hundred tons of food. Processing and polishing would reduce that hundred tons of brown rice to 70 tons of white polished rice.[10]

The aftermath was startling, incredible. Dr. Scharff had originally gone to Singapore with the mission of reducing infant mortality from malaria. When he arrived, the mortality rate was 420 per 1,000 births. He used herculean but orthodox medical methods. In less than a decade, the program had reduced the death rate of infants to

160 per 1,000, almost on a par with the existing rate in Britain. However, after a year on the brown rice diet enforced by military decree, there was a dramatic shift in vital statistics. Instead of 160 infants dying in their first year of life, only 80 died. The figure was cut in half without medical efforts.

"It seems to me that here is a phenomenon which should make every statesman think," the eminent British physician Dr. L. J. Picton, O.B.E., wrote some years later. "At a stroke of the pen, hundreds of thousands of lives were saved."

Was Dr. Scharff awarded a Nobel prize? Did the World Health Organization spread the news? Perhaps prenatal clinics, pediatricians, and white hospital ships of hope spread the story to the rest of the world? Surely the answer is obvious. What fees can the medical profession earn by selling brown rice? A vogue for natural grains could raise havoc with the vitamin pushers, the sugar pushers, the pharmaceutical companies, and their partners in the diseasestablishment. The Singapore story seemed buried for keeps in secret files or perhaps at the Ministry of Health.

". . . We are left to wonder," mused Dr. Picton, "in what proportion caprice and unthinking custom are mixed with the wisdom that governs us."[11]

The combination of white sugar and white rice— especially among people whose principal food is rice— is lethal. The removal of the B vitamins, among others, from the rice, causes imbalance, for as the body seeks what it lacks, more B vitamins are leeched from the system in order to digest the white rice. Refined white sugar leeches the same vitamins for the same reason. The combination of refined flour and refined sugar spells double trouble: beriberi is that final stage of weakness, that exhaustion which is the body saying "Enough, no more." The health problems that physicians now call subclinical scurvy and subclinical beriberi cover all the escalating stages of malnutrition and weakness in between. Subclinical beriberi is an officious hermetic way of describing beriberi that is not sufficiently severe or classical in its symptoms to alert the average physician into diagnosing the symptoms.

The U.S. adventure in Viet Nam was, by world consensus, a folly on many levels. Perhaps, on the basic level of human nutrition, it was one of the sorriest stories of all. Viet Nam was one of the world's biggest rice bowls. For decades, Viet Nam exported rice to many parts of the world. Whole rice was the principal food of the Vietnamese. For years, the guerilla bands of the Viet Minh and Viet Cong sustained themselves with a food supply system as simple and primitive as that of the Roman legions of Julius Caesar. Each man carried a little sack of whole rice and some salt. They added manioc leaves, from the jungle, and fish when possible. For years, they stymied the elaborately equipped and lavishly rationed armies of the West.

When Western military forces finally withdrew, the world was told in copious detail about the Vietnamization of the war. One heard far less about the Americanization of the South Vietnamese Army's food supply.

Since the late 1960s, perhaps longer, the allied armies of South Vietnam—one of the major rice producing areas on this planet—were supplied with white, instant rice from America. The cost to the American taxpayers was almost a million dollars a month.

A Pentagon official explained:

The Vietnamese, being a "backward" people, do not have rice-processing facilities of their own. (To put it another way, somebody decided there was more profit to be made by selling the South Vietnamese processed rice from the U.S. than by selling them the machinery.)

Homegrown Vietnamese rice is "useless to a soldier in the field since it would have to be cooked in the field." (That must have been breathtaking military intelligence for the Viet Cong.)

"American instant rice is perfect for the situation," Robert Graff of the Defense Personnel Support Center in Philadelphia explained to Associated Press on April 17, 1971. The Pentagon had been supplying instant rice to Viet Nam since 1968 at a rate of one and a half million 65-cent bags per month, he noted.

At the same time, of course, the U.S. had been supplying the South Vietnamese sugar by the ton, soda by the ocean. Now that South Viet Nam was permanently hooked to a Westernized diet of sugar and polished rice—each stripped of their life-sustaining B complex vitamins—it is no surprise that the South Vietnamese have developed many entirely new diseases. U.S. medical officials in Viet Nam professed to be stumped by the outbreak of new fevers which afflicted children principally. Radio and TV broadcast warnings; leaflets were dropped from the air; the hospitals were overrun. U.S. doctors were ordered to search for a vaccine. Intravenous adrenal fluids and blood plasma were airlifted in and everything blamed on the mosquitos.[12]

When the victorious Viet Cong armies overran Saigon, they were exposed for the first time—like the Crusaders arriving in the Holy Land centuries before—to the pause that refreshes, the Coke machine, the candy counter. It is their turn to accustom themselves to gluttony, and La Dolce Vita and to eat and drink sugar openly in the street without shame.

Isn't this where we came in?

Dead Dogs and Englishmen

Millions of tons of sugar could hardly have been floated across oceans for centuries without some bizarre misadventures. One such occurred when a vessel carrying a cargo of sugar was shipwrecked in 1793. The five surviving sailors were finally rescued after being marooned for nine days. They were in a wasted condition due to starvation. They had subsisted by eating nothing but sugar and drinking rum. (As many people can testify, including me, it is perfectly possible to survive comfortably for nine days or longer without food or water. With a little water, but no food, it is possible to survive much longer than that.) The eminent French physiologist F. Magendie was inspired by that incident to conduct a series of experiments with animals which he published in 1816. He fed dogs a diet of sugar or olive oil and water. All the dogs wasted and died.[1]

The shipwrecked sailors and the French physiologist's experimental dogs proved the same point once and for all. As a steady diet, sugar is *worse than nothing*. Plain water can keep you alive for quite some time. Sugar and water can kill you. "Human subjects were unable to subsist on a diet of sugar."[2] There is on record, the saga of a young girl, seriously injured in a plane accident, who kept alive for well over a month on nothing but melted snow. Two men afloat in an overturned sailboat in the Pacific survived for seventy-two days in the summer of 1973 with nothing but a cup of rainwater every five days, a cup of salt water, a tablespoon of peanut butter a day, and a few sardines.[3] In late 1970, a nine-year-old boy ran away from home and kept alive for ten days in the Wyoming wilderness without food in temperatures that dropped occasionally to 40 degrees. At the end, he was in remarkably good condition.[4]

Refined sugar is lethal when ingested by humans because it provides only that which nutritionists describe as empty or naked calories. In addition, sugar is worse than nothing because it drains and leeches the body of precious vitamins and minerals through the demand its digestion, detoxification, and elimination make upon one's entire system.

So essential is balance to our bodies, that we have many ways to provide against the sudden shock of a heavy intake of sugar. Minerals such as sodium (from salt), potassium and magnesium (from vegetables), and calcium (from the bones) are mobilized and used in chemical transmutation; neutral acids are produced which attempt to return the acid-alkaline balance factor of the blood to a more normal state.

Sugar taken every day produces a continuously over-acid condition, and more and more minerals are required from deep in the body in the attempt to rectify the imbalance. Finally, in order to protect the blood, so much calcium is taken from the bones and teeth that decay and general weakening begin.

Excess sugar eventually affects every organ in the body. Initially, it is stored in the liver in the form of glucose (glycogen). Since the liver's capacity is limited, a daily intake of refined sugar (above the required amount of natural sugar) soon makes the liver expand like a balloon. When the liver is filled to its maximum capacity, the excess glycogen is returned to the blood in the form of fatty acids. These are taken to every part of the body and stored in the most inactive areas: the belly, the buttocks, the breasts, and the thighs.

When these comparatively harmless places are completely filled, fatty acids are then distributed among active organs, such as the heart and kidneys. These begin to slow down; finally their tissues degenerate and turn to fat. The whole body is affected by their reduced ability and abnormal blood pressure is created. Refined sugar lacks natural minerals (which are, however, in the sugar beet or cane). Our parasympathetic nervous system is affected; and organs governed by it, such as the small brain, become inactive or paralyzed. (Normal brain function is rarely thought of as being as biologic as digestion.) The circulatory and lymphatic systems are invaded, and the quality of the red corpuscles starts to change. An overabundance of white cells occurs, and the creation of tissue becomes slower.

Our body's tolerance and immunizing power becomes more limited, so we cannot respond properly to extreme attacks, whether they be cold, heat, mosquitos, or microbes. Excessive sugar has a strong mal-effect on the functioning of the brain; the key to orderly brain function is glutamic acid, a vital compound found in many vegetables. The B vitamins play a major role in dividing glutamic acid into antagonistic-complementary compounds which produce a "proceed" or "control" response in the brain. B vitamins are also manufactured by symbiotic bacteria which live in our intestines. When refined sugar is taken daily, these bacteria wither and die, and our stock of B vitamins gets very low. Too much sugar makes one sleepy; our ability to calculate and remember is lost.

Shipwrecked sailors who ate nothing but sugar and rum for nine days surely went through some of this trauma; the tales they had to tell created a big public relations problem for the sugar pushers. The dead dogs in Professor Magendie's laboratory alerted the sugar industry to the hazards of free scientific inquiry.

From that day to this, the sugar industry has invested millions of dollars in behind-the-scenes, subsidized science. The best scientific names that money could buy have been hired in the hope that they could one day come up with something at least pseudoscientific in the way of glad tidings about sugar.

It has been proved, however, that (1) sugar *is* a major factor in dental decay; (2) sugar in a person's diet *does* cause overweight; (3) removal of sugar from diets *has* cured symptoms of crippling, world-wide diseases such as diabetes, cancer, and heart illnesses. However, the story of the public relation attempts on the part of the sugar manufacturers began in Britain in 1808, when the Committee of West India reported to the House of Commons that a prize of twenty-five guineas had been offered to anyone who could come up with the most "satisfactory" experiments to prove that unrefined sugar was good for feeding and fattening oxen, cows, hogs, and sheep.[5] Food for animals is often seasonal, always expensive. Sugar by then was dirt cheap. People weren't eating it fast enough.

Pigs thrive on garbage because they know their way around. Sheep are no dopes either. When artificial fertilizer was first introduced into Britain, one skeptical farmer divided his largest meadow into two parts. He had heard all the new scientific propaganda from Germany about the wonders of store-bought chemical fertilizer, but he had some respect for the intelligence and instinct of his four-legged friends. That fall, he used the new manufactured stuff on one half of his meadow; on the other side, he used plain old manure. The following spring, he removed the dividing lines and turned his sheep loose. Within a few days, they were all grazing on the side of the meadow that had been treated in the old-fashioned way. That was scientific evidence enough for him. He never used manufactured fertilizer again.

Sir Frederick Banting, the codiscoverer of insulin, noticed in 1929 in Panama that among sugar plantation owners who ate large amounts of their refined stuff, diabetes was common. Among native cane cutters, who only got to chew the raw cane, he saw no diabetes. Naturally, the attempt to feed livestock with sugar and molasses in England in 1808 was a disaster. When the Committee on

West India made its fourth report to the House of Commons, one Member of Parliament, John Curwin, reported that he had tried to feed sugar and molasses to calves without success. He suggested that perhaps someone should try again by sneaking sugar and molasses into skimmed milk. Had anything come of that, you can be sure the West Indian sugar merchants would have spread the news around the world. After this singular lack of success in pushing sugar in cow pastures, the West Indian sugar merchants gave up.

With undaunted zeal for increasing the market demand for the most important agricultural product of the West Indies, the Committee of West India was reduced to a tactic that has served the sugar pushers for almost two hundred years: Irrelevant and transparently silly testimonials from faraway, inaccessible people with some kind of "scientific" credentials. One early commentator called them "hired consciences." The House of Commons committee was so hard-up for local cheerleaders on the sugar question, they were reduced to quoting a doctor from faraway Philadelphia, a leader of the recent American Colonial rebellion: "The *great* Dr. Rush of Philadelphia is *reported to have said* that 'sugar contains more nutrients *in the same bulk* than any other known substance.'" At the same time, the same Dr. Rush was preaching that masturbation was the cause of insanity.

If a weasel-worded statement like that was quoted, one can be sure no animal doctor could be found in Britain who would recommend sugar for the care and feeding of cows, pigs, or sheep.

While preparing his epochal volume *A History of Nutrition*, published in 1957, Professor E. V. McCollum of Johns Hopkins University (sometimes called America's foremost nutritionist, certainly a pioneer in the field) reviewed approximately 200,000 published scientific papers, recording experiments with food, their properties, their utilization, and their effects on animals and men. The material covered the period from the mid-eighteenth century to 1940. From this great repository of scientific inquiry, McCollum selected those experiments which he regarded as significant "to relate the story of progress in discovering human error in this segment of science [of nutrition]." Professor McCollum fails to record a single controlled scientific experiment with sugar between 1816 —when Professor Magendie was inspired by the ship-wrecked sailors of 1793 to feed sugar and water to the dogs who subsequently died in his laboratory—and 1940. Although he does not mention early medical alerts on sugar from such medical writers as Rauwolf, Willis, and Hurt, the good professor had time and space to record this kind of pro-sugar flimflam which hasn't changed from that day to this: "That eminent physician Sir John Pringle remarked that the plague *had* never been known in any country where sugar composes a material part of the diet of the inhabitants." (Emphasis added.) Just which plague, or sickness, neither writer classified.

"Thomas Thompson writing in 1838 said: 'Sugar has now become an essential part of the food of the Euro-peans. It contains *perhaps* a greater proportion of nourish-ment than any other vegetable substance *in the same bulk. . . . If we believe Dr. Rush,* the plentiful use of it is *one of the best* preventatives of the disease occa-sioned by worms. It has long been supposed to have a tendency to injure the teeth; but this prejudice is now given up.' " (Emphasis added.)

While the italics are mine, the tongue in cheek has got to be Professor McCollum's. Is he telling us what-ever is, is OK? Is he telling us that two hundred years of science has missed the boat? If sugar can kill dogs, as Professor Magendie seems to have proven, it certainly ought to be able to kill worms. There has been no out-break of leprosy in Ashtabula, Ohio, since the establish-ment of a Coca-Cola plant there in 1922. How about turning that into a scientific fact and hiring some doctor to cite it in the *Ladies' Home Journal?*

Unhappily, we must remind ourselves that scientists today, and always, accomplish little without a sponsor. Official scientific facts—as distinguished from plain gar-den variety facts like the one the British farmer came by in his own meadow with his own sheep—are expensive to come by. The protocols of modern science have com-pounded the costs of scientific inquiry. We have no right

to be surprised when we read the introduction to Mc-
Collum's *A History of Nutrition* and find that "The
author and publishers are indebted to The Nutrition
Foundation, Inc., for a grant provided to meet a portion
of the cost of publication of this book."

What, you might ask, is The Nutrition Foundation,
Inc.? The author and the publishers don't tell you. It
happens to be a front organization for the leading sugar
pushing conglomerates in the food business, including
the American Sugar Refining Company, Coca-Cola, Pepsi-
Cola, Curtis Candy Co., General Foods, General Mills,
Nestles Co., Inc., Pet Milk Co., and Sunshine Biscuits;
about forty-five such companies in all.

Perhaps the most significant thing about McCollum's
1957 history was what he left out: A monumental earlier
work described by an eminent Harvard professor as "one
of those epochal pieces of research which makes every
other investigator desirous of kicking himself because
he never thought of doing the same thing."

In the 1930s, a research dentist from Cleveland, Ohio,
Dr. Weston A. Price, traveled all over the world—from
the lands of the Eskimos to the South Sea Islands, from
Africa to New Zealand. His *Nutrition and Physical Degeneration: A Comparison of Primitive and Modern Diets
and Their Effects*, which is illustrated with hundreds of
photographs, was first published in 1939.

The work of Dr. Price took the whole world as his
laboratory. His devastating conclusion, recorded in horri-
fying detail in area after area, was simple: People who
live under so-called backward primitive conditions had
excellent teeth and wonderful general health. They ate
natural, unrefined food from their own locale. As soon
as refined, sugared foods were imported as a result of
contact with "civilization," physical degeneration began
in a way that was definitely observable within a single
generation.

Any credibility the sugar pushers have is based on
our ignorance of works like that of Dr. Price. Sugar manufacturers keep trying, hoping, and contributing generous
research grants to colleges and universities; but the research laboratories never come up with anything solid

the manufacturers can use. Invariably, the research results are bad news.

"Let us go to the ignorant savage, consider his way of eating and be wise," Harvard professor Earnest Hooten said in *Apes, Men and Morons.* "Let us cease pretending that toothbrushes and toothpaste are anymore important than shoebrushes and shoepolish. It is store food that has given us store teeth."

When the researchers bite the hands that feed them, and the news gets out, it's embarrassing all around. In 1958, *Time* magazine reported that a Harvard biochemist and his assistants had worked with myriads of mice for more than ten years, bankrolled by the Sugar Research Foundation, Inc., to the tune of $57,000, to find out how sugar causes dental cavities and how to prevent this. It took them ten years to discover that there was no way to prevent sugar causing dental decay. When the researchers reported their findings in *Dental Association Journal*, their source of money dried up. The Sugar Research Foundation withdrew its support.

The more scientists disappointed them, the more the sugar pushers had to rely on the ad men.

"It is a rule of thumb," wrote Paul Hawken, "the more you see a product advertised, the more of a ripoff it is." Hawken, author of *The Magic of Findhorn*, spent several years building a natural food business which used no advertising and no sugar.

A product like Coca-Cola which contains known poisons and destroys teeth and stomach has one of the most stunning ad campaigns in the history of the Western world.

It is really fantastic: This unreal amount of money creating an illusion—the illusion that "Coke is the real thing." Now Coke executives have learned from extensive research that young America is searching for what is real, meaningful in this plastic world, and one bright ad executive comes up with the idea that it is Coke. Yep, Coke is the real thing and this is drilled into the minds of 97 percent of all young people between the age of six and nineteen until their teeth are rotting just like their parents' did.

There is nothing truthful about advertising. Imagine a

young pimply faced kid in front of a camera telling folks how clear his complexion was before he started drinking Coke; and even though he knows it's bumming his social life, he just can't seem to get off the stuff. That would be truth in advertising. Or how about a young girl holding up a can of orange drink made in New Jersey saying the reason it's orange is because of the food coloring. The reason it is bad is because we use coal-tar artificial flavors, and the reason we would like you to try it is because we want to make money. Truth in advertising would be the end of three major networks, 500 magazines, several thousand newspapers, and tens of thousands of businesses. So there will never be truth in advertising.

After scanning fifty years of sugar advertising, it's hard to disagree with Hawken.

When calories became the big thing in the 1920s, and everybody was learning to count them, the sugar pushers turned up with a new pitch. They boasted there were 2,500 calories in a pound of sugar. A little over a quarter pound of sugar would produce 20 percent of the total daily quota.

"If you could buy all your food energy as cheaply as you buy calories in sugar," they told us, "your board bill for the year would be very low. If sugar were seven cents a pound, it would cost less than $35 for a whole year."

A very inexpensive way to kill yourself.

"Of course, we don't live on any such unbalanced diet," they admitted later. "But that figure serves to point out how inexpensive sugar is as an energy building food. What was once a luxury only a privileged few could enjoy is now a food for the poorest of people."

Later the sugar pushers advertised that sugar was chemically pure, topping Ivory Soap in that department, being 99.9 percent pure against Ivory's vaunted 99.44. "No food of our every day diet is purer," we were assured.

What was meant by purity, besides the unarguable fact that all vitamins, minerals, salts, fibers, and proteins had been removed in the refining process? Well, the sugar pushers came up with a new slant on purity.

"You don't have to sort it like beans, wash it like rice. Every grain is like every other. No waste attends its use. No useless bones like in meat, no grounds like coffee."

Pure is a favorite adjective of the sugar pushers because it means one thing to the chemists and another thing to the ordinary mortals. When honey is labeled pure, this means that it is in its natural state (stolen directly from the bees who made it), no adulteration with sucrose to stretch it and no harmful chemical residues which men may have sprayed on the flowers. It does not mean that the honey is free from minerals like iodine, iron, calcium, phosphorus, or multiple vitamins. So effective is the purification process which sugar cane and beets undergo in the refineries, that sugar ends up as chemically pure as the morphine or the heroin a chemist has on his laboratory shelves. What nutritional virtue this abstract chemical purity represents, the sugar pushers never tell us.

Beginning with World War I, the sugar pushers coated their propaganda with a preparedness pitch. "Dietitians have known the high food value of sugar for a long time," said an industry tract of the 1920s. "But it took World War I to bring this home. The energy building power of sugar reaches the muscles in minutes and it is of value to soldiers as a ration given them just before an attack was launched." The sugar pushers have been harping on the energy building power of sucrose for years because it contains *nothing else.* Caloric energy and habit forming taste, that's what sucrose has and nothing else. All other foods contain energy plus. All foods contain *some* nutrients in the way of proteins, carbohydrates, vitamins, or minerals—or all of these. Sucrose contains caloric energy—period.

The "quick" energy claim the sugar pushers talk about, which drives reluctant doughboys over the top and drives children up the wall, is based on the fact that refined sucrose is not digested in the mouth or the stomach but passes directly to the lower intestines and thence to the bloodstream. The extra speed with which sucrose enters the bloodstream does more harm than good.

Anyway, in World War I, while sucrose was rationed for the folks back home, it flowed freely and unrationed to the fighting doughboys. They not only had it in their candy and chewing gum before attacks, it was available for breakfast, lunch, and dinner. Perhaps the army was consciously using sucrose as a stimulant for the troops about to go over the top (hashish was used in the same way by the Assassins against the Crusaders.) Refined sucrose might have worked as a stimulant through World Wars I and II; but by the time of Korea and Viet Nam, the troops were so glutted with sugar that many turned on to hashish . . . pot . . . grass and even stronger addictive drugs.

Much of the public confusion about refined sugar is compounded by language. Sugars are classified by chemists as carbohydrates. This manufactured word means a substance containing carbon with oxygen and hydrogen.

If chemists want to use these hermetic terms in their laboratories when they talk to one another, fine. The use of the word carbohydrate outside the laboratory—especially in food labeling and advertising lingo—to describe both natural, complete cereal grains (which have been a principal food of mankind for thousands of years) and man-refined sugar (which is a manufactured drug and principal poison of mankind for only a few hundred years) is demonstrably wicked. This kind of confusion makes possible the flimflam practiced by sugar pushers to confound anxious mothers into thinking kiddies need sugar to survive.

In 1973, the Sugar Information Foundation placed full page advertisements in national magazines. Actually, the ads were disguised retractions they were forced to make in a strategic retreat after a lengthy tussle with the Federal Trade Commission over an earlier ad campaign claiming that a little shot of sugar before meals would "curb" your appetite. "You need carbohydrates. And it so happens that sugar is the best-tasting carbohydrate." You might as well say everybody needs liquids every day. It so happens that many people find champagne is the best tasting liquid. How long would the Women's Christian Temperance Union let the liquor lobby get away with that one?

The use of the word *carbohydrate* to describe sugar is deliberately misleading. Since the improved labeling of nutritional properties was required on packages and cans, refined carbohydrates like sugar are lumped together with those carbohydrates which may or may not be refined. The several types of carbohydrates are added together for an overall carbohydrate total. Thus, the effect of the label is to hide the sugar content from the unwary buyer. Chemists add to the confusion by using the word sugar to describe an entire group of substances that are similar but not identical.

Glucose is a sugar found usually with other sugars, in fruits and vegetables. It is a key material in the metabolism of all plants and animals. Many of our principal foods are converted into *glucose* in our bodies. Glucose is always present in our bloodstream, and it is often called blood sugar.

Dextrose, derived synthetically from starch, also called "corn sugar."

Fructose is fruit sugar.

Maltose is malt sugar.

Lactose is milk sugar.

Sucrose is refined sugar made from the sugar cane and the sugar beet.

Glucose has always been an essential element in the human bloodstream. *Sucrose* addiction is something new in the history of the human animal. To use the word sugar to describe two substances which are far from being identical, which have different chemical structures, and which affect the body in profoundly different ways compounds confusion. It makes possible more flimflam from the sugar pushers who tell us how important *sugar* is as an essential component of the human body, how it is oxidized to produce energy, how it is metabolized to produce warmth, and so on. They're talking about glucose, of course, which is manufactured in our bodies. However, one is led to believe that the manufacturers are talking about the sucrose which is made in their refineries. When the word sugar can mean the glucose in your blood as well as the sucrose in your Coca-Cola, it's great for the sugar pushers but it's rough on everybody else.

People have been bamboozled into thinking of their bodies the way they think of their checking accounts. If they suspect they have low blood sugar, they are programmed to snack on vending machine candies and sodas in order to raise their blood sugar level. Get it up. Actually this is the worst thing to do. The level of *glucose* in their blood is apt to be low because they are addicted to sucrose. People who kick sucrose addiction and stay off sucrose find that the glucose level of their blood returns to normal and stays there.

Since the late 1960s, millions of Americans have returned to natural food. A new type of store, the natural food store, has encouraged many to become dropouts at the supermarket. Natural food can be instrumental in restoring health. Many people, therefore, have come to equate the word "natural" with "healthy." So the sugar pushers have begun to pervert the word "natural" in order to mislead the public.

"Made from natural ingredients," the television sugar pushers tell us about product after product. The word *from* is not accented on television. It should be. Even refined sugar is made *from* natural ingredients. There is nothing new about that. The natural ingredients are cane and beets. But that four letter word *from* hardly suggests that 90 percent of the cane and beet have been removed. Heroin too could be advertised as being made *from* natural ingredients. The opium poppy is as natural as the sugar beet. It's what man does with it that tells the story.

The back of the box of Quaker 100% Natural Cereal reads, "Leaving well enough alone is the secret to the delicious taste. Every ingredient is natural. Nothing has been processed in. No artificial flavoring. No preservatives." Sounds great, doesn't it?

The box lists the proteins and the carbohydrates, the fats and vitamins. But nowhere does it tell you that it's about 20 percent sugar. That's hidden under the umbrella word carbohydrate. Nothing has been processed *in*. Everything *has* been processed *out* of the sugar but the calories.

Unfortunately, the examples are endless. If you want to avoid sugar in the supermarket, there is only one sure way. Don't buy anything unless it says on the label prominently, in plain English: "No sugar added." Use of the word *carbohydrate* as a "scientific" word for sugar has become a standard defense strategy with sugar pushers and many of their medical apologists. It's their security blanket.

On April 12, 1973, three prominent doctors, two of them representing the American Medical Association's Council on Food and Nutrition, were testifying before a Senate Committee on Nutrition and Human Needs.

Senator Schweiker of Pennsylvania tried valiantly to get the doctors to make the distinction between "sugar" and "carbohydrate." Here's what happened (italics added):

SENATOR SCHWEIKER. . . . one of the points apparently at issue here medically [in the AMA report] . . . saying it is inaccurate to state that sugar has high antinutrient properties. I wonder is this an accurate expression and who might comment on this for me?

DR. VAN ITALIE. When *we* talk about antinutrient properties, we *usually* refer to a substance in the diet or a drug that is antagonistic to a nutrient, interfering in some way with its use or its metabolism. Carbohydrate is metabolized or "burned" with the help of certain enzymes which contain thiamin and other B vitamins. Thus, there is an increased need for these vitamins when more carbohydrate in the diet is consumed. This is why people on very high carbohydrate diets in the Far East who also have a low vitamin B_1 intake develop beriberi. The fact that the requirement for vitamin B_1 and certain other B vitamins will increase somewhat when you take more carbohydrate does not justify the statement that carbohydrates—or sugar—is an antinutrient.

SENATOR SCHWEIKER. I am not talking carbohydrate; I'm talking sugar. Let's keep it on the sugar track.

DR. VAN ITALIE. There is no difference between sugar or carbohydrate with respect to vitamin B_1.

[This is inaccurate, unless refined carbohydrates are specified.]

SENATOR SCHWEIKER. Well, we have had a number of dentists just come before us recently and tell us how bad sugar, not carbohydrate, was on dental cavities.

DR. VAN ITALIE. That is correct, but that's not what I am talking about. Sugar is lacking in vitamins. That's agreed and it's *probably* bad for teeth. . . . I was addressing myself to one specific statement . . . which affirms sugar to be an antinutrient. This is scientifically not a correct statement. Sugar and all other carbohydrates increase the need for vitamin B_1. That's the only statement I made.

[Once again, the statement is inaccurate. Natural carbohydrates supply their own B vitamins; refined carbohydrates don't.]

DR. VAN ITALIE. An antinutrient is a substance that interferes with the utilization or metabolism of a nutrient. Something that actually antagonizes its metabolic use. It might be, let's say, an excess of certain toxic metal that might interfere with metabolism. Certain drugs interfere with the nutrients and are called antinutrients. The antifertility pill may have antinutrient properties.

SENATOR SCHWEIKER. And you are saying that something that increases the need for nutrients in terms of quantity is not an antinutrient?

DR. VAN ITALIE. That is correct.

SENATOR SCHWEIKER. Are you sure we are not getting into a semantic argument here?

DR. VAN ITALIE. It's misleading to say that there is something bad about carbohydrate because it increases the need for a vitamin. . . .

[It is even more misleading to talk about natural carbohydrates such as grains interchangeably with refined carbohydrates such as sugar.]

DR. VAN ITALIE. After all, exercise increases the need for certain vitamins. That doesn't mean that exercise is "antinutrient."

SENATOR SCHWEIKER. If we market a cereal and say we presweetened the cereal and added sugar, we are working against ourselves. A customer buys a pack of cereal, nutrients added, presweetened. Here we have both in the same ingredients. That increases the nutrients and who are we kidding? If we hadn't had the sugar we might not need the nutrients.

DR. VAN ITALIE. I am not defending sugar, Senator Schweiker. I am not in favor of an excessive intake of sugar. [Is anybody ever in favor of excess?] I was merely objecting to the term of antinutrient in the context it was used. I agree with you that when you add sugar to a product you may make people eat it because it is sweeter but it certainly adds no nutritional property other than energy.

SENATOR SCHWEIKER. Right. That is all the questions I have, Mr. Chairman. Thank you.

DR. BUTTERWORTH. Sugar is a carbohydrate.

SENATOR SCHWEIKER. It is one of the carbohydrates but to say that the whole range of carbohydrates and sugar are the same thing is not true. Dental cavities are caused by sugar, not by carbohydrates. That's exactly the differentiation I am trying to make.

DR. BUTTERWORTH. That is correct but I didn't want to leave the hearing with the impression that sugar is an antinutrient. Now, sugar may cause dental caries and, certainly, there is excellent evidence for that.

SENATOR SCHWEIKER. There is no doubt about that.

DR. BUTTERWORTH. No doubt. But it is not an antinutrient. Sugar is a nutrient and sugar is a carbohydrate.

SENATOR SCHWEIKER. But it does substantially increase the need for nutrients.

DR. VAN ITALIE. No more than other forms of carbohydrates. . . .

[He keeps repeating and repeating that inaccuracy. How many medical practitioners realize that some carbohydrates come *with* vitamins, whereas other carbohydrates are available only as "empty" calories, stripped of their vitamins.]

DR. VAN ITALIE. I think it is important to point out that any carbohydrate you take, no matter what it is, if it's going to be absorbed by the intestine, has to be reduced to "sugar" before it can be absorbed. [The difference between glucose made in the body from natural carbohydrates and refined white sugar can be the difference between life and death.] When you take starch, any form of starch, it's digested in the intestinal tract and ends up as glucose or one of the other simple sugars. Thus sugar or sucrose is really a "predigested" type of carbohydrate.

[More confusion. Sucrose is a refined carbohydrate; refinement removes 90 percent of its bulk and all its vitamins and minerals. This is precisely where the major damage to the body from refined sugar arises. To absorb this "predigested carbohydrate," the body has to deplete its store of vitamins and minerals; imbalance is created. Since the stress is continual if the diet is sugar-heavy, the eventual results are chronic ill health.]

SENATOR SCHWEIKER. Now, the FTC made the sugar associates quit advertising that sugar was an energy builder and nutrient. Now, say carbohydrate is an energy builder but to say sugar is an energy builder nutrient, the FTC made them cease and desist, so we are getting in a very close area here of what impression the public has.

DR. ADAMSON. I would like to examine the credentials of those who made this recommendation. It is certainly hard for me, not being a nutritionist, to accept that anybody who is qualified to make a judgment and testify to your committee could make a statement that sugar is not an energy deliverer—energy giver.

DR. VAN ITALIE. I think the reason that the FTC cracked down on that sugar ad was that the sugar people were suggesting there was something unique about sugar as an energy source. If this was the case, I believe the Federal Trade Commission was justified in their criticism of this kind of advertising approach.

SENATOR SCHWEIKER. But it was getting to the semantics of what the layman understands. It is very well for us to define the dimensions of what we mean but if the effect is the opposite on the public that is what the FTC was complaining about. They implied it was a nutrient. Now, when *you* say it's inaccurate to call it an antinutrient, we are getting awfully close to the same thing. That's two negatives making a positive.

DR. VAN ITALIE. Any food that contains readily available calories is a good source of energy. I think that's what the FTC was saying. [Really?]

SENATOR SCHWEIKER. When you say it's inaccurate to call it an antinutrient, you are really saying it is a nutrient, by any kind of deductive reasoning.

DR. VAN ITALIE. Sugar is a nutrient.

SENATOR SCHWEIKER. And that is just what the FTC said you can't say because they don't believe it.

DR. VAN ITALIE. I'm sorry, but I don't agree with that. I

think the FTC was objecting to possibly misleading information that the advertisers were using in the promotion of sugar.

SENATOR SCHWEIKER. Well, I'll be glad to show you the ad. I have a copy of it.

At that point the Chairman of the Senate Select Committee, Senator McGovern, said they were running out of time. The argument and the hearing were adjourned. Of course Senator Schweiker was right all along the line, as far as he went.

Some months later, a five-member arbitration panel of the National Advertising Review Board found that the claim that sugar was a nutrient was without foundation. The sugar pushers promised to stop making the claim until they could back it up. However, millions more people were misled before the ad was suspended. It cost nothing for the sugar manufacturers to promise not to use a similar advertising campaign.

While one arm of government was slapping the wrist of the sugar manufacturers, another arm of the government was rushing to the rescue. A brand new, multi-colored comic book which comes free on request (at taxpayer's expense) has been prepared by the U.S. Department of Agriculture and Health, Education and Welfare in cooperation with the Grocery Manufacturers of America and the Advertising Council. It does exactly what the FTC bagged the sugar pushers for doing; the comic implies that sugar is a nutrient. Sugar is listed under the major nutrients, and public confusion is compounded by the failure to make the basic and crucial distinction between natural carbohydrates such as those in whole grains, vegetables, and fruit and refined carbohydrates such as those in sugar and white flour. Even the elementary warning about what sugar does to your teeth is missing; its cautions on sugar are confined to quantitative warnings for overweight teenagers.

As the U.S. populace has learned in the 1970s, the years of Watergate, government from the White House down does not even pretend to be embarrassed when caught lying. This is progress, as Russell Baker of *The New York Times* says, no matter what the moralists tell you. Government lies are most dangerous when they are believed to be the truth.

Their credibility is based on our ignorance.

Almost twenty years ago, Dr. William Coda Martin tried to answer the question: When is a food a food and when a poison? His working definition of poison was:

Medically: Any substance applied to the body, ingested, or developed within the body, which causes or may cause disease.

Physically: Any substance which inhibits the activity of a catalyst which is a minor substance, chemical, or enzyme that activates a reaction.[6]

The dictionary gives an even broader definition for poison: "To exert a harmful influence on, or to pervert."

Dr. Martin classified refined sugar as a poison because it has been depleted of its life forces, vitamins, and minerals.

What is left consists of pure, refined carbohydrates. The body cannot utilize this refined starch and carbohydrate unless the depleted proteins, vitamins, and minerals are present. Nature supplies these elements in each plant in quantities sufficient to metabolize the carbohydrate in that particular plant. There is no excess for other added carbohydrates. Incomplete carbohydrate metabolism results in the formation of "toxic metabolite" such as Pyruvic acid and abnormal sugars containing 5 carbon atoms. Pyruvic acid accumulates in the brain and nervous system and the abnormal sugars in the red blood cells. These toxic metabolites interfere with the respiration of the cells. They cannot get sufficient oxygen to survive and function normally. In time some of the cells die. This interferes with the function of a part of the body and is the beginning of degenerative disease. With over 50 percent of our diet today composed of these refined carbohydrates [refined sugar, white flour, polished rice, macaroni, and most breakfast cereals], does it require a million dollars for research to find out why this generation is developing more and more degenerative diseases?

Things have changed very little in three hundred years.

When Dr. Thomas Willis's warning on sugar was published in 1685, it took almost forty years for the sugar industry to find a doctor to defend them. Finally, *Vindication of Sugar Against the Charge of Dr. Willis* was published in London. It was not written in Latin, as it might have been had it been addressed to the fellows of the Royal Society of which Willis was a founder. It was written in English and "dedicated to the ladies." Its author conceded that sugar was the subject of continuing controversy inside the medical profession; for he boasts of having outlived "many bitter enemies of that most delicious and nourishing balsamic preparation, fine sugar."

This was a jab at Willis, who died young—perhaps he had found out about the dangers of sugar the hard way. It's hard to read this so-called *Vindication* without suspecting that the author might have been offered a few shares in the British West Indian Company. It was no vindication at all. It was an all-out blurb:

I have frequently recommended the Ladies well-chosen morning repast, called Break-Fast, as consisting of good materials, namely bread, butter, milk, water, and sugar. Chocolate and tea are also endowed with uncommon virtues when warily and discreetly used; nor do I decry and condemn coffee tho' it proved very prejudicial to my own health. Coffee to some people is of good use when taken in just proportions, and for some particular disease, especially when they join it with a quantity of fine sugar. . . .

One caveat or caution, to those that are inclining to be too fat, namely that sugar being so very high a nourisher may dispose them to be fatter than they desire to be, who are afraid of their fine shapes, but then it makes amends by supplying a very wholesome and goodly countenance and sweetens peevish and cross humors where they unhappily prevail. . . .

More particularly in praise of sugar. It is sugar we call upon to correct the harshness of remaining sourness in our most sweet and delicate fruits, even in their ripe state, even the sweetest strawberries and raspberries are mended by strowing sugar on them, and currants are scarce tolerable without it. Sugar may be proved to be a lower sort of Vice

Regent to the Glorious Planet, the Sun, by anticipating the ripening virtue of this most illustrious Star.[7]

The author was Dr. Frederick Slare, Fellow of the Royal College of Physicians and the Royal Society. He sounds for all the world like Dr. Frederick Stare of the Harvard School of Nutrition, writing assurances about sugar today for the sugar-pushing magazines with large circulation.

In a recent interview with *W*, the bi-weekly version of *Women's Wear Daily*, Dr. Stare managed to bring things full circle, back to where the sugar pushers began years ago. He now finds the world energy crisis the imperative for *doubling* our intake of sugar:

We have to cultivate foods that require as little land as possible to produce a maximum amount of energy. For instance, it takes 0.15 acres of land to produce a million calories of sugar; it takes 17 acres of land to produce a million calories of meat. Calories are energy, and I would recommend that most people could healthily double their sugar intake daily.

Sugar is the cheapest source of food energy, and I predict it will become much more prevalent in the diets of the world.

People say that all you get out of sugar is calories, no nutrients. Like many foods, I expect it to be fortified more and more in the future. There is no perfect food, not even mother's milk.[8]

Stare's statement is one of those effective lies that contains truth, but does not express it. Again, its credibility is based on the reader's ignorance. The choice between sugar and meat is desperate and false. The raising of cane for sugar and beef for steak are both appallingly wasteful.

Sugar may offer the cheapest calories in the supermarket, until you count the total hidden cost. One estimate of the current cost of doing the backlog of repair and replacement of America's teeth runs to $54 billion.

The U.S. has already doubled its intake of sugar a few times since 1909, with the consequences in physical degeneration all around us.

"*People* say sugar is only calories, no nutrients," (emphasis added) says Dr. Stare. Whether this is true or false, he doesn't say. But by saying *people* instead of medical authorities like himself, it becomes an authoritative put down, hinting (without promising anything) that we will all find out better one day.

Meanwhile, Stare expects sugar to soon be fortified. The FDA will have to reverse itself again. "Enrichment" of devitalized sugar with a few synthetic vitamins will be the ultimate perversion.

If Dracula drains your blood with his teeth and gives you a vitamin B_{12} shot before he flies out the window, would you say you'd been had or enriched?

Sugar is not perfect, Stare admits. But, he continues, what food is, not even mother's milk.

Whose mother's milk is he talking about?

Sugar is a constant. Its lack of perfection as a food is total.

On any scale of nutrients, it would rate less than zero.

Mother's milk is as infinitely variable as life itself; it depends muchly—like the future of the human race—on the judgment each mother displays in her selection of food.

In an address on Food Faddism published by the Sugar Research Foundation on May 16, 1951, Dr. Stare is quoted as saying:

"I should certainly say before closing that the food industries, the Sugar Foundation, the Nutrition Foundation, and a number of food companies as individual companies have certainly done a lot in helping to support basic nutrition, and a lot in helping to support our department [of nutrition at Harvard] for which we are certainly appreciative."

Between 1950 and 1956, according to Open Letter II of the Boston Nutrition Society, January 22, 1957, these same groups contributed almost a quarter of a million dollars to Dr. Stare's Harvard Department of Nutrition.

Medical authorities on sugar, such as Dr. G. D. Campbell, physician to the Diabetic Clinic of King Edward VII Hospital, Durban, South Africa, have suggested urgent restriction—under the aegis of the World Health

Organization—of highly slanted and at times virtually untrue statements issued by sugar authorities and their medical agents to promote the sale of sugar. Campbell suggested a code of ethics banning the intrusion of interested or sugar-subsidized scientists in nutrition societies to debar them from using societies and academic titles in the interests of their employers or sponsors. "Disinterested scientists should be particularly guarded in acceptance of any form of financial assistance from the sugar authorities, specially those given with 'no strings attached'; more than one nutritionist has already had cause to regret such a course." Highly interesting versions of interim results have appeared from time to time in sugar publications, without the knowledge or sanction of the actual workers sponsored.[9]

Codes of Honesty

The Pure Food and Drug Laws are frequently regarded as landmarks in the history of social legislation. Certainly, government can have no higher aim than to attempt to protect the health of the people. Perhaps biological decline was well along when it became *necessary* to pass laws to prevent people, out of excessive devotion to moneymaking, from poisoning one another.

"When people lost sight of the way to live," wrote Lao Tsu, "came codes of love and honesty."

Keeping sugar out of beer had been a burning public barroom issue in England for centuries. Finally, Parliament passed an act in 1816 making it illegal for a brewer to have sugar in his *possession*. A brewer would be presumed guilty of intent to "sophisticate" if he so much as had sugar around. Where once knavish brewers had been dragged around town in a cart in which privy refuse had been collected, Parliament settled for fines and warnings. Sophisticators were handled in a "civilized" fashion. They were taken to court. The lawyers took over. The brewers organized and lobbied Parliament for twenty years until they were finally allowed to make—for their use only—a syrup from sugar for darkening their beer. So much for progress.

By that time an anonymous British consumerist had created a public uproar in 1830 with his book, *Deadly Adulteration and Slow Poisoning Unmasked,* or *Disease and Death in the Pot and the Bottle,* in which the blood-empoisoning and life-destroying adulterations of wines, spirits, beer, bread, flour, tea, *sugar,* spices, cheese-mongery, pastry, confectionary, medicines, etc., etc. are laid open to the public.

In 1850, a British physician had the happy idea of looking at suspected foods through that new invention the microscope. When he read a paper before the Botan-nical Society of London in 1850, on the shocking dis-coveries the microscopic examination had revealed in the sugar, there was uproar in the papers and among the populace. Dr. Arthur H. Hassall was in consequence commissioned by the owner of the eminent British medical periodical *The Lancet* to extend his microscopic examination to other foods. The pendulum of public panic swung all the way. *The Lancet* published Hassall's reports for four years, providing unassailable chapter and verse on the appalling state of the food supply. They pulled no punches. Names and addresses of hundreds of thousands of manufacturers and suppliers of adulterated food were laid bare. The figures were horrendous: Out of 34 sample coffees, only 3 were pure; of 49 loaves of bread, all contained alum; of 56 cocoa samples, only 8 were satisfactory; of 26 milks, 15 were adulterated; out of some 100 sugared confections, practically all con-tained one or more harmful chemicals.[1]

Parliamentary commissions were appointed; there were Watergate-type hearings for years. In the end, tough laws were passed; and the litigation went on for years. By 1899, however, much of Britain's food production had become industrialized, which created a fresh problem. Manufacturers were able to deceive the unsuspecting public. Then, a major disaster occurred in 1900. Some 6,000 people fell ill of a strange new disease for which nobody had a name. It was alternately labeled alcoholism, peripheral neuritis; or multiple neuritis.

Before any great medical brains could find a foreign bacterium, an exotic insect, or an obscure amoeba to hang this on, it was discovered that most of the victims— including some seventy who died—had one thing in common. All were beer drinkers. Many worked in breweries—models of modern breweries. Eventually, an investigation revealed dangerous amounts of arsenic in the suspected brew. The beer was hauled off the market; the epidemic was no more. It was as simple as that. All the breweries implicated in the epidemic had been using brewing sugars—glucose and invert sugars—supplied by a single firm. The brewing sugars from this source were found to have been contaminated by arsenic in the course of their manufacture. Some specimens contained as much as 2.6 percent!

A royal commission was appointed to get to the bottom of the British beer barrel. In the course of their investigation, frightening details were uncovered about sugar refining: carbonic acid gas was passed through the liquid juice of the cane or beet to precipitate other impurities like lime and strontia used in a previous stage of refinement. When this carbonic acid gas is obtained from coal, sugar often shows traces of arsenic! When arsenical malt or sugar additives are fermented, as in brewing, the yeast precipitates upon itself a considerable proportion of the impurity, thus partly cleansing the beer, but all preparations made from this yeast are thus exposed to contamination from arsenic.

The royal commission discovered what the country people had known intuitively when they rode knavish brewers out of town. On the continent, beer was still made in the old fashioned way—malt was not dried in kilns with combustion gases but on floors heated from below. The slow traditional process was safe. German and other continental beer did not contain arsenic. This lethal substance had only been found in the beers of industrialized, progressive Britain! This discovery opened up alarming possibilities. The dangerous brew of invert sugars was not only used in beer—after Parliament gave in and permitted it in 1847—but in a host of other "sophisticated" products like honey, jam, marmalade, and candy.

With fine understatement, the *Encyclopaedia Britannica* confirms the axiom of Lao Tsu: "It is difficult to say in the present state of the law whether such admixture amounts to adulteration. It was clearly made originally for fraudulent purposes, but usage and high court decision have gradually given the practice an air of respectability." The epitaph for pure food legislation in an industrial society was written in Britain before the United States ever got moving on the question. The battle began in Britain over beer. In the U.S., it arose over whiskey and Coca-Cola.

In both countries, then as now, government was an annex to trade. Political corruption was an offshoot of business corruption. From the whiskey scandals at the time of President Grant in the 1870s to Teapot Dome in the 1920s to the Watergate in the 1970s, the public is often better informed on political corruption than on business corruption. Government cannot be conducted wholly in the dark; business can, in the words of John Jay Chapman. That's especially true of the food business. When a man runs for Congress, his life becomes an open book. Even though in 1975 other foods have to be labeled clearly to show their ingredients, consumers who want to know the ingredients of ice cream find it's none of their business.

The U.S. government, through the Department of Internal Revenue, has had its mitts in the whiskey business from the earliest days of this republic. A heavy excise tax was levied on manufactured alcohol, both for industrial use and for imbibing in the pursuit of happiness. For years, whiskey was whiskey: a distillate, in a pot still, of the fermented mash of a cereal or a mixture of cereals. All the natural elements of the grain were contained in it, as well as ethyl alcohol and its congeners, which were volatile at the temperature of distillation. The whiskey also contained coloring matters and other soluble products extracted from the oak storage casks, and any new compounds arising during storage. Potable whiskey was kept in storage for four years. Whiskey was an Irish and Scotch version of the Latin *aqua vitae,* water of life, which the French made from the grape and called *eau de vie.* Its Scottish Gaelic name was *uisge beatha,* and then *usquebaugh,* and finally Anglicised as *whiskey.*

Then came the invention of the continuous still, a device which—like the sugar refinery—revolutionized production. Cheap, distilled, untaxed alcohol could now be manufactured. Mixed with genuine whiskey with flavoring and coloring added, the mixture could be passed off as whiskey. Fake whiskey was described as "rectified." Overnight, the manufacture of the cheap alcohol became a tremendous new business. The fake stuff was put on the market under the name and appearance of the regular natural stuff. Congress was persuaded to go along with this palpable fraud in return for taking its cut in taxes. Drunkenness and alcoholic poisoning were now within reach of everyone, rich and poor. Alcoholism soon became a national disease and eventually, in its turn, created the antidote: the crusade for prohibition of all booze, real and fake.

It was an era of anything goes in the food, drink, and drug department. Heroin, morphine, and cocaine were sold over the counter in drugstores and shops. Patent medicines, based on addictive drugs, were a billion dollar mail-order business. Rectified whiskey was for sale in the country store and the saloon. Makers of addictive nostrums were the largest single advertisers in the newspapers and magazines. During the Spanish American War, suppliers of bully beef to the armed forces went too far. Fighting men sickened and died from eating rotten meat. The meat scandal created a public uproar. Crusading magazines began exposing the shocking use of additives, fake flavorings, and colorings in canned and bottled food. Upton Sinclair did a job on the meat packers; his novel *The Jungle* shocked the public and created a clamor for government action.

The chief of the Department of Agriculture's Bureau of Chemistry, Dr. Harvey W. Wiley, was the Ralph Nader of his time. After crusading for pure food and drug legislation for decades, he finally undertook a public experiment in 1902 which caught the imagination of the populace. Male volunteers were drafted into teams (which the newspapers soon called "The Poison Squad"). Young, healthy men were fed the old-fashioned American diet. One by one, the new fangled food additives, which manufacturers were adding to ketchup, canned corn, bread, and meat, were introduced to their diet. Food processors trembled, the public cheered, and followed the experiment—which was reported in the newspapers daily—with avid interest. For five years, the Poison Squad was given regular doses of the food preservatives, adulterants, and coloring matter then in general use by food processors: boric acid, borax, salicylic acid, salicylates, benzoic acid, benzoates, sulfur dioxide, sulfites, formaldehyde, sulfate of copper, and saltpeter. Periodically, Dr. Wiley published bulletins detailing the serious physical effects of these chemicals then being used in food. The newspapers soon made Wiley's name a household word. The Poison Squad was as famous in their heyday as the astronauts were in theirs.

The combined forces of the food lobby, the drug lobby, and the rectified whiskey lobby were routed. After twenty-five years of public agitation for reform, pure food and drug laws were piloted through Congress. The combined vote of Senate and House was 304 for; only 21 against. On January 1, 1907, Dr. Wiley's Bureau of Chemistry was empowered to police the U.S. food industry: To legislate, to inspect, and to take offenders to court.

Wiley and his bureau began enforcing the law to the letter. Casks of fake whiskey were seized and manufacturers were dragged into court. Shipments of Coca-Cola across state lines were seized for being adulterated and misbranded.[2]

What was Coca-Cola?

Well, in the early seventeenth century, an Italian voyager to South America found the Indians there constantly chewing on the leaf of the coca plant; at work, on trips, they carried it in small pouches and kept it in their mouths with a small amount of ground lime or ashes of the quinine plant. "Having it, they work happily and walk a day or two without refreshing themselves or otherwise eating anything," wrote Francesco Carletti in his journal of 1594-1606.

Three or four times a day, everything stopped for the coca break. For the Peruvian Indians, it had been the pause—from time immemorial—that refreshes, stimulates, sharpens the mind, and increases physical prowess. Through refinement of the South American coca leaf, a constellation of alkaloid drugs, which are called cocaine, were derived. The coca plant is now cultivated in the West Indies, Java, Sumatra, and other parts of the tropical world.

In North America, the Indians chewed or smoked tobacco. However, in West Africa, the natives had a habit of getting high from chewing kernels of the cola nut. The nut contained caffeine (found in lower concentrations in coffee) and another stimulant, which found its way into Western medicine as the heart stimulant kolanin.

In the good old days in the South, when many highborn ladies routinely "doctored" themselves with daily doses of laudanum and other addicting opium syrups, Coca-Cola began as a patented headache remedy. Drug pushing was a multibillion dollar, wholly legitimate, and legal business in those days. Opium, cocaine, morphine, and later heroin were advertised on the front pages of newspapers and magazines as a cure for everything from syphilis to bad breath. The patented headache remedy, like most sugared medicines on the market, was habit-forming by definition and design. The Coca-Cola habit became the basis of a multimillion dollar business in the South. In the 1890s, Coca-Cola advertising described the product as "A Wonderful Nerve and Brain Tonic and Remarkable Therapeutic Agent." The federal government took its first official look at the "tonic" after passage of the first Pure Food and Drug Law in 1906. In carrying out provisions of the law, the Bureau of Chemistry of the U.S. Department of Agriculture analyzed Coca-Cola. Charges were brought against the company by the Bureau of Chemistry, who seized an amount of Coca-Cola in interstate transit and recommended that criminal charges for adulteration and misbranding be brought against the manufacturers and dealers.

"Those who adulterated our food and drugs foresaw that if they could cripple the activities of the Bureau of Chemistry," its founder and chief Dr. Harvey W. Wiley wrote some years later, "they could save themselves from indictments. They proceeded along successful lines to effect this paralysis." It proved impossible to have any of the bureau's accusations against Coca-Cola endorsed by higher authority. Finally the Bureau of Chemistry was ordered, over the signature of the secretary of agriculture, "to cease and desist in its activities in trying to get the Coca-Cola company to the bar of justice."

The fix was in, everybody thought, at the highest level, like Watergate and ITT in the 1970s. And then a gutsy newspaper owner from Atlanta, Mr. Seeley, came up to Washington and paid a visit to Dr. Wiley. He wanted to know why the bureau was pressing criminal charges against the manufacturers of ketchup and string beans and laying off Coca-Cola. Dr. Wiley calmly showed him his signed orders from the secretary of Agriculture. Mr. Seeley blew his top. "He was greatly astonished that the secretary of Agriculture had thus interfered with the administration of justice," said Dr. Wiley.

The angry visitor immediately bounced over to the office of the secretary of Agriculture and "entered a vigorous protest against the policy of the department in protecting adulterators and misbranders of foods."

He threatened to publicize all the gory details in his Atlanta newspaper unless the secretary recalled the order. The Bureau of Chemistry was directed to go ahead with the prosecution. Publicly, the Department of Agriculture gave the go-ahead. They had no choice. Privately, they did everything possible to scuttle the case from the inside. The bureau wanted to bring the case to the District of Columbia; transporting experts and assembling evidence would be simpler, as well as less expensive for the government. However, the top echelons in the department were determined that the case should be tried in Chattanooga, Tennessee. Coca-Cola had its chief bottling works there, and the company also owned a great deal of real estate including the principal hotel—and perhaps a judge or two. "The whole environment in Chattanooga was favorable to the Coca-Cola industry," said Dr. Wiley. "The department was put to a large expense to send its scientific officers so far away from base. It was equivalent to trying the case in Atlanta."

The trial was long, drawn-out, and hotly contested. An array of experts testified on both sides. The attorneys for Coca-Cola finally moved to dismiss the case on a technicality: caffeine, the chief injurious substance in Coca-Cola, was not an added substance under the law because it was in the original formula. The Chattanooga judge promptly obliged and that was supposed to be the end of that. Finally, the Bureau of Chemistry appealed that decision, eventually to the Supreme Court.

Chief Justice Charles Evans Hughes wrote the unanimous opinion reversing the Chattanooga judge and upholding the Bureau of Chemistry in September 1917. "We can see no escape from the conclusion that [caffeine] is an added ingredient within the meaning of the statute . . . the claimant has always insisted and now insists that its product contains both [coca and cola]. . . . We conclude that the Court erred in directing a verdict . . . judgment is reversed. . . ."[3]

The Supreme Court decision had demolished the contentions of Coca-Cola by deciding that caffeine was an added substance and that Coca-Cola was a descriptive and not a distinctive name. Coca-Cola was in trouble. As would happen later, when Supreme Court decisions on enforcement of the Harrison Drug Control Act of 1914 were perverted by the executive branch of government, the court was unable to enforce its decisions. The judicial—like the legislative—branch of government has no troops. T Men and G Men and agents for the Department of Agriculture work for the White House and the Executive. Defiance of law and order is a game at which government can beat you. What Coca-Cola undertook to do behind the scenes to save its corporate life, we can only surmise. When brought back into court in Chattanooga in 1917, Coca-Cola pleaded *nolo contendere,* no contest.

On motion of the district attorney, the court passed sentence which, at face value, seemed severe enough to satisfy the most belligerent newspaper editor from Atlanta. The company was ordered to pay all costs of the action; forty barrels and twenty kegs of seized Coca-Cola were to be released to the company with the provision that Coca-Cola "shall not be sold or otherwise disposed of contrary to the provisions of the federal Food and Drugs Act, or the laws of any state, territory, or district, or insular possessions of the United States."

That would seem to be clear enough. Coca-Cola cannot be sold outside of Georgia. But the judge's decision also included a safety valve clause: ". . . Judgment of forfeiture shall not be binding upon the said Coca-Cola Company or its product, except as to this cause, and the particular goods seized herein. . . ."

In other words, Coca-Cola could not sell the forty barrels and twenty kegs, but they were free to go ahead and sell other barrels and other kegs in other places. The government would have to bring action through the Bureau of Chemistry under the Pure Food and Drug Law again and again, barrel by barrel, keg by keg, bottle by bottle. A few innocent, little judicial words provided a loophole big enough to accommodate a tank car.

The secretary of Agriculture had to be blackmailed into enforcing the law against Coca-Cola in the first place. Secure in the belief that the public, preoccupied with preparedness for a war of survival against the beastly Hun, would settle for the symbolic gesture, and not the reality, he forbade the Bureau of Chemistry from bringing in any more action against the Coca-Cola Company. By this time, the valiant Dr. Wiley had been the subject of retaliatory investigations and phony charges—of the kind that General Motors tried to use in the 1960s against Ralph Nader.

As Wiley wrote in his book:

No attempt was made by the executors of the food law to inforce the decree of the courts by beginning action against Coca-Cola products every time they crossed a state line.

Under the opinions of the Supreme Court, such proceedings would have been uniformly successful.

Owing to a lack of these proceedings, the Coca-Cola Company has its stock now listed on the New York Stock Exchange. Its sales have been enormously increased, invading the North, as they previously invaded the South. The effect of drinking caffeine on an empty stomach and in a free state are far more dangerous than drinking an equal quantity of caffeine wrapped up with tannic acid in tea and coffee. The threat to health and happiness of our people is reaching far greater proportions due to this expansion of trade. The governors of the New York Exchange have admitted the stock of the Coca-Cola Company, the products of which have been condemned by a United States court as both adulterated and misbranded. This baleful condition could have been easily avoided if the enforcing officers had raised their hands to protest against the further development of this business by seizing its products and bringing criminal action against its manufacturers. Another interesting story would have been clarified if the Supreme Court could have passed an opinion on the immunity granted the Coca-Cola Company by the Court.

The campaign for passage of the Pure Food and Drug Laws had been conducted out in the open. Its undoing was accomplished in the dark. Food processors and rectified whiskey makers formed a united front to sabotage Wiley and his bureau. Representatives of the food business camped on the doorsteps of legislators, cabinet officers, and the president of the United States, complaining that sacred capital was being confiscated, praying, begging, and blackmailing for relief from the policies of Wiley and his bureau. But Wiley had become a symbol of incorruptible service in the public interest, so they had to proceed gingerly, deviously.

When the ketchup makers and the canners of corn visited the White House, President Teddy Roosevelt listened to their woeful pleas. Then he summoned his secretary of Agriculture and Dr. Wiley to listen to the complaints. After their pitiful recital of restrictions that hampered their moneymaking activities, the President turned to his secretary of Agriculture and said: "What is your opinion about the propriety of enforcing the rulings of your Chief of Bureau?" (No presidential tapes exist of this encounter, only Wiley's notes—and history is fortunate to have even these.)

The secretary replied that the law was the law. Substances added to food for any purpose which are deleterious to the health shall be forbidden. "Dr. Wiley made extensive investigation in feeding benzoated foods to healthy young men and in every instance he found that their health was undermined."

Then Teddy turned to Wiley and asked him what he thought.

"Mr. President," Wiley replied, "I don't *think,* I *know* by patient experiment that benzoate of soda or benzoic acid added to human food is injurious to health."

The President banged the table with his fist and told his important corporate visitors: "This substance that you are using is injurious to health and you shall not use it any longer."

That would seem to be that. But one of the emissaries —perhaps the most prestigious—was an important political figure, a man about to be elected vice president of the United States to replace Roosevelt (who had succeeded to the presidency on the assassination of McKinley). James S. Sherman was high in the counsels of the Republican party, although that day he was representing his own firm, Sherman Brothers of New York.

"Mr. President," he began, "there is another matter that we spoke to you about yesterday that is not included in what you have just said about the use of benzoate. I refer to the use of saccharin in foods. My firm last year saved $4,000 by sweetening canned corn with saccharin instead of sugar. We want a decision from you on this question."

Dr. Wiley was no politician. All the others were. He was no intimate of the President's, as were the others. If he had ever had tea or coffee with the President he might have known what they knew. He walked into a trap. Violating presidential protocol, instead of waiting for the President to ask his view, he was so outraged at this bare-faced political appeal, he blurted it out.

"Every one who ate that sweet corn was deceived," Wiley declared. "He thought he was eating sugar, when in point of fact he was eating a coal tar product totally devoid of food value and extremely injurious to health."

As Wiley recalled later, the President changed abruptly from Dr. Jekyll to Mr. Hyde. Turning angrily to Wiley, he said:

"You tell me that saccharin is injurious to health?"

"Yes, Mr. President," said Wiley, "I do tell you that."

"Dr. Rixey gives it to me every day," the President replied.

"Mr. President, he probably thinks you may be threatened with diabetes," said Wiley.

"Anyone who says saccharin is injurious to health is an idiot." The President was angry. The meeting broke up. Wiley never saw the President again. Dr. Wiley dates the dismantling of the enforcement of the Pure Food and Drug Laws to that incident that day in the White House Cabinet Room, during the first year of enforcement of the law.[4]

Teddy Roosevelt had been an ailing, sickly youth. Overcoming these physical shortcomings, he had become a crusading New York police commissioner, a tough Rough Rider War Hero, an authentic American hero. Low glucose in the blood had not yet been officially called hypoglycemia. It was the custom for doctors with potentially diabetic patients to prescribe saccharin instead of sugar. Wiley hadn't known that the President may have been one of those. You can bet that the food lobbyists, especially the chap who was about to be nominated as vice president, were better briefed than the chief of the Bureau of Chemistry.

Wiley had contravened the advice of the President's own doctor. He stood convicted of *lèse majesté*. Who knew that the former First Lady, Ida McKinley, was prone to have epileptic fits at state dinners? Who knew that President Kennedy's doctors were giving him cortisone and/or amphetamines, or that President Franklin Roosevelt's doctors were giving him morphine toward the end? Excessive devotion to the public health had turned a minor gaffe into a major political crisis. Wiley never ceased to blame himself for unwittingly providing the trigger for undoing the pure food laws which he fought for all his life.

The very next day, Teddy Roosevelt staged an executive coup by appointing a referee board of consulting scientific experts. He made sure his new board would uphold him and his White House physician by appointing as its chairman Dr. I. Remsen, the man who had been given a medal as the discoverer of saccharin. The chairman was empowered to select other members of the panel. This was the beginning of the end of Dr. Wiley and his Bureau of Chemistry. The manufacturers of ersatz whiskey took their case to the White House; another board was appointed to supersede Dr. Wiley. Wiley was totally occupied fighting bureaucratic battles inside his office. A phoney investigation brought silly charges in an attempt to discredit him. He was gagged by executive decree. His scientific bulletins warning against new food additives went unpublished. Eventually, he was forced to resign in order to be able to speak out in public and before the Congress.

It was the plain provision of the act, and was fully understood at the time of enactment, as stated in the law itself, that the Bureau of Chemistry was to examine all samples of suspected foods and drugs to determine whether they were adulterated or misbranded and that if this examination disclosed such facts the matter was to be referred to the courts for decision. Interest after interest, engaged in what the Bureau of Chemistry found to be the manufacture of misbranded or adulterated foods and drugs, made an appeal to escape appearing in court to defend their practices. Various methods were employed to secure this end; many of which were successful.

One by one I found that the activities pertaining to the Bureau of Chemistry were restricted and various forms of manipulated food products were withdrawn from its consideration and referred either to other bodies not contemplated by the law or directly relieved from further control. A few of the instances of this kind are well known. Among these may be mentioned the manufacture of so-called whiskey from alcohol, colors, and flavors; the addition to food prod ucts of benzoic acid and its salts, of sulfurous acid and its salts, of sulfate of copper, of saccharin, and of alum; the manufacture of so-called wines from pomace, chemicals, and colors; the floating of oysters in polluted waters for the purpose of making them look fatter and larger than they really are for the purposes of sale; the selling of moldy, fermented, decomposed, and misbranded grains; the offering to the people of glucose under the name "corn syrup," thus taking a name which rightfully belongs to another product made directly from Indian corn stalks.

The official toleration and validation of such practices have restricted the activities of the Bureau of Chemistry to a very narrow field. As a result of these restrictions, I have been instructed to refrain from stating in any public way my own opinions regarding the effect of these substances upon health, and this restriction has interfered with my academic freedom of speech on matters relating directly to the public welfare.[5]

Upton Sinclair's book *The Jungle* had helped turn the tide in favor of the Pure Food and Drug Laws. After he left government, Dr. Wiley wrote a book telling the whole sordid story of how those laws had been scuttled from within government. He knew where the bodies were buried, and he resolved to tell it all and let the American people get riled up once again. However, he was no politician. Again he underestimated the forces arrayed against him. Wiley, undertaking to finance his book, turned his precious manuscript over to a printer. That manuscript mysteriously "disappeared" and has never been found to this day. Just how these things are done is rarely uncovered.

Shattered but unbroken, Dr. Wiley valiantly returned to work, rewriting his book from scratch. This chore occupied him totally for ten years. He tried to update matters, but by 1929 many of his shocking revelations were already old hat. Some of the villains were dead. Most of the politicians had passed on or at least out of power. Still, his volume *The History of a Crime Against the Food Law* was a primer on government corruption, quite unlike anything that had ever been written before. This time, he tried to protect himself. He took no chances on the manuscript getting lost again. Every facet of its production and printing was personally supervised by Wiley. When distribution began in 1929, it looked like a best seller. Books disappeared rapidly from bookstore shelves. Yet no letters were received from readers, no congratulations, no kudos, and virtually no reviews. The books kept on disappearing, yet copies could not be found anywhere.

In desperation, Dr. Wiley put the few remaining books in libraries around the country—they disappeared from libraries as quickly as they had vanished from the stores. Try your neighborhood library today and see if you can find a copy. It should surprise no one today that these things can happen, when the advertising budget for one food conglomerate is larger than the entire annual budget of the government agency charged with policing the industry. Dr. Wiley's valedictory on the last page of his exposé was prophetic in 1929. Today it is shattering.

If the Bureau of Chemistry had been permitted to enforce the law as it was written and as it tried to do, what would have been the condition now? No food product in our country would have any trace of benzoic acid, sulfurous acid or sulfites, or any alum or saccharin, save for medicinal purposes. No soft drink would contain any caffeine, or theobromine. No bleached flour would enter interstate commerce. Our foods and drugs would be wholly without any form of adulteration and misbranding. The health of our people would be vastly improved and their life greatly extended. The manufacturers of our food supply, and especially the millers, would devote their energies to improving the public health and promoting happiness in every home by the production of whole ground, unbolted cereal flours and meals.

The resistance of our people to infectious diseases would be greatly increased by a vastly improved and more wholesome diet. Our example would be followed by the civilized world and thus bring to the whole universe the benefits which our own people had received.

We would have been spared the ignominy and disgrace of great scientific men bending their efforts to defeat the purpose of one of the greatest laws ever enacted for the protection of the public welfare. Eminent officials of our government would have escaped the indignation of outraged public opinion because they permitted and encouraged these frauds on the public. The cause of a wholesome diet would not have been put back for fifty or a hundred years. And last but least, this History of a Crime would never have been written.

The Bureau of Chemistry was finally legally dismantled. In its place, the Food and Drug and Insecticide Administration, precursor of the Food and Drug Administration, was established. The Poison Squad, that group of healthy young men on whom Dr. Wiley had tested proposed new food additives *before* allowing the foods to be turned loose on the public at large, was ultimately replaced by the FDA's GRAS (Generally Regarded as Safe) list—a list of food colorings, additives, and adulterants. Manufacturers and food processors were given carte blanche to use practically anything in its products *until* evidence turned up that it might be injurious to the public health. The whole intent of the Pure Food and Drug Laws had been turned on its head.

The Poison Squad was enlarged to include everybody in the country. Today, the GRAS list has become so lengthy that the average American ingests five pounds of chemical additives every year, together with approximately another fifty pounds of hidden sugar.

Like the British admiralty two hundred years ago, the FDA spends much of its time acting as unofficial cheerleader for the food industry, telling us that the average American diet, whatever that is, is the best in the world's history. Dr. Wiley was posthumously honored by his government: A stamp bearing his name and face was issued. Eventually, he was nominated for the U.S. Hall of Fame. He won't make it in the 1970s. But one day, perhaps the day after the FDA tells us that Wiley was absolutely right about saccharin (among other things), and the pendulum of public panic really swings, his statue will surely be rushed to the pantheon of American heroes.

In 1971, saccharin was quietly removed from the GRAS list by the FDA. That quiet validation of Wiley's views took sixty odd years. Now the FDA has begun to restrict its use, but not in so-called low-calorie or sugarfree drinks, which are the biggest users of saccharin. The sugarfree, diet-food business booms as more and more Americans discover they have the *sugar blues:* It now grosses more than a billion dollars a year with diet soda as the top seller. In the last fifty years, plenty of alarms have been registered on the subject of America's addiction to sugar. How many of them have come from our official watchdogs in the Food and Drug Administration? None that I have been able to discover. In fact, when the operatives of the government bureau become unwillingly trapped in any facet of the sugar controversy, they seem to be telling us that everything is A-OK.

In 1961, an Ohio food company came up with a real marketing coup. They introduced a new product, fortified sugar. For years, grains, flours, and bread—gutted of vitamins and minerals in the refining process—had been sold as "fortified" and "enriched," after addition of a few synthetic vitamins. The FDA kept telling us that enriched flour was just as good as the real stuff. Billions of dollars in advertising had programmed the American housewife into grabbing for enriched this and fortified that. So why not enrich white sugar? Suddenly somebody did. "Fortified sugar" appeared on the market with a list of vitamins and minerals on the package: Iodine, iron, vitamin C, four B complex vitamins, and 400 units of vitamin A.

What were the sugar pushers to do? They could lick them or join them. Joining presented certain problems. If the peddlers of refined white sugar were going to compete by listing their vitamins and minerals on the package, they would have nothing to reveal except a string of zeroes. If the sugar pushers rose to the bait and began fortifying their refined white sugar with vitamins and minerals, they were between the devil and the deep. Some of their biggest customers like Coca-Cola and the soft drink makers might regard this as distinctly unfair.

Whatever happened in the higher councils of the sugar industry we shall never know. The FDA rode to the rescue. Whose rescue? Government inspectors seized quantities of fortified sugar and declared by administrative fiat that the product was "misbranded." Misbranding, a blunderbuss FDA regulation, usually means a charge that will have to do until they can dig up something else.

In other FDA raids, misbranding has been construed to mean that if a natural food store has a book on display which says that brown unpolished rice is good for what ails you, and better than white rice, the book has to be fifty feet away from the rice or it can be construed as a label "misbranding" the rice. The FDA can then proceed either to seize and burn the book or the rice. Since book burning reminds some sensitive people in the Western world of Hitler, the FDA has opted in favor of burning the rice, as has been done in Viet Nam, which strikes some people as OK.

The manufacturers of fortified sugar thought they had a good thing going for them. After all, the U.S. is a free country, and they did have the money and lawyers to take the matter to court. The litigation went on for two years before a decision was reached. During the court proceedings, the FDA contended that listing of vitamins and minerals on the packages of enriched sugar was misbranding in that they were "not nutritionally significant because adequate amounts of these nutrients are available in the average American diet."

Was the FDA saying that you don't need enriched sugar because you've already got enriched bread? The federal judge threw the FDA case out of court with legal scolding. "If the government's case were valid," he said, "any vitamin fortified product could be singled out and challenged on the ground that . . . these nutrients are available everywhere in the food supply . . . the government's position is clearly untenable."

The enriched sugar people won their court case. But they got the message. How long has it been since you've seen any singing commercials for fortified and enriched sugar?

In 1951, a doctor who had been in charge of nutritional research for the U.S. Navy during World War II testified before a congressional committee. (When the Navy discovered the amount of money their men were spending on Coca-Cola, all cola beverages were studied. It was found they contained about 10 percent sugar.) The soft drink industry was given sugar rationing certificates so they could collect on all sugar sold to the armed forces. The Navy nutritionist, Dr. McCay, began studying these certificates:

"I was amazed to learn," he testified, "that the beverage contained substantial amounts of phosphoric acid. . . . At the Naval Medical Research Institute, we put human teeth in a cola beverage and found they softened and started to dissolve within a short period."

While the congressmen gaped, the doctor went on:

"The acidity of cola beverages . . . is about the same as vinegar. The sugar content masks the acidity, and children little realize they are drinking this strange mixture of phosphoric acid, sugar, caffeine, coloring, and flavoring matter."

A congressman asked the doctor what government bureau had charge of passing on the contents of soft drinks.

"So far as I know, no one passes upon it or pays any attention to it," the doctor replied.

"No one passes on the contents of soft drinks?" asked the congressman.

"So far as I know, no one."

Another congressman asked if the doctor had made any tests of the effect of cola beverages on metal and iron. When the doctor said he hadn't, the congressman volunteered: "A friend of mine told me once that he dropped three tenpenny nails into one of the cola bottles, and in forty-eight hours the nails had completely dissolved."

"Sure," the doctor answered. "Phosphoric acid there would dissolve iron or limestone. You might drop it on the steps, and it would erode the steps coming up here. . . . Try it."[6]

"Since soft drinks are playing an increasingly important part of the American diet and tend to displace foods such as milk, they deserve very careful consideration," the doctor suggested.

That was in 1951. Today it's gone from bad to worse. Figures suggest that 25 percent of the sugar consumed in the U.S. reaches the American gullet in the form of soft drinks of all kinds.

Between 1962 and 1972, coffee drinking dropped, as did the consumption of milk, while the consumption of soft drinks almost doubled—in excess of 30 gallons per person per year for 1972 as against 16.2 gallons for 1962.

Beer and tea are fourth and fifth on the list of favorite American drinks. Both registered an increase in a decade. The boost in tea sales was largely attributed to the sale of teas ready to drink, some with lemon and sugar already added. Tea has been turned into a sugared soft drink, so it begins to compete with other flavors. Virtually everything Americans drink—coffee, soft drinks, milk, beer, tea, juices, distilled spirits, and wine—is loaded with sugar or artificial sweeteners.

Our addiction to drink—from the cradle to the grave— is an addiction to sugar.

Centuries ago, the country people got into an uproar over knavish sophisticators adding sugar to their beer in tiny amounts as a fermenting agent. Way back in the 1920s, fighting Senator Robert La Follette, the populist senator from Wisconsin went to bat against the sugar lobby. He concluded that the sugar trust not only controls prices, it controls the government.

Today the sugar pushers and cola tycoons have presidents and prime ministers in their pocket. The famous kitchen debate between former Vice President Nixon and Premier Khrushchev in Moscow in the 1960s was in large part a promotion stunt to photograph the premier with a bottle of Pepsi-Cola. Nixon had been Pepsi's lawyer. The president of Pepsi-Cola, Inc., became President of the Nixon Foundation after his lawyer became President of the United States. In 1972, Pepsi obtained the first Russian franchise to peddle its products in the Soviet Union in exchange for distribution rights here for Soviet wines and spirits.

The billion-dollar, sugar-pushing, soft-drink industry deserves very careful consideration, as the World War II Navy nutritionist suggested to Congress.

You can be sure that's what they got.

What the Specialists Say

Whether it's sugared cereal or pastry and black coffee for breakfast, whether it's hamburgers and Coca-Cola for lunch, or the full "gourmet" dinner in the evening, chemically, the average American diet is a formula that guarantees bubble, bubble, stomach trouble.

Unless you've taken too much insulin and, in a state of insulin shock, need sugar as an antidote, hardly anyone ever has cause to take sugar alone. Humans need sugar as much as they need the nicotine in tobacco. Crave it is one thing—need it is another. From the days of the Persian empire to our own, sugar has usually been used to hop up the flavor of other food and drink, as an ingredient in the kitchen or as a condiment at the table. Let us leave aside for the moment the known effect of sugar (long-term and short-term) on the entire system and concentrate on the effect of sugar taken in combination with other daily foods.

When Grandma warned that sugared cookies before meals "will spoil your supper," she knew what she was talking about. Her explanation might not have satisfied a chemist but, as with many traditional axioms, from the Mosaic law on kosher food and separation in the kitchen, such rules are based on years of trial and error and are apt to be right on the button. Most modern research in combining food is a labored discovery of the things Grandma took for granted.

Any diet or regime undertaken for the single purpose of losing weight is dangerous, by definition. Obesity is talked about and treated as a disease in twentieth-century America. Obesity is not a disease. It is only a symptom, a sign, a warning that your body is out of order. Dieting to lose weight is as silly and dangerous as taking aspirin to relieve a headache before you know the reason for the headache. Getting rid of a symptom is like turning off an alarm. It leaves the basic cause untouched.

Any diet or regime undertaken with any objective short of restoration of total health of your body is dangerous. Many overweight people are undernourished. (Dr. H. Curtis Wood stresses this point in his 1971 book, *Overfed But Undernourished*.) Eating less can aggravate this condition unless one is concerned with the quality of the food instead of just its quantity.

Many people—doctors included—assume that if weight is lost, fat is lost. This is not necessarily so. Any diet which lumps all carbohydrates together is dangerous. Any diet which does not consider the quality of carbohydrates and makes the crucial life-and-death distinction between natural, unrefined carbohydrates like whole grains and vegetables and man-refined carbohydrates like sugar and white flour is dangerous. Any diet which includes refined sugar and white flour, no matter what "scientific" name is applied to them, is dangerous.

Kicking sugar and white flour and substituting whole grains, vegetables, and natural fruits, in season, is the core of any sensible natural regime. Changing the *quality* of your carbohydrates can change the quality of your health and life. If you eat natural food of good quality, quantity tends to take care of itself. Nobody is going to eat a half dozen sugar beets or a whole case of sugar cane. Even if they do, it will be less dangerous than a few ounces of sugar.

Sugar of all kinds—natural sugars, such as those in honey and fruit (fructose) as well as the refined white stuff (sucrose)—tends to arrest the secretion of gastric juices and have an inhibiting effect on the stomach's natural ability to move. Sugars are not digested in the mouth, like cereals, or in the stomach, like animal flesh. When taken alone, they pass quickly through the stomach into the small intestine. When sugars are eaten with other foods—perhaps meat and bread in a sandwich, they are held up in the stomach for a while. The sugar in the bread and the Coke sit there with the hamburger and the bun waiting for them to be digested. While the stomach is working on the animal protein and the refined starch in the bread, the addition of the sugar practically guarantees rapid acid fermentation under the conditions of warmth and moisture existing in the stomach.

One lump of sugar in your coffee after a sandwich is enough to turn your stomach into a ferment. One soda with a hamburger is enough to turn your stomach into a still. Sugar on cereals—whether you buy it already sugared in a box or add it yourself—almost guarantees acid fermentation. Since the beginning of time, natural laws were observed, in both senses of that word, when it came to eating foods in combination. Birds have been observed eating insects at one period in the day and seeds at another. Other animals tend to eat one food at a time. Flesh-eating animals take their protein raw and straight.

In the Orient, it is traditional to eat yang before yin. Miso soup (yang-fermented soybean protein) for breakfast; raw fish (more yang protein) at the beginning of the meal; afterwards comes the rice (which is less yang than the miso and fish); and then the vegetables which are yin. If you ever eat with a traditional Japanese family and you violate this order, the Orientals (if your friends) will correct you courteously but firmly. The law observed by Orthodox Jews prohibits many combinations at the same meal, especially flesh and dairy products. Special utensils for the dairy meal and different utensils for the flesh meal reinforce that tabu at the food's source in the kitchen. Man learned very early in the game what improper combinations of food could do to the human system. When he got a stomachache from combining raw fruit with grain, or honey with porridge, he didn't reach for an antacid tablet. He learned not to eat that way. When gluttony and excess became widespread, religious codes and commandments were invoked against it. Gluttony is a capital sin in most religions; but there are no specific religious warnings or commandments against refined sugar because sugar abuse—like drug abuse—did not appear on the world scene until centuries after holy books had gone to press.

"Why must we accept as normal what we find in a race of sick and weakened human beings?" Dr. Herbert M. Shelton asks. "Must we always take it for granted that the present eating practices of civilized men are normal?"

"Foul stools, loose stools, impacted stools, pebbly stools, much foul gas, colitis, hemorrhoids, bleeding with stools, the need for toilet paper . . . are swept into the orbit of the normal."[1]

When starches and complex sugars (like those in honey and fruits) are digested, they are broken down into simple sugars called monosaccharides, which are usable substances—nutriments. When starches and sugars are taken together and undergo fermentation, they are broken down into carbon dioxide, acetic acid, alcohol, and water. With the exception of the water, all these are unusable substances—poisons. When proteins are digested they are broken down into amino acids, which are usable substances—nutriments. When proteins are taken with sugar, they putrefy, they are broken down into a variety of ptomaines and leucomaines, which are nonusable substances—poisons. Enzymic digestion of foods prepares them for use by our body. Bacterial decomposition unfits them for use by our body. The first process gives us nutriments, the second gives us poisons.

Much that passes for modern nutrition is obsessed with a mania for quantitative counting. The body is treated like a checking account. Deposit calories (like dollars) and withdraw energy. Deposit proteins, carbohydrates, fats, vitamins, and minerals—balanced quantitatively—and the result theoretically is a healthy body. People qualify as healthy today if they can crawl out of bed, get to the office, and sign in. If they can't make it, call the doctor to qualify for sick pay, hospitalization, rest cure—anything from a day's pay without working to an artificial kidney, courtesy of the taxpayers.

But what doth it profit someone if the theoretically required calories and nutrients are consumed daily, yet this random eat-on-the-run, snack time collection of foods ferments and putrefies in the digestive tract? What good is it if the body is fed protein only to have it putrefy in the gastrointestinal canal? Carbohydrates that ferment in the digestive tract are converted into alcohol and acetic acid, not digestible monosaccharides.

"To derive sustenance from foods eaten, they must be digested," Shelton warned years ago. "They must not rot."

Sure, the body can get rid of poisons through the urine and the pores; the amount of poisons in the urine is taken as an index to what's going on in the intestine. The body does establish a tolerance for these poisons, just as it adjusts gradually to an intake of heroin. But, says Shelton, "the discomfort from accumulation of gas, the bad breath, and foul and unpleasant odors are as undesirable as are the poisons."[2]

I don't know what you were doing during Digestive Disease Week in May 1973, but I celebrated by watching a seminar on David Susskind's television talk show. Three eminent New York gastroenterologists and a psychiatrist talked about ulcers for an hour and a half. I made myself a bet that these three distinguished specialists could go on for the entire ninety minutes without ever mentioning the word sugar. So I had to hang on every word before I could collect.

True to form there were the learned quotations from the classics. ("Iago gnawed within.") There were seductive psychiatric discussions of the ulcer personality (taxi drivers, airport control men, women after menopause).

There were historic footnotes: A nod for William Beaumont the father of gastroenterology who studied the man with the shotgun hole in his stomach; glancing blows at underlying predisposition and familial tendency (frustration eats at you); an exposition of symptoms in a constellation (hunger-like pains, relieved by eating, vomiting of blood, then see your doctor and get a barium enema and X-ray for sure).

There were incidental warnings. Aspirin can inflame ulcers and cause bleeding in 70 percent of ulcer cases. How many commercials have you ever seen with live doctors relaying that warning? "I hate aspirin," said one of the specialists, "my mother-in-law lives on it but hidden aspirin is a cause of ulcers." What is aspirin hidden in? They didn't tell us.

Certain hopeful developments on the horizon were pointed out. Neil Miller at the Rockefeller Institute has a medication that will control stomach acidity; the Japanese have perfected minute instruments that can spot ulcers. There were generous admissions of past medical errors—in the past, mutilating surgery was resorted to prematurely with the removal of all or part of the stomach.

Finally, the doctors got down to cases; acid in the stomach causes ulcers; no acid, no ulcers. Most of us, we were told, have acid stomach. What causes acid stomach? Well, acid. The stomach as a checking account again.

Do you refer ulcer patients to a psychiatrist, Susskind wanted to know. Not usually, they said. Antacids are better. They make him feel better quicker. However, drugs to accelerate healing do not exist. We all have to live with stress.

Acid causes pain, they told us. To relieve pain, one doctor suggested the standard bland diet. Palatable, but not too appetizing. Three meals and a snack on a regular schedule. Cut down acid by cutting out curries. Ever seen a TV commercial for curry? Caffeine is acid; black coffee is out, have it with cream. They were getting close to the point where I might lose my bet, but that passed. Nobody mentioned sugar or Coca-Cola, which has caffeine and sugar built in.

As a strict diet for those with severe pain, they suggested a thermos of milk, cream of wheat, custard, and Jello. These last two have their sugar built in. Nobody mentioned that. After staying on these diets for two to six weeks, the average ulcer patient should find some relief. What then?

Then, said a doctor (without argument from the others), "Eat anything you want." No doctor can cure ulcers at the present time, we were told. Surgery is the ultimate answer, at a price. In place of the "mutilating" surgery practiced in the not-so-distant past, the surgeons now have a new kind of operation which does not call for removal of the stomach, it merely cuts off the nerves and blocks registration of pain. Some 50 percent of ulcer patients may expect a recurrence in two years; 75 percent in four years.

Pain is the God-given warning signal from nature that something is wrong. So you have an operation that turns off your alarm signal. That's cool, very cool. . . . Imagine our reaction if we turned in a fire alarm and the fire engine roared to the scene and turned it off without bothering to do anything about the fire. By that standard, abortion is a contraceptive.

Well, twenty million Americans have ulcers, the good doctors told us. Here was a seminar of leading New York specialists telling us how little they know in the most convincing way possible. What is the answer? More money from the federal government for more research. In ninety minutes, they were unable to come up with a single constructive suggestion for the average person to manage their diet in a way that might prevent ulcers. They were able to talk for ninety minutes without a single mention of sugar.

A month later, three gastroenterologists told a Senate subcommittee that aspirin and patent medicines containing aspirin, like Alka-Seltzer, can aggravate the stomach disorders they are supposed to relieve.

Dr. J. Donald Ostrow, an associate professor of medicine at the University of Pennsylvania, suggested that the Alka-Seltzer pushers should be ordered to put on television "a guy vomiting blood and a gastroscope being put down" the fellow's throat. Dr. Ostrow noted that during the past eighteen months, he had observed eighteen patients at the VA Hospital in Philadelphia "in whom gastrointestinal hemorrhage was engendered by ingestion of aspirin preparations. In five of these patients, the preparation was Alka-Seltzer, repeatedly taken over a short period of time to treat symptoms of gastric distress which were in fact related to underlying disorders of the stomach."[3]

Ostrow talked about the vicious circle which begins when people take Alka-Seltzer to relieve stomach distress: Temporarily it seems to work. As the antacid effects subside, the pain returns, more severe than before. This leads to another dose of Alka-Seltzer and so on, with more pain, more Alka-Seltzer, until the patient ends up bleeding and in the hospital. Using the figures supplied by the Alka-Seltzer makers, the doctor estimated that every four months in this country some 600,000 individuals use Alka-Seltzer to excess, ending up worse off than they were before.

Another doctor assured that Senate Subcommittee that aspirin does not induce massive bleeding in the stomachs of normal people. Of course not. However, healthy people don't take the stuff. So where does that leave us?

Interesting things often happen when physicians attempt to cure themselves. If you find a doctor who practices unorthodox medicine, chances are his eyes and mind were opened when he tried to cure himself by the book. When that didn't work, he threw away the book and began experimenting with himself. Pain and suffering tend to erode one's faith in conventional treatment. After a while, one is willing to try anything. Even something as sensible as watching what you eat. That's been the story among the great unorthodox healers like Dr. Tilden, Dr. Hal Beiler, and many more in America and abroad.

In *Sweet and Dangerous,* Dr. John Yudkin, the eminent British physician, biochemist, and Emeritus Professor of Nutrition at London University, tells how he had been diagnosed as having ulcers twenty-five years ago. He was given the standard advice: Take it easy, don't get exhausted, avoid spicy foods, eat small meals more frequently, delay having surgery unless it becomes imperative. He took antacid preparations whenever he had distress. Then, he started putting on weight, like so many men of his age. So he put himself on a regime for weight reduction. He cut down sugar, among other things. In a few months, he discovered his stomach symptoms had almost entirely disappeared.

Dr. Yudkin undertook stringent experiments for the next two years, getting together information on forty-one patients. The results were quite clear. Two claimed to be worse off on a low carbohydrate diet, eleven said they found no appreciable difference, but a decided majority of twenty-eight said they were much better off. Many vowed they would stay on the low carbohydrate regime for keeps. The patients included men and women with gastric or duodenal ulcers, and some with hiatus hernia.

"Now it can no longer be said that diet does not relieve severe dyspepsia," Dr. Yudkin says. "The right diet will, only the wrong diet will not."

Why does the right diet work? "Sugar irritates the lining of the upper alimentary canal, the esophagus, stomach, and duodenum. . . ." The diet Yudkin put his patients on contains little sugar.[4]

Dr. Yudkin was working with patients who could not be completely controlled, since they were not hospitalized. Physicians had to take the patients' word for what they were eating and how closely they were following instructions. Under controlled conditions, in the army or in a prison, this kind of experiment with a sugarfree diet might be even more conclusive.

Dr. Yudkin reports another recent experiment which pointed the other way. He persuaded seven young men each to swallow a tube first thing in the morning so that samples could be obtained of their gastric juices at rest; then, at fifteen minute intervals—after they had swallowed a bland test meal consisting mainly of pectin—further samples were taken. Samples were analyzed in the usual way, measuring the degree of acidity and digestive activity. Then the patients were put on a high-sugar diet for two weeks and tested again. Results showed that two weeks of a sugar-rich diet was enough to increase both stomach acidity and digestive activity of the gastric juices, of the kind one finds in people with gastric or duodenal ulcers. The rich diet of sugar increased stomach acidity by 20 percent or so and the enzyme activity was increased almost three times. (These effects were observed in the morning, before breakfast.)

This is probably much too simple to interest the ulcer specialist. Most of the nutritional regimes being promoted today still concern themselves with quantitative things. They talk about calories. Eat your protein, watch your fats, maybe cut down on carbohydrates. Occasionally one hears about a qualitative difference between vegetable and animal fats, polysaturated and polyunsaturated. However, carbohydrates are still lumped together and protein is protein. The whole subject of mixing foods together in unholy indigestible combinations is left to Fannie Farmer and the people who dream up cookbooks and television dinners. We learn nothing from our hangovers and our heartburn, except to reach for that Alka-Seltzer.

Reach for a Lucky
Instead of a Sweet?

The biggest sugar customer in this country is the food processing industry. That figures. Who is number two and trying harder? Would you believe, the tobacco industry? Exact figures are called trade secrets. The Surgeon General is permitted to tell you on every package and in every advertisement that cigarette smoking is dangerous to your health. Cigarette manufacturers, however, are not required to give you any further information.

Manufacturers of candy kisses are required to tell you on the wrapper that sugar is their principal ingredient. Cans of oyster stew have to list their ingredients also. The manufacturer of an ice cream sandwich has to tell you every single item that goes into the wafer, but he's not even allowed to say what's in the ice cream. So it is with tobacco. About the tar and nicotine they tell you; about the filters they go on and on, but about anything else in the tobacco? Nothing. One American tobacco industry authority told *Medical World News* in March 1973, that an average of 5 percent sugar is added to cigarettes, up to 20 percent in cigars, and as much as 40 percent in pipe tobacco, mostly in the form of molasses and such.

The sugar-in-everything craze reached such a peak in this country that, during one four-year period in the 1960s, the amount of sugar used in processed food increased a whopping 50 percent. Has this type of increase also occurred in the tobacco industry's use of refined sugar? According to a television documentary aired by the British Broadcasting Corporation in the fall of 1972, it has indeed and for quite some time. Since this particular TV show may not be picked up for rebroadcast in America, you may as well know that it amounted to an indictment of sugar in tobacco as a possible source of lung cancer, based on chemistry and experimental studies. Interesting statistics compared lung cancer figures in countries where sugar-cured cigarettes are smoked with lands where cigarettes are made with unadulterated tobacco—that is, not sugar-cured tobacco.

Tobacco, of course, is almost as new to Western civilization as man-refined sugar. Native American Indians have been blowing peace pipes for centuries, for all we know, but tobacco was unknown to the white man until Columbus caught the Cuban natives chewing and smoking it in 1492. Smoking was found to be bound up with the most solemn tribal religious ceremonies. Some say tobacco was the Mexican-Indian word for the herb; others claim it was the name of the y-shaped, wooden tube apparatus the natives fitted into their nostrils.

The tobacco plant itself was first brought to Europe in 1558 by a physician dispatched by Philip II of Spain to investigate the flora and fauna of Mexico. The French Ambassador to Portugal brought tobacco seeds to his queen, Catherine de Medici. His name, Jean Nicot, eventually became the basis for the Latinized name of the plant *Nicotinia.* Like sugar, nicotinia was thought to possess healing medical powers. It became the miracle drug of its time and its boosters went all out, calling it *herba panacea, herba santa,* divine tobacco, healthy holy herb, holy all-purpose herb. During the seventeenth century, tobacco addiction spread like wildfire through all

European nations, despite the opposition of statesmen and clergy who invoked ultimate penalties of excommunication and death. When the death penalty didn't work, most governments settled for taxes.

Tobacco was eventually cultivated all over the world, but the prime producers and growers were in the U.S. In the beginning, tobacco was cured the way the Indians had done it from time immemorial: Wilted tobacco leaves were suspended on racks in the sun. Eventually barns and sheds were built to protect crops from the rain.

Air curing—tobacco is hung in a barn where the air circulates freely during dry weather—was similar to sun drying. In cold weather, artificial heat was used. Most cigar tobacco today is air cured. Air curing takes about three months and only traces of natural sugars are left in the tobacco after that time.

In flue curing (also known as the Virginia cure), fires are set outside the barn, and the heat is led via iron pipes or flues into the building in which the tobacco is hung fresh from the fields. Since the temperatures reach up to 170 degrees, this process speeds the cure. Time is money in the tobacco business—and all business—so this saves money. However, the intense heat inactivates natural enzymes which would otherwise cause the natural tobacco sugars to ferment. So flue-cured tobacco can contain as much as 20 percent sugar by weight.

To complicate things even further, sugar (sucrose) is added to air-cured tobacco during the blending process. How long has this been going on? Practically forever. At the turn of the century, the British claimed that pure water alone was used to dampen tobacco leaves in the United Kingdom, whereas in America "certain sauces are employed which consist of mixtures of aromatic substances, sugar, liquorice, common salt and salt petre etc. dissolved in water. The use of sauces is to improve the flavor and burning qualities of the leaves."

Anyone who has ever smoked a French cigarette and put it down after a few puffs will have noticed how it extinguishes itself in the ash tray. Put down an American cigarette and it smokes itself. In France one can buy cigarettes in yellow, unbleached paper. The first time I offered an American cigarette to a Frenchman, he accepted with pleasure. He then sliced the cigarette laterally with a knife, removed the tobacco from the white paper, and re-rolled it in yellow paper. When he lit the white American paper with a match and burned it under my nose, I choked.

I must confess that the idea that tobacco had been treated with sugar all this time came as something of a surprise to me. In England, in the 1970s, the controversy over the sugar content of cigarettes is often front page news. When the British government announced in the fall of 1972 that it would publish a table of tar and nicotine levels in British cigarette brands—as had been done in the United States—the *London Sunday Times* went to bat on page one. They charged that this kind of list might be misleading and cited studies which showed that British cigarettes—made from flue-dried tobacco (which has a high sugar content) may increase the risk of serious lung disease, even though the tar and nicotine ratings are relatively low.

The late Dr. Richard D. Passey of London's Chester Beatty Research Institute had spent twenty years investigating smoking and cancer. Intrigued by the lower incidence of cancer in cigar smokers as compared with cigarette smokers, he studied the difference between the two types of tobacco and the smoke they produced. He pointed out that most British cigarette tobacco is flue-cured whereas cigar tobacco is air-cured. In many countries, cigarettes are blends of the two types of tobacco, as in the U.S., or are entirely of air-cured tobacco as in most of Eastern Europe and Asia.

Smokes produced by burning the two types of tobacco are very different, according to Dr. Passey. High sugar content tobacco produces strongly acid smoke. Low sugar tobacco produces smoke that is weakly acid or alkaline.

This thesis is supported by America's Dr. G. B. Gori, associate director of the National Cancer Institute and chairman of their Tobacco Working Group which spends $6 million yearly searching for a "safer" cigarette. "One would tend to inhale more when the smoke is acidic, and that's why I believe that flue-cured tobacco may be more dangerous, in the long run, than the burley or air-dried type," says Dr. Gori.

Dr. Passey, the British tobacco expert, has compared European cigarette and cancer rates country by country:

England and Wales have the world's highest rate of lung cancer for men. British cigarettes have the highest sugar content of any in the world, 17 percent.

Frenchmen smoke about two-thirds as many cigarettes per capita as Englishmen. Their lung cancer rate is one-third as high and their cigarettes are made of air-dried tobacco with only 2 percent sugar.

American men smoke more cigarettes per capita than Britons, but their lung cancer rate is only half what it is in Britain. American cigarettes are a blend of both kinds of tobacco—with an average sugar content of 10 percent.

In Russia, China, Formosa, and other countries where cigarettes are made of air-dried tobacco—close to the kind the American Indians used before the invention of sugar sauces—they are unable to find any correlation at all between smoking and lung cancer.[1]

Although Mao's government ceaselessly encourages people to keep themselves fit, China is one of the few countries in the world where there is no official anti-smoking campaign. Chinese cigarettes are said to have extremely low nicotine and tar content, as well as being low in sugar.[2]

In India, where coronary disease is common enough among the well-to-do, though rare in the masses, R. P. Malhotra and N. S. Pathania showed, in a 1958 article in a British medical journal, that coronary disease was equally common among the Sikihms who do not smoke as it was among the Hindus who do.

The British medical publication *The Lancet* took serious exception to Dr. Passey's theory and his data. The National Cancer Institute's Dr. Gori insists: "I don't think one should pinpoint sugar in particular." One thing all experts agree upon, the question is worth exploring.

The National Cancer Institute of America is not only studying the effect of different fertilizer used in tobacco growing, as well as many chemicals now used in finished cigarettes, they are also moving into the sugar question.

"We are now planning to study this issue in detail," Dr. Gori wrote me in 1973, "and determine inhalation patterns of smokers that use cigarettes prevalently made of air-cured (low sugar, high pH) or flue-cured (high sugar, low pH). If relationships are uncovered, then it may be possible to connect the level of sugar in tobacco with the smoking dynamics of the smoker and therefore to higher or lower risks."

My friends from the Far East, like Sakurazawa Ohsawa and Herman Aihara, find the official U.S. doctrine that smoking causes lung cancer very amusing. They are confident that, in another decade, the National Cancer Institute will be compelled to admit that the tremendous excess of sugar and artificial chemicals in our food, as well as the excess of chemicalized animal protein eaten, are involved in causing lung cancer.

They claim that the cause of cancer is excess yin—sugar and artificial chemicals.

Smoking is very yang and as such it is preferable to eating too much fruit, fruit juices, soda, and other carbonated, caffeinated, sugar concoctions.

It is more important to cut out drugs and sugar and cut down on fruit than it is to stop smoking completely.

Tobacco was used by the American Indians in its natural state as a cure for many diseases.

Commercial cigarettes contain unnatural chemicals and sugars, so avoid them and roll your own from naturally grown tobacco—if you can find it—and use wrapping paper not chemically treated.

People with weak lungs, kidneys, or liver are constitutionally weak and should not smoke very much.

Smoking is not a necessity, like eating. It is a pleasure.

The question with pleasure is always finding a healthy balance between the pleasure and its effects.

Many years ago, when weight-watching first became an American preoccupation, especially among women, a cigarette slogan advised: Reach for a Lucky instead of a sweet.

Perhaps that slogan was wiser than we know.

Despite all the injunctions from the Surgeon General and the diseasestablishment, smoking in the U.S. has decreased little. The lone individual today can do very little to improve the quality of the air he breathes, but he does have some control over what he puts in his stomach, and what *kind* of tobacco smoke he admits to his body. Sugared cigarettes are unnecessary. If smokers start asking for non-sugared cigarettes, the market supply would match the demand.

In the 1970s, it became official U.S. policy to discourage cigarette smoking. Trains and buses have always had nonsmoking compartments. Now the same option exists on planes. In bars and restaurants, nonsmokers still take their chances. In department stores, offices, theaters, hospitals, and some public buildings, however, no-smoking rules are posted and enforced. Fire regulations provide heavy sanctions in many places. Tobacco is heavily taxed everywhere. In some countries, Sweden, for instance, a sky-high cigarette tax is used not so much to raise revenue as to raise conscious social policy to discourage smokers.

Nonsmokers have some elements of law and custom behind them. If they smell smoke, they can holler, plead, take refuge, threaten, or move. Violators are easily detected as long as people preserve some vestige of the sense of smell. Hazards and unpleasantness may always lurk around the corner for the nonsmoker, but his plight is a cool, unpolluted breeze compared with the lot of the diabetic, the hypoglycemic, or a plain sensible soul trying to keep his body sugarfree.

The conscientious objector to sugar is alone, moving through the day like a drunk navigating minefields. The twilight zone is entered every time one opens one's mouth. Stumbling out of bed in the morning, you reach for the toothpaste. How do you know it doesn't contain sugar? The high-powered commercials tell you how great toothpaste tastes and what it does for your breath, as well as unintelligible details on the chemical cavity fighters that have been built in. But what tube actually tells you its contents? Even if you examine the fine print, you're still on your own. For an answer you can believe, send it to an independent laboratory and have it analyzed. The only sure ways are to forget them all and use an unadvertised brand of powder that doesn't taste sweet, or bring some unadulterated toothpaste in from Europe when you travel, or make your own out of sea salt and charred eggplant.

In March 1974, Lt. Hiro Onoda emerged from the jungles of the Philippine Islands after living a precarious, marginal existence for almost thirty years. Onoda had been holding out all that time for a direct order from his superior officer to surrender. He flew home to a hero's welcome in Tokyo. After doctors examined him, it was announced: No cavities! No Crest! No Fluoride! Certainly no sugar. And no cavities! Sugar-drunk Americans the same age as the Japanese lieutenant have lost, on the average, half of their teeth. By the age of 55, one American out of every two has lost all his teeth. Sugar blue is the color of the solution where they park their dentures for the night.

The New York Times reported in June 1975 that "44% of Scots over 16 Found to be Toothless." The article noted that the Scottish state-operated health services had statistics for 1974 showing that 44 percent of Scots aged 16 or more had lost all their teeth. Only 2 percent of the people surveyed could be called dentally fit. The report concluded that significantly "Scotland has one of the highest sugar-consumption rates in the world, 120 pounds per person annually."

In the 1973 issues for February and August, *Esquire* magazine published two lengthy articles, one on weight-loss dieting, the other on the high cost of dental care without a single mention of the word sugar—the major cause of obesity and tooth decay. In another article on weight-loss dieting by a doctor, the word sugar was mentioned exactly once, to tell us that "sugar is pure carbohydrate." In the article on tooth decay, the word sugar never appeared. *Esquire* called "carbohydrates a major contributor to tooth decay."

Sugar-eaters may brush their teeth between every bite and see their dentist three times a day, but there's no escape from the sugar blues.

The avant garde of dentistry has rediscovered that the body and the teeth are not two separate entities; the teeth are part of the body. There was an entire period during which the teeth were thought to be "inactive organs"; tooth decay was taken to be a local development on the surface of the teeth. Dentists were considered in the league with barbers, as mechanics, cosmeticians, tinkerers. If a dentist talked to a patient about anything except cavities or choice of filling, he was treading on the jealously regarded terrain of the medical man.

All that is over. Dental researchers have proven that the teeth are subject to the same metabolic processes that affect other organs of the body. The entire body is one.

By adapting a technique originally developed to study movement of fluid within organs like the liver and kidneys, two researchers from the Loma Linda School of Dentistry have found that subtle changes in the internal activity of the teeth, *caused by sugar*, can be an early sign of later decay.

In their report to a Chicago meeting of the International Association for Dental Research, Doctors R. E. Steinman and John Leonora showed that the principal change, caused by sugar, is in the movement of fluid within the teeth. Hormonal chemicals are carried from the pulp to the enamel through tiny channels in the dentin.

Resistance to tooth decay involves the health of the entire body: Complex physiological processes are involved in maintaining and protecting the health of the teeth. The two researchers found that:

—A high sugar diet can slow the rate of transport of hormonal chemicals by as much as two-thirds *even in one week*.

—Teeth with sluggish internal activity have a high incidence of decay.

—A hormone released by the hypothalamus stimulates the release by the salivary or parotid gland of a second hormone. This second hormone increases the rate of fluid flow in the teeth.

—A high sugar diet upsets the hormonal balance and

reduces the flow in the internal system. This w
the tooth and makes it more susceptible to decay.

—Healthy teeth are normally invulnerable to the
microbes that are always present in the mouth.

Who wants to get rid of friendly germs in the mouth
except those crazy people selling mouthwash?

Postponing the first of the day's quandaries, standing
in the bathroom, you might reach for the consolation
of that first cigarette. Will it pass the sugarfree test?
The Surgeon General's message tells you it's dangerous
to your health. But one man's hazard may be another
man's dish. Quantity changes quality. What's in it? Some
cigarettes list their tar and nicotine. But which tobacco
is cured with sugar and which is not? If you want an
imported, sugarfree cigarette a double tax is imposed.
Should you want to roll your own, buy imported tobacco
and imported paper without chemicals and saltpeter.
Freedom of choice is a farce if one has to be a tobacco
expert or send your favorite weed to a testing lab.

Back in the bathroom, maybe you stub out that cigarette and reach for a bottle of vitamins. On the one
hand, the government informs us that smoking depletes
our systems of certain vitamins. On the other hand, the
government assures us we don't have to worry since
the average U.S. diet supplies these essential items in
quantity aplenty. To be sure, without developing a vitamin pill habit, one takes a few from time to time. How
can you tell which ones are coated with sugar? Manufacturers are compelled to list all sorts of things on the
label. But where is the news that the little pills are sugar-
coated or not? Ask your neighborhood merchant, write
to the manufacturer, what do you do?

Airplanes have smoking and nonsmoking sections now
so you can make your seating choice as you board. However, if you hope for something sugarless to eat or drink,
you can bring your own lunch or telephone the airline
48 hours in advance and ask for a dietetic meal. I've
always wanted to try one, but I never have that much
advance notice. So it's a treat I've missed.

Despite the advertising and hoopla about choosing
among competing airlines, air travel only involves a slim

3 percent of the U.S. population. Those millions of flights primarily involve the same small percentage of the traveling public. Mass traveling in America happens on the superhighway, in the automobile. The superhighway has virtually eliminated the picnic ground, the roadside inn, the roadside stand, the truck stop diner, and the home cooked meal in regional restaurants.

The hungry auto traveler today is a captive customer. Officially franchised restaurants with their standard architectural fixtures offer similar menus, coast to coast, from Maine to California. They're pushing ice cream in umpteen delicious flavors (although—more doubletalk—usually only three, vanilla, chocolate, plus one unusual flavor, are truly available), soft drinks and cola of every kind, sugared snacks in every conceivable alluring package to set the children screaming. If you expect sustenance without sugar, you're in for a rough time.

It's the same old story. Bread, rolls, and pastries, crackers and cookies, donuts and waffles, pancakes and toast, jellies and jam, relish and ketchup, vegetables and fruit, meat and potatoes, soup to nuts, everything is frozen, prepared, pepped up with sugar. In the morning, you may pass over the sugar-laden packaged breakfast foods in favor of a bowl of plain old oatmeal. If you're persistent, they may find you some honey to put on it, but even the honey may be filtered and stretched with sugar. The oatmeal is usually salted during cooking and the salt may have sugar in it, too. If you're daring, you may inquire. The baked beans are loaded with sugar. The bacon is sugar-cured.

As your eyes run down the menu, focusing on the items least likely to have sugar in them, you breathe a sigh when you discover clam chowder on the menu. You hold your breath, expecting the waitress to tell you, with a smile of pleasure, that it's been discontinued or is out of season. If you're lucky, you negotiate a bowl of chowder made with canned clams, tired vegetables, and not too much else, you hope. You congratulate yourself on your acumen. The chowder, like everything else, reminds you how good clam chowder used to be in some long ago lost time. As you wait in line to pay the cashier, you find—among the sugared goodies—a display of cans of clam chowder for the take-home trade. The stuff isn't worth carrying to the car but you pick it up and look at the label. Your stomach gurgles sharply . . . the first ingredient listed is the sugar you've been trying to escape. More sugar than clams. You've been had. The only way out is to carry breakfast, dinner, and lunch

The time has come to bring back the dinner pail. I have an old-fashioned one with a thermos snapped in the top. I never get in a car anymore without a full thermos and something substantial in the way of emergency rations. The last time I did any coast-to-coast driving, I discovered the wonders of a simple emergency ration called a rice ball. Cook a bowlful of unpolished brown rice, and let it cool. Then hold sheets of the Japanese sea vegetable, nori, known in the West as laver, over low heat until they are crinkly crisp. Pit some umeboshi salted plums. Then, dipping your hands in cool sea-salted water so the rice doesn't stick to them, shape a handful of rice into a ball. Push half a plum into the center, wrap the rice ball in the toasted seaweed, tearing it and fitting the seaweed into place. Put each rice ball in a waxed paper sandwich bag and keep them in your lunch box or a brown paper bag. Don't wrap them too tightly, the air should circulate around them a little. The salted plum keeps the rice from turning green for three or four days, sometimes longer, it depends on the climate. The toasted sea vegetable wrapper stops the rice from drying out. Whenever you feel hungry as you drive, take a rice ball and munch it, chewing every mouthful for a good minute or so. This is important for your digestion. The seaweed absorbs the moisture from the rice, and makes it soft and chewy. The plum flavors the rice sharply. Your driving will be excellent—and even. One seems to develop eyes in the back of the head. You drive without the ups and downs of discomfort or hunger pangs. Most important of all, you're capable of handling the vagaries of those careless drivers on the highway.

The carnage on America's highways exceeds all deaths in all wars. Year by year, despite the billions of dollars spent for highway safety, construction, education, and policing, it goes up and up. The real causes of fatal auto accidents are usually buried with the victims. There have been studies on top of studies. Radar, computers, and behavioral scientists have all searched for answers. Shocking, agonizing appeals on television attempt to bring the horror right into our laps. Reformed drunks appeal to us to get the drunken driver off the road. At holiday time, drivers are urged to skip that last drink and have a cup of coffee for the road. How many television appeals have you seen suggesting that the sugar drunk be gotten off the highways?

It has to come. It can't be swept under the rug much longer. In 1971, in one of the most comprehensive studies of highway accidents ever compiled, Dr. H. J. Roberts, a specialist of internal medicine, devoted a thousand pages of text and charts attempting to emphasize the fact that highway accident research on "causes" of traffic accidents needs to be completely revamped. Strictly speaking, events such as accidents are misnamed. An accident is, simply, an occurrence with a hidden cause. What does it mean if somebody missed a stop sign, ran through an intersection, got in the wrong lane, passed another motorist on a hill, speeded around a curve, or lost control of his car? *Why* did the driver do it?[3]

One learns in army combat, in automobile accidents, in drownings, in every physical crisis that a few seconds can be an eternity which spells the difference between survival and doom: The ability to react speedily, promptly, and precisely to any challenge or danger—this is the thing one measures in service comrades, in taxi drivers, in skiing, mountain climbing, or any hazardous physical activity. This is one of the most important indices to one's own health. When one is truly healthy, it means one has this ability to react spontaneously. If an American steps off the sidewalk into London traffic during those first few days in an unfamiliar city where the traffic flow is reversed from one's normal pattern, an alert person catches such an error. If the steep rocks you're climbing present a hazard, you rapidly evaluate moves around them. So it is driving on the highway.

In his comprehensive study, published in 1971, that

entailed years of research, Dr. Roberts concluded that a "significant source" of many unexplainable accidents is that "millions of American drivers are subject to pathological drowsiness and hypoglycemia due to functional hyperinsulinism." He estimates that there may be as many as ten million drivers like that on the road of America today.

In other words, low glucose level in the blood gums up brain functioning, perceptions, and reactions. What causes this condition? The doctor's answer: "The apparent increased incidence of hyperinsulinism and of narcolepsy [abnormal attacks of drowsiness] during recent decades can be largely attributed to the consequences of an enormous rise in sugar consumption by a vulnerable population."[4]

Today, Americans eat 1 out of every 5 meals in restaurants, where no one is required to tell the customer, on the menu or elsewhere, whether or not there is sugar in your supper.

Some people can handle the only food available to captive customers on the superhighways—the sugar-in-everything menu from the look-alike establishments smeared across the country, plus the ice cream, the Coca-Cola, the coffee, the candy, the chewing gum, and dazzling array of sugared snacks at the check-out counter. Some people can't. Of course, some people can handle it right up to the point they can't. They never find out what is enough until they find out what is more than enough and end up hospitalized, maimed, or dead.

Hyperinsulinism or low glucose level in the blood can be aggravated by other factors, according to Dr. Roberts. One is age. Roberts cites a number of studies which show that three out of four elderly people have faulty sugar metabolism. Another complicating factor is the wide use of medications such as tranquilizers and antihistamines which have a marked tendency to induce drowsiness. To combine these drugs with a heavy sugar habit can be devastating. Another complicating factor is alcohol. A drink or two may be unimportant by itself. The Breath-o-lator test may tell only part of the story. With someone who has problems with sugar metabolism, it depends on the kind of alcoholic beverage. After all, whiskey, beer, and wine contain more than alcohol. Their sugar content varies widely. Alcohol combined with a sugar load adds to the drain on the brain. Even more scary is the fact that many, if not all, alcoholics are also hypoglycemics or victims of hyperinsulinism, people with low glucose levels in their blood. Roberts cites other studies which show that alcoholics have an exceptionally high rate of auto accidents—*even when they are sober*.

If you've gone without sugar as long as I have, you learn to detect it by simple signs. When you have eaten at a restaurant or some place where control of the actual content of the food is out of your hands, taste is not always infallible. However, if you get sleepy after such a meal, you can be sure something had sugar or honey in it. Many fruits, especially sugar rich tropical fruits, make me sleepy. Honey can do the same thing. I know a Japanese lady who, when she came to the U.S. for the first time, had never tasted sugar in her life. When a kind soul gave her a loaf of whole wheat bread as a gift, she ate some and promptly went to sleep and missed her plane. The bread had been made with honey—that was enough to do it.

For highway safety, Dr. Roberts suggests that drivers avoid glucose and sucrose. In other words, if you want to get there and back, travel sugarfree. I've been sugarfree since the 1960s, by which I mean that I eliminated refined sucrose from my diet. I have come to know hundreds of young people who have found that illness or bingeing on drugs and sugar became the doorway to health. Once they reestablished their own health, we had in common our interest in food. If one can use that overworked word lifestyle, we shared a sugarfree lifestyle. I kept in touch with many of them in campuses and communes, through their travels here and abroad and everywhere. One day you meet them in Boston. The next week you run into them in southern California. In all that time, with hundreds of friends more or less constantly on the road, I have known only two who were involved in auto accidents.

I made a point of personally investigating each incident.

In both cases, each was driving alone. One had had a history of epilepsy. He had cured himself in a couple of years by adhering to a sugarfree diet, with lots of whole grains, vegetables, sometimes a little fish, and even less fruit. He got so frisky he forgot his old malady. It had been a year since he had had a mild seizure. When he was visiting a retired priest in a Catholic rectory in Boston, he was invited for dinner—a trap of a meal rich enough for an archbishop and topped off by a sugar-bomb dessert. Even though he stayed away from the wine, returning home on the freeway, he went blank—an epileptic seizure. The resulting accident left both legs in plaster casts.

The second friend involved in a highway accident had been a diabetic since the age of sixteen. He had been on insulin for ten years. Through trial and error, booze and marijuana, he had learned enough about his own metabolism to find a regime that worked for him. He has since been able to cut down his insulin by more than half by adhering to what quantitative nutritionists would call a high-carbohydrate diet of mostly whole grains and vegetables. Before he managed that, during the time he was combining insulin and marijuana, he blacked out on a back road in California and crashed into a ditch. The highway patrol took him to the hospital. When they found the card, "I am a Diabetic" in his back pocket, his driver's license was suspended.

When you apply for a driver's license today, a big-to-do is made over your skill at backing into a parking place; a written test in which you display your memory for traffic regulations is obligatory. An inspector rides around the block with you to see how you handle stopping and starting, and other elements of driving. Your vision is tested. Computers keep track of your driving violations. But until we figure out a way of screening out the sugar drunks, highway safety will continue to be a sometime thing.

Kicking

Kicking a sugar habit isn't going to be easy, but it can be lots of fun. If you live alone, kicking cold turkey is probably the best way to go. Collect everything in your abode that has sugar in it; throw it in the garbage and start over. This way, if you yen to start bingeing, you haven't made it easy for yourself. You can make one decision at the store instead of fighting temptation full-time at home. It may take a month or so to change the way you shop, cook, and entertain. The details of your daily struggle are not important but the general direction in which you're headed is vital.

If you have a heavy ice cream habit, don't try to cut out ice cream entirely. Great ice creams made with honey only are available almost everywhere. Shiloh Farms in the East makes a fine one entirely without sugar; natural emulsifiers and honey are used. They also distribute the Danish Haagen Das ice cream. But watch it. Haagen Das makes two kinds—one with honey *and* sugar, the other with honey only. Honey on the label means nothing unless it also says absolutely no sugar. Once you've weaned yourself onto honey ice cream, *then* cut that amount in half and taper off gradually. Save ice cream as a reward for special occasions; buy it pint by pint. Keeping records of what you eat and where you buy supplies can be a major part of the fun. Then when your friends want to know exactly what you did and how, your experiment is documented, day by day, chapter and verse.

If your coffee habit is heavy, with lots of sugar and cream, you may want to do as I did: Cut out the coffee altogether. I felt that if I couldn't have my café au lait with two or three lumps of sugar, I didn't want it at all. Fortunately, I preferred tea straight and plain—so I switched to tea. If you think you don't like tea, maybe it's because you have been trapped into the use of tea bags. Throw out the tea bags and invest in some fresh Japanese or Chinese tea. Japanese bancha tea—either leaf or twig, or combination of both—is miles from Lipton shavings in a bag. One roasts bancha tea lightly in a pan and then brews it in a Pyrex pot on the stove for fifteen or twenty minutes. Make a huge pot and reheat it when you want it. The tea can even be used twice or fresh tea added. It's a whole new experience if you haven't tried it—and worth the adventure.

If you work in an office or factory where the coffee break, the coffee cart, or the trek to the vending machine is a ritual of the day, do what I did: Invest in a chic thermos, and take your own tea. Nothing beats it as a conversation piece. Don't be exclusive! Make a vow to share your sugarless bliss with someone every day. One day is plenty to each customer. After that, let them get their own thermos.

After you've gotten used to taking tea plain, *then* try black coffee, or coffee with a slice of lemon peel. Experiment with one of the great European coffee substitutes. Some are made with roasted grains; others with dandelion. After a long coffee famine, these brews can taste great. I've enjoyed a German one, Pero; another, Bambu; a great one made in Canada, Dandylion. Use these just like instant coffee. Try them in your thermos with a slice of lemon peel. You'll learn very quickly that everything changes, including tastes, yens, and habits you thought were yours for a lifetime. All your food tastes so much better once you eliminate refined sugar; at first you think it's the food, then you realize it's you, your body.

For years, many health food stores have sold light brown, dark brown, and so-called "raw" sugar along with the vitamins and the wheat germ. Cakes, pastries, cookies —even bread—sold in health food stores were made with "partially refined" sugar. The impression given was that it was somehow superior to the white stuff at the supermarket.

If one inquired, one was often led to believe that the sugars traditionally used by the health food industry had been snatched from the mechanical jaws of sugar refineries sometime before the ultimate processing turned them into refined white sugar.

Then, in the late 1960s, when young people were questioning everything they'd been sold and natural food stores and co-ops began springing up everywhere, a young pioneer of the natural food movement in northern California had his doubts about brown sugar.

Fred Rohe had been selling "raw" and brown sugars at his New Age Food Stores in north California. When he couldn't get any straight answers about where the sugar came from and what had been done to it, he took the trouble to visit sugar refineries in Hawaii and California.

He soon had the answer. Light brown, dark brown, and raw sugar are all made the same way: Molasses is added to refined sugar. "Brown sugar is nothing more than white sugar wearing a mask," he concluded. For Kleenraw 5 percent molasses is added; for light brown, 12 percent molasses; and for dark brown, 13 percent. The raw-like illusion is a result of a specially designed crystallization process which produces this aesthetic effect. Fred Rohe threw all the colored sugars out of his store; he helped found an organization of natural food stores owners called Organic Merchants. One of the basic tenets of the organization was to refuse shelf room to all kinds of sugar or any product containing sugar. He wrote a devastating two-page pamphlet, *The Sugar Story,* to educate his customers.

"Our intention is not to take the pleasure out of anyone's life," said *The Sugar Story,* "but to play a part in upgrading the quality of American food. If enough of us stop buying junk—even the better junk—the food manufacturers will listen."

Organic merchants sell honey and recommend substituting half the amount for the sugar called for in recipes. Some sell carob molasses, carob syrup, unrefined sugar cane syrup, sorghum molasses, and date sugar. Erewhon now sells a natural glucose syrup made from rice and barley. Natural food stores today have become educational institutions—teaching by example. Man-refined sucrose—white or colored—is one place where they draw the line.

In kicking sugar, the most helpful extra hint I can give you is the one that worked for me. Kick red meat at the same time. It's easier now that meat has been priced out of sight. You'll discover very soon what the Orientals have known since time immemorial. Meat (which is masculine yang) sets up a powerful yen in your system to be balanced with its opposite—something very sweet and feminine and yin, like fruit or sugar.

Just switching from red meat to fish or fowl reduces your desire for a sweet concoction at the end of the meal—makes it easier to settle for natural fruit or for no dessert at all. The more vegetable protein used in place of animal protein, the easier it becomes to forget about sugar, pastries, and such. I learned, from a savvy young lady, a trick that brings people together. When invited out for dinner, she would order maybe the appetizer, sometimes the soup, then the entree. Then, instead of saying "Wouldn't you like to come home for a drink?" she would invite her companion to drop by for a homemade, sugarfree dessert and tea, or ersatz coffee.

If you don't live alone, kicking a sugar habit can be quite a production. Doing it together can be delightful. If you're a mama or a papa, the same theory applies. If mama and papa can agree to give it a try, especially when young kids are involved, it can be a ball. Young children can be the greatest little guinea pigs you ever saw. The results with children are often so dramatic that it supplies motivation and example for their elders. Remember, no medical authority on this planet will stand up and say that sugar is necessary for anybody. No medical authority on this planet will even claim that sugar is good for children. And no medical authority on this planet will say that a sugarfree diet is at all dangerous. All the medical authorities dare to say is that sugar tastes good and has calories. If you have a child at home between, say, two and five, kicking sugar together can be a fantastic adventure.

Few places exist in society where an experiment in nutrition can actually be controlled. The first place, obviously, is prison. Another is an army unit under isolated conditions. Even a hospital is not a place where total control can be exercised unless rooms are isolated and guarded. But if you have a child in a crib, or one young enough so that you can control the diet, the opportunity is unique.

If your child is used to a certain level of sugar (i.e., that already in baby food, soft drinks, desserts, or treats), don't do anything drastic at first. When you throw out the sugar intended for the adults, leave the baby's food alone. Record carefully the infant's behavior. Is your baby cranky when awakening? Happy at play? Watch activity, moods, and spells. Watch the baby like a warden for three or five days while the diet is sugared—and that means sugar in the baby food, cereal, vegetables, soft drinks, juices, desserts, and ice cream. Then reverse your field completely. Cut out all the sweets. Eliminate everything with sugar in it. Offer apples, pears, nuts, raisins, and juice that is labeled "unsweetened."

Watch the child's behavior for at least ten days. The difference will amaze you. It may be all the scientific proof you need to continue the experiment with yourself and the rest of the family. I have seen sugarfree babies in Europe and America. It is incredible. They seem to be a different breed altogether from average, sugar-glutted children. The wonderful thing is, if raised completely without sugar, when children are exposed to the multiple temptations of a sugared culture, they have already developed natural immunity. Given sugar candy or sweetened soft drinks, they reject them. The younger your children are, the easier it can be to eliminate sugar from their diet.

If your children are older, weaning may be a problem. In many cases, sugar has to be removed slowly and carefully. Offer unsweetened apple juice instead of cola or soft drinks. If tantrums are thrown, let it go. Bake them honeyed cookies and offer plenty of homemade desserts—which they will claim to detest. Buy honey ice cream instead of the heavily sugared kind. Bring children into the act by letting the girls worry about their complexion or their menstrual cramps enough to try the results from sugarfree cookies or pies which they can help bake. Sometimes, boys also are concerned enough about their complexion or other problems (unnecessary bosoms, perhaps) to interest themselves in the family experiments. If your kids are seventeen or over, the shoe may be completely on the other foot. Many teenagers today are more interested in natural food and know a lot more on the subject than their parents.

A family is a group of people having the same blood. A mother feeds her child with her own blood and milk for the first months of its life. From then on, a person's blood is created anew daily when the family eats together. Eating the same food together every day helps make the family a group of the same blood. In earlier times, the kitchen and the dining area were sacred places in the home. The mother kept the family together with the food she cooked. No other earthly ceremony surpassed it in importance.

It is no wonder most American families are fragmented today. In the twentieth century, family could be characterized as a group having the same address and telephone number. During the first days of life, the infant feeds via a hospital assembly line. Then sugared meals come out of supermarket jars. As soon as the child is able to crawl, sugared delights are rewards; punishments mean the cola is taken away. For good behavior, the child may select sugared cereal in an individual box containing a plastic prize. Drinks are the milk of cows never seen, the frozen juice of fruit never touched. The Good Humor Man is in the street with iced sugar delights. What used to be birthday party food—pizza, sugar cake, cookies, ice cream, and cola—have become frozen proxies for the daily bread. Before children have developed judgment other than at the tip of their tongues, brother and sister feed themselves with toasted waffles out of a box, pancakes out of a jug. The words treat and snack are drained of meaning; the children treat themselves when the impulse moves them: At the refrigerator, the freezer, the candy store, the school cafeteria, the vending machine. If grace was said before eating, praying would be intermittent, all day long.

Mother takes her weight watchers' concoctions out of a box; downtown, Daddy has a two-martini, credit-card lunch. The kids at school are fed at the pleasure of almighty government or they squander their allowance at the candy store. After school, the never-ending birthday party bingeing is taken up again. Kids spoil their suppers with supermarket snacks and sugared drinks. If frozen TV dinners on individual trays are too much for mother, if she deserves a break today, the family rattles off to the nearest drive-in, where it's each to his own.

I've been conducting a survey.

Every young female sugar addict I know has confessed the same thing: They don't know now—and never have known—what it was to have a normal menstrual period, without pain, cramps, or extreme discomfort. No wonder the TV commercials show mother introducing their teenage daughters to the wonders of pain-killing drugs "for those very special days of feminine discomfort."

I got turned onto this subject when I met a young actress. When the day came for her big scene, she started acting as temperamental as Marilyn Monroe. When I guessed what was ailing her, she let it all out. I showed her how to kick sugar. She was willing and ready to do anything to relieve the three-day torture that had occurred monthly since she had reached puberty. Her next period was noticeably better, and within two months, she had completely forgotten her menstrual period was due, because she had been accustomed to having 24 hours of warning pain before the onset of menstruation.

After this experience, I began to feel like Dr. Kildare. My beautiful patient spread the message through fitting rooms and dressing rooms from New York to California. Subsequently, I've discovered that many doctors—especially in France—have been wise for decades to the lethal effects of sugar on feminine metabolic balance.

In the magazine *La Vie Claire*, Dr. Victor Lorenc wrote:

With women, sugar causes pains during menstruation. Here is the case of Sophie Z . . . she used to take a daily consumption of approximately 100 grams of industrial sugar. At the age of thirty her menstruation became extremely painful. This discomfort disappeared completely with the suppression in 1911 of this "murderous food."

Since that time we have been able to observe many analogous cases. This fact ought to be known and spread abroad by workers with women. Sugar abstinence rids women of what is known as a "natural weakness," that is to say, of nervousness and incapacity to work which are often the result of difficult menstruation.

Do you have freckles? If you do, chances are you have a big sugar habit. After you have kicked sugar for a year or so, you begin to notice big changes in the way your skin takes to the sun. Sitting in the hot sun covered with chemical sauce to get a beautiful tan is looking for trouble—especially for women. After you've kicked sugar you will discover that *sunbathing without any protective lotion* is usually possible with little or no risk of burning or peeling. Should your skin turn red, one usually doesn't burn. I never peel. As a child, I used to have painful sunburn on the first exposure to the sun. After ten years of being sugarfree, I am able to loll in the desert for an hour, pick up an instant tan and never have any redness, itching, pain, or any of the old sunburn symptoms. Try it and see. Remember, take it easy with sun experiments. It's not that it's not *nice* to fool mother nature, it's impossible. Some people are better off avoiding the sun, sugarfree diet or not.

You're having a picnic at the beach or in the park; the typical American family arrives. The kids explode out of the station wagon before Dad has turned off the ignition. Mother starts unloading the car and informing Papa where to put the blanket. Before the soft drink cooler is sprung open, Mother attacks the air, sand, and greenery with lethal insecticide spray. Massive retaliation against the insect world that had beleaguered them on the last country jaunt. Mother has forgotten, if she ever knew, that just as spilled sugar in our kitchens attracts ants and insects, so does sugar in our bloodstreams attract mosquitos, microbes, and parasites.

One of the great joys of being sugarfree is to be able to lie on the beach or loll in the mountains without being bothered by mosquitos or other creatures. Once off sugar for a year or so, try it and see if it isn't true for you too. If you take along a guest who's still addicted to sugar, lie side by side. See who the mosquitos go for and who is left alone.

After all, it's no accident that the first cases of mosquito-borne yellow fever—in the Western Hemisphere—occurred in the sugar island of Barbados in 1647. In the beginning it was called *nova pestis*. Yellow fever spread from one sugar center to another: Guadalupe, St. Kitts, Jamaica, Brazil, British Guinea, Spain, Portugal, New Orleans, and, finally, Cuba, where the U.S. Army mounted a massive campaign at the turn of the twentieth century to make our sugar colony of Cuba safe from the mosquito.

Sugar addiction is a worldwide phenomenon today. World production in 1975 will exceed 150 billion pounds. Prices have zoomed but per capita consumption ranges from over a hundred pounds per person per year in rich countries like the U.S. to less than ten pounds per capita in underdeveloped lands.

Sugar pushers have their eyes on Asia and Africa. If

just a few million there can be hooked on coke, a per capita increase of a few pounds a year in these giant markets would amount to a boom. If that happens, the current food crisis can turn into catastrophe.

The mark of slavery still sticks to cane cutting in many tropical lands. Many militant blacks want no part of raising cane in the hot tropical sun. To newly independent nations hungering to join The Haves, sugar is a symbol of La Dolce Vita. It's tough to ask anybody to give up something they've never had. White people have had their sugar for centuries without sweating in the hot sun.

The Chinese have gone from the ox cart to the jet, skipping many stages between. But adaptation to technology is one thing. Adaptation of the human body to a sugar-ridden environment is something else. Today, people who never tasted sugar in their lives can move—like suburban children fooling around with drugs—from innocence to dependency overnight. When that happens—whether in suburbia or Siberia—the result is the same: documented disaster.

While hordes of scientists whoring for the sugar industry work in their expensive laboratories looking for shreds of pseudoscientific solace for the sugar pushers, a trio of British scientists have again blown the whole game wide open by studying mankind as a whole, making the entire planet their globalaboratory, as Dr. Price did in the 1930s.

The sun never sets on the Coca-Cola sign today, so the British doctors have taken that as their cue: their book ranges over the lands of the one-time British empire and beyond. They see man as a part of an environment with a history (as physician-botanist Rauwolf did centuries ago in the 1500s), not symptoms on a chart, data from a computer. Their work is Darwinian in scope and produces a synthesis of Eastern experience with Western knowledge. Their findings support the warnings our friends from the Orient have journeyed to the West to share with us. Their exploratory range covers the Zulu in his tribal lands contrasted with his suddenly urbanized cousins; U.S. blacks, contrasted with other Africans; Indians in India compared with Indians in South Africa;

Cherokee Indians compared with East Pakistanis; Eskimos stacked against Icelanders; Yemenites in their own lands compared with Yemenites who have jetted to a new life in Israel. Sugar consumption is related to physical degeneration on a global scale.

This prophetic and devastating work is the work of Surgeon-Captain T. L. Cleave (retired from the Royal Navy); Dr. G. D. Campbell, of the Diabetic Clinic of King Edward VIII Hospital in Durban, South Africa; and Professor N. S. Painter of London's Royal College of Surgeons.

The second edition of *Diabetes, Coronary Thrombosis, and the Saccharine Disease*, published by John Wright and Sons, Ltd., in England, came out in 1969. Here are some of their conclusions:

The different symptoms of arsenic poisoning, syphilis, or other diseases (due to a single cause) are not normally treated as separate diseases, so why should the multiple symptoms caused by sugar be so treated? Of all foods processed by man, refined carbohydrates like sugar and white flour are altered the most: 90 percent of the cane or beet is removed, 30 percent of the wheat. Changes produced by cooking food are trifling in comparison.

This perversion of natural food is so recent in the total history of man that it dates only to yesterday. Man is fully able to live on plants—millions of whole rice eaters in the Orient have done so for centuries. Where men live on whole foods, sugar diseases are strikingly absent. Refinement of carbohydrates like white sugar and white flour affects the human body in three main ways:

1. Man-refined sugar is eight times as concentrated as flour, and eight times as unnatural—perhaps eight times as dangerous. It is the unnaturalness that deceives the tongue and appetite, leading to overconsumption. Who would eat 2½ pounds of sugar beets a day? Yet the equivalent in refined sugar is a mere 5 ounces. Overconsumption produces diabetes, obesity, and coronary thrombosis among other things.

2. Removal of natural vegetable fiber produces tooth

decay, diseases of the gums, stomach trouble, varicose veins, hemorrhoids, and diverticular disease.

3. Removal of proteins causes peptic ulcers.

It would be extraordinary if sugar and white flour, known to wreak havoc on the teeth, did not also have profound repercussions elsewhere in the body.

Coronary disease has heretofore been regarded as a "complication" of diabetes. Both coronary disease and diabetes have a common cause: White sugar and white flour.

Indians in Natal, South Africa, consume nine times the amount of sugar that Indians in India consume, and the former have suffered a veritable explosion of diabetes—it is believed to be the highest anywhere in the world. If the masses in India ever have that much sugar available, the consequences within a decade or two are "too frightening to contemplate."

Emphasis of public health programs should shift from detection of sugar disease to preventive nutrition—principally, the substitution of natural carbohydrates for refined ones.

Preventive nutrition may also have to include, temporarily, the "theoretically incorrect" use of artificial sweeteners which the authors of *Diabetes, Coronary Thrombosis, and the Saccharine Disease* compare to the use of the contraceptive pill as "undesirable but often unavoidable."

Heroin was first introduced as a harmless nonaddictive substitute for morphine. More recently, methadone was introduced as a harmless nonaddictive substitute for heroin. It was only a matter of time until the synthetics were discovered to be as perilous as the old-fashioned narcotics.

So it is with the synthetic sweeteners touted and marketed as harmless substitutes for sugar. Saccharin and the cyclamates have many defenders in the medical profession. When compared with sugar, a scientific case can always be made for them as the lesser of two evils. Scientists are working frantically to come up with new formulae for new synthetic sweeteners. Other scientists are at work, often with the help of the sugar industry, to prove that the new synthetics are potentially hazardous.

The trouble with all synthetic sweeteners, aside from their potential danger to our health, is that the longer we depend on them, the more difficult it becomes to appreciate the natural sweetness of natural food. Dependence on synthetic sweeteners, like dependence on sugar, deadens our sense of taste to the point where it almost disappears.

The best advice I've found on the subject of artificial sweeteners comes from Dr. A. Kawahata, a leading Japanese nutritionist from Kyoto University, who quotes an early Buddhist axiom:

If you look for sweetness
Your search will be endless
You will never be satisfied
But if you seek the *true* taste
You will find what you are looking for.

Soup to Nuts

It is a miracle if one finds a canned soup at the store without sugar or chemical preservatives in it. If you're kicking sugar, you're on your own in this department. Homemade soup is a cinch to create. The only work is in foraging for the good ingredients.

I keep on hand a supply of dried split peas, pinto beans, and lentils. They combine beautifully with staple vegetables like onions, leeks, carrots, and celery. Variations are possible with the seasonal vegetables—pumpkin, squash, sweet corn, beets, turnips, and parsnips.

Soak dried peas or beans overnight in cool water. If you want to be adventurous, try soaking a small piece of dried wakame—a Japanese sea vegetable available in many natural food stores—with them. The minerals in the wakame help reduce the cooking time and add a savory flavor.

Soups are simplicity itself.

Start with a good vegetable oil, unfiltered sesame or corn oil, or a combination of the two. Sauté a chopped onion in a heavy pot. Add chopped celery, perhaps carrots. Slowly pour in the soaked peas and water. Bring to a low boil and simmer slowly for an hour, until the soaked vegetables are soft and edible but not mushy. Let the soup rest. When it's time to serve the soup, warm it again. Pour into individual bowls and add tamari, a traditional soy sauce which has sea salt in it. (Traditional Japanese soy sauce tamari is a live food, naturally fermented and aged in wood for two years and made without chemicals or preservatives. Its ingredients are water, soybeans, wheat, and sea salt. The brand I use is imported and sold in America under the Erewhon label. Many other soy sauces on the U.S. market are made with sugar and other chemicals to reduce the fermentation time.)

This is the basic recipe. The variations are endless.

If good onions are available, onion soup will stand on its own. Or, go heavy on celery, put it through the blender after it's cooked, and you have cream of celery. Use chopped beets and beet tops, with a little cabbage, and you have a kind of borscht. Add slices of pumpkin and/or butternut squash to the onion, sauté it until soft, add water—and you have pumpkin soup. When I use pumpkin or squash, I prefer a heavy soybean oil instead of sesame. Combined with onion and butternut squash, this tastes—to me anyway—like cream of tomato.

If you can find leeks, use them in addition to or in place of the onion, then you are moving in the direction of what used to be called vichyssoise; thicken it with oat flour. I avoid tomatoes and potatoes in soup. I also avoid using most grains in my soups except barley. A little barley added to almost any combination of vegetables gives a completely different texture and flavor.

I make a beautiful double corn soup which is a meal in itself. Sauté chopped onions in oil. When the onions are golden, stir a half cup or more of stone ground yellow or white corn meal into the oil and onion and gently sauté. (Chopped green pepper adds color and flavor.) After the corn meal has gently simmered in the oil, water is added gradually as if making a gravy. As it thickens, more and more water is added. This simmers for almost an hour. Shortly before serving, add kernels of fresh corn off the cob and serve with tamari. Off season, one can use frozen corn (cook it until it is thawed and chewy).

With soups like this you never have to write down a recipe.

Go Italian by making an onion and celery stock and adding slices of romaine or escarole. Decorate the soup bowls with tiny slices of chopped scallion, as the Japanese do. Use carrot tops and the roots of leeks—as the French do—if you chop them fine and sauté them well. Go heavy on the cabbage like the Russians and the Irish. You can use rolled oats—or oat flour—instead of corn, as the Scotch and Irish do. Or use onion stock and add chopped uncooked vegetables and end up the Mediterranean way. The point is, if you can find decent vegetables, you'll have great soup. The tamari takes care of the seasoning.

Among American sugar-pushing people killers, Fannie Farmer is certainly the queen. Whether she reflected the Victorian era or influenced it, we'll never know. Certainly her cookbooks were bibles in the American kitchens at the turn of the century. She started out as a pupil at the Boston Cooking School, perhaps many of her recipes were stolen from the headmistress Mrs. Lincoln, whose less successful cookbook was published years before that of Fannie Farmer.

For decades, women have been stealing recipes from Fannie. Perhaps she was encouraged by the Sugar Lobby! We do know that it is fitting she was immortalized as the face on a candy box. For she was one—if not *the*—originator of the deadly idea of adding sugar to practically everything: Bread, vegetables, salads, and their dressings.

In the salad section of the Fannie Farmer cookbook, published in 1896, recipes for salad dressing advocated pouring in the sugar. As successive editions came along, tomato aspics were made truly lethal by adding sugar. Sugar was used to speed up the leavening of bread. Fannie went way beyond that to the point that Europeans tasting

American bread thought of it as cake. And that's what it was.

Her mania for adding sugar culminates in the 1965 edition of her cookbook, which suggests taking commercial mayonnaise (already sugared) and adding two parts of it to one part of sugar and two parts of lemon juice and other seasonings. Then she says "Shake well." It certainly will.

It is virtually impossible today to buy bottled mayonnaise or salad dressing of any kind without finding it already loaded with sugar. If you begin messing around with Jello and flavored gelatin (which is heavily sugared) and add canned fruit in sugared syrup, one ends up with a typical American salad. Many women eat nothing but this kind of sugarbomb and imagine they are "dieting." Small wonder they complain that their menfolks resist those colorful concoctions they use to dress up the table. Everyone would be much better off eating the flowers in the centerpiece.

Ketchup, mayonnaise, and the various combinations thereof called Russian dressings are loaded with sugar. Sugar is in everything, including the pickles. If you want to kick sugar, you may have to rethink the whole subject of salads. Remember, in 1905, the Japanese licked the Russians, perhaps you will try a Japanese salad. Easy to make and great for your stomach, it combines well with almost any other food. Compact enough to be carried in a small jar, it keeps practically forever. Pressed salad is made by adding pieces of salted vegetables to a crock covered with a weighted, fitted board. If you have a crock and a rock, fine. If not, a couple of bowls, one fitted inside the other are perfect. Use a jug of water as a weight.

Oriental vegetables like Chinese cabbage or bok choy are great for pressed salad, but practically any vegetables will do. Lettuce, escarole, romaine, dandelion greens, beets, celery, onions, turnips (don't forget to use the tops of celery, beets, radishes, carrots, and turnips), scallions, chives, mustard greens, and radishes—both white and red; I avoid strong leaves like spinach and kale. Cucumbers combine with almost any green vegetable and are great alone. I start by washing off the dirt and grit from leaves. (Whenever I wash vegetables that are particularly full of earth, I remember the American woman in Paris. When we agreed it was great to be able to buy fresh vegetables in the French open air neighborhood markets, she made a terrible face and said, "But they're so *dirty*.") If you're lucky enough to have vegetables (perhaps from your own garden or someone else's) grown without chemicals and insecticides, on composted soil, they have real taste. If they have real taste, chances are they have dirt on them. After you wash and dry them, cut into small pieces. Then put into a bowl (or a crock if you have one) in layers, dusting each layer with a small amount of sea salt. In France, one buys sea salt at the supermarket in a plastic bag, you then roast slightly and grind. Most natural food stores or gourmet shops have quality, finely ground sea salt. I won't touch the kind that pours when it rains; it contains sugar. After dusting the layered vegetables, place the smaller bowl inside the larger bowl, which contains the vegetables. Put something heavy inside the top bowl in the way of a weight. When I'm traveling, I often use a wooden cutting board on top of the bowl, onto which I pile books, on a traveling iron, or lamp, or whatever I lay eyes on. If you have an open crock, have a woodworking friend make you a fitted wooden lid and bring home a very Zen rock from the beach to serve as a permanent weight.

After an hour in the crock, the pressed salad is usually ready. Remove the weight, pour off the liquid, and serve with a dash of tamari soy sauce. If you like, add a little unrefined sesame oil. If fibrous vegetables like turnips and carrots are stiff, return them to the crock (or whatever) for more squeezing. The Japanese make gorgeous pickles the same way, sometimes a sprinkling of rice bran and herbs is added. The vegetables stand in the brine for days, even weeks. The action of the salt on the vegetables makes for a complete transformation, a totally different taste.

A pressed salad can become a main dish: Cook a bowl of whole wheat or buckwheat macaroni, drain it, mix in a little sesame oil and soy sauce, and then add to the vegetables. You'll hardly miss the commercial sugared mayonnaise. If you do, some natural food stores have mayonnaise made from fertile eggs, decent oil, and a little honey instead of sugar. Mayonnaise can be thinned with soy sauce and lemon juice; use it until you have weaned your family off commercial mixtures they think they can't live without.

Tomatoes and avocados are tropical fruits. I do not use them in salads at all. If you are in the tropics and want an avocado, I found the best to do is eat it all by itself, with a little soy sauce or tamari. Tomatoes and potatoes I skip altogether. You can make a potato salad with pressed vegetables, using them in the same way you use whole wheat or buckwheat pasta. Buckwheat pasta, by the way, is a Japanese delicacy called soba, not much appreciated in America. Buckwheat is full of rutin—the stuff one pays an arm and a leg for when buying vitamin pills. (I know women who examine themselves periodically for signs of visible broken veins or unsightly tiny, blue capillaries. As soon as they find anything like this they head for the buckwheat. Try it and see. If your doctor has varicose veins in his nose, tell him about buckwheat. Never let a doctor examine you without examining him just as carefully. Many of them need all the help one can offer.)

No salad makes sense to me anymore without a dash of homegrown sprouts. In the Orient they were sprouting grains, beans, and legumes for centuries before anyone ever heard of vitamin C. Today, when decent fresh vegetables and greens cost an arm and a leg, everybody who can has his or her own garden. For sprouts, one doesn't need a compost heap, a patch of earth, or a sunny windowsill. One can even grow them in jail. All you need is a Mason jar, fresh water, and seeds: Alfalfa, mung beans, or lentils. Many natural food stores and gourmet shops have tricky little devices for sprouting seeds painlessly. Some are crockery contraptions; others are simply Mason jars with removable screened tops. Follow the instructions and within hours or days, you'll have more sprouts than you can eat. (They keep in the refrigerator for days.) Add sprouts to salads or use them in more complicated dishes. The seeds and legumes can be bought in bulk in any natural food store.

Once you've had success with sprouts, you're ready to grow herbs, wheat grass, and buckwheat lettuce on the windowsill. When one of your house plants gives up the ghost, don't pitch out the earth with the plant. Keep it, water it, and when the earth is good and moist, scatter the soil with wheat berries or unroasted buckwheat groats that have been soaked for a few hours in fresh water. Keep the earth moist and within a few hours the wheat berries will send out little tentacles, root themselves, and begin shooting up straight green grass. When the wheat grass is 6 to 8 inches high, just cut a handful of grass, as you do with chives. Use the buckwheat lettuce like watercress. Chew it instead of chewing gum. You'll be astonished at the natural sweetness. You chew and you chew. Then there comes a point on which there are two schools of thought. Either you swallow the grass or you spit it out. It's loaded with vitamins and minerals and better than drugstore items for any ailments. Animals cure themselves using certain kinds of grass as medicine. When they feel ill, they quit eating and chew nothing but certain grasses until they have recovered. This makes a great game for kids—especially if you're trying to help them kick chewing gum or candy. Here is a natural sweet they can grow themselves.

After collecting almost fifty million dollars a year for umpteen years, promising the donors that if they give and give someone could find a cure for heart disease in their lifetime, the American Heart Association has belatedly admitted that nobody can stop you from digging your grave with your teeth.

The Heart Association published, with great hoopla, an official cookbook for "fat-controlled" eating. It tells you how to count cholesterol the way people used to count calories. We hardly needed them to tell us after all these years that Safflower, sesame, and corn oil are better than lard, margarine, butter, and some of the other gooky cooking fats on the market. They have come up with some other helpful hints (a low cholesterol omelet made with one egg yolk and three whites) but they still don't differentiate between eggs and eggs. Natural fertile eggs, in England these are free range eggs laid by chickens allowed to pick their own food, and sterile eggs, the kind laid by zombic chickens trapped in assembly line prison hatcheries. If a hen sits on a fertile egg (the kind you used to be able to get in the country), it will turn into a baby chicken. If a hen sits on a sterile egg, it will turn into a stinking mess. A good egg is hard to find. The other kind are usually available at the supermarket.

The *Reader's Digest* got on the bandwagon by publishing with great fanfare excerpts from the American Heart Association's Cookbook as *The Fat Controlled Diet.* I couldn't resist skimming through their recipes to see what all the noise was about. Despite all the scientific work that has been published connecting high sugar intake with heart disease, the American Heart Association approaches the subject of sugar gingerly.

"Eat foods that will satisfy your daily needs for protein, vitamins, minerals, and other nutrients. Your appetite will then be satisfied to a greater degree by usable food elements, rather than by empty calories, such as those found in sugar."

They still can't seem to move beyond the old, discredited notion that sugar is merely harmless, empty or naked calories. Grains and cereals, we are told, do not contain cholesterol. What they do contain, they don't tell us. Don't load up on rich dairy products like butter, ice cream, and whole milk. Convenience foods may be inconvenient for fat-controlled eating. Desserts can be adapted in a way to cut down butter and egg yolks.

When it comes to the recipes, it's fat-free, low-cholesterol, Fannie Farmer all the way. Sugar in the bread, the pancakes, the coffee cake, the muffins, and the rolls. Grape jelly and cranberry sauce with hamburgers; mayonnaise with mousse; cornflakes, and cooked (sugared) fruits with main course. All this sugar before one reaches dessert. When you do get to the fat-controlled desserts, all except one is laced with sugar.

I am grateful to the AHA Cookbook for one thing. I don't like their recipe much but the garbanzo dip reminded me of a great dish actually based on an Arab delicacy called *hummus tahina*. Two kinds of tahini exist: The blonde tahini made from peeled seeds, and the dark variety made from roasted seeds which is called sesame butter. It is close in taste to the familiar peanut butter. Without the tahini (as the AHA suggests)—a blonde paste made out of crushed sesame seeds which has been a staple in the Middle East for centuries—the dip is a pale thing indeed. Canned garbanzos are suggested. I prefer to start with dried chick peas from a natural food store. Who needs to buy all that canned water? Soak the dried garbanzos in water overnight and then simmer them in the same water over a low flame until soft. I use a small piece of Japanese seaweed called kombu in the soaking and cooking. It speeds things up and adds cholesterol-free nutrients of its own.

Now we come to the garlic. Nobody can pretend to tell you how much garlic to put in the dish. It depends on your taste. It also depends on the garlic. I used to think I knew something about garlic. That was before I visited the ancient town of Fleurance in Gascony, southwestern France. Here is garlic such as you've never tasted before—grown without chemical fertilizer or insecticides. The mayor of Fleurance is the famous natural healer and herbalist Maurice Messegué (see Chapter 3). His goal in life is to make the name of his town synonymous with the greatest natural food in Europe, if not the world. (The incomparable chickens from Fleurance are on the menu—complete with billing—at Maxim's in Paris.) The garlic grown around Fleurance is so rich and juicy it explodes with flavor and juices when sliced open. Messegué says garlic is a great tonic and healer but dangerous if grown synthetically because toxic chemicals tend to be concentrated in the cloves. I returned from Fleurance with garlic in blue sacks tied with green ribbons. One large clove of garlic from Fleurance might suit your taste for the dish. If you have to settle for the tired dried stuff peddled in most cities, you might need a whole bulb. Eventually, Neiman Marcus in Dallas will carry Fleurance garlic. Others will not be far behind once the quality is made known. Ask for it and look for those blue and green sacks.

Several kinds of blonde tahini are on the market. The one I prefer is imported and packaged by Erewhon of Boston and Los Angeles. Put the cooked garbanzos in your blender, with enough cooking water to cover. Add the tahini, garlic, and a good dash of tamari soy sauce. Mix it, then taste. If it doesn't grab you, adjust the flavor by adding either beans, tahini, soy sauce, or garlic.

It's a great dip and a fabulous open-faced sandwich. Use it to stuff celery instead of some fattening cheese. This dip is loaded with everything that's good for you and, unlike dips made with mayonnaise, it's completely sugarfree.

Once you begin to develop respect for the food you cook and eat, you come to have the same respect for the precision of the French language. No wonder French was the language of diplomacy; its economy and precision also made it the language of international cuisine. In French, for instance, *Riz complêt* is rice with all the natural minerals and vitamins intact, unpolished, and unprocessed. In English, one has to make do with the appelation brown rice—an inexact description of its color. This makes all sorts of hanky panky possible. A little coloring is added to polished rice, and it's sold in the supermarket as brown rice. It's brown, all right, but nowhere near being complete.

In French, the word for grape is *raisin*. What we call the raisin in English, the French call *raisin sec*. Dried grape. We need to be reminded that the raisin is a dried grape. The concentrated grape sugar of the raisin makes it an ideal natural sweetner. The dried currant is not quite so sweet, but it has a tart flavor all its own. Then there are dried apples, peaches, pears, plums (called prunes, which is French for plum), apricots, cherries, and raspberries. Of course, one can buy dried bananas and pineapples but I have learned to leave tropical fruits to the tropics and concentrate on native fruits. What's natural for the Eskimo is different from what's natural for the Fiji Islander, right?

Try the marvelous dried and salted Japanese plum, the

umeboshi. It's virtually unknown in this country outside Japanese stores. Used traditionally in Japanese herbal medicine, umeboshi is also a great ally in the kitchen, especially with other dried fruit.

Drying fruit in season to keep it for the long winter months is an old custom. Fruit that's been sun dried without chemical preservatives has a spectacular flavor. It's quite different from sugared, canned fruit. It keeps well and takes up little space. With a few jars of dried fruit, umeboshi plums, and nuts on hand, you're ready for some sensory discoveries. When you give up man-refined sugar you open yourself to an entirely new range of flavors—many of which, ironically, predominated in the old-fashioned goodies! Another accessory I use all the time is dried lemon and orange peel (stored in a glass jar).

The combinations are endless. Start with dried apples, raisins, and a little lemon peel. Soak a handful of dried apples in cool water. If they absorb all the water, add more. Chop the raisins with a knife, so that their sweetness is let loose through the whole compote. Add dried lemon peel and bring to a slow simmer. Let the mixture bubble for some twenty minutes, then turn off the heat and let the pot stand. Use the concoction as it is; or put it through the blender and call it applesauce; or thicken it with a little arrowroot and use it for pie or tart filling. Next time, add dried chestnuts. Chestnuts and apples combine beautifully. Or use currants instead of raisins.

For a different fruit compote, combine currants, apricots, and lemon peel. Or currants and pears. Each of these combinations is enhanced by the addition of salted umeboshi plum (remove the pit if you wish). The salted plum acts as a catalyst, coverting flavors.

I usually keep a jar of stewed fruit in the refrigerator. With that on hand I can turn out a pie, a compote, or a mysterious fruit pudding in an instant. Put the fruit through the blender, add a little arrowroot-water mixture, and turn it into a sherbet glass where it cools and jells like you know what.

Most of the canned and packaged puddings on the

market are loaded with sugar. Kids are used to the texture and the color. I've had some success weaning youngsters off sugared puddings by making a whipped mixture out of stewed dried fruit and tahini (the latter has been used as a milk substitute for centuries in Arab countries). Soak a cup of dried apricots or apples in water with lemon peel and an umeboshi plum. Stew slowly over a low flame for several minutes, then cool. Put the mixture into the blender with several tablespoons of tahini and blend. Pour this into individual dishes to serve. I sometimes add a dash of coconut on top.

With pie crust, like everything else, the trick is finding the perfect ingredients: Organically grown, stone-ground, whole wheat pastry flour; organically grown, stone-ground, whole corn meal; sesame oil made from the first pressing, without the application of external heat, free from chemicals, unrefined, and unbleached; sea salt.

I use a combination of about one-third corn meal and two thirds pastry flour. The corn meal is for variety, texture, and flavor. If the corn texture is too primitive for your taste, cut down the amount or use only pastry flour.

Mix the flours in a bowl with a pinch of sea salt. If you insist on exact measurement, start with a cup of flour in total. Dribble two or three tablespoons of sesame or corn oil into the flour. Mix thoroughly until the oil has permeated the flour. Add a little cold water, dribbling it into the mixture gradually until the dough can be rolled into a ball. Set the ball aside for a half hour or so. Dust a wooden board with flour, get out your rolling pin (a clean beer bottle works well), and roll the dough until it is thin and flat. Shape it to a pie plate, trimming off excess, patching if necessary.

The combination toaster-ovens are great for baking pie shells. Use a low heat and bake for a few minutes, then set aside to cool. If you have to use a stove oven, pre-heat to around 300 degrees; then bake the pie shell until it's crisp and golden. Suggesting an exact amount of baking time is futile because every oven is different. Twenty minutes should do it at the outside. Try making individual pies occasionally; they're easier and more attractive to serve.

I rarely use fresh fruit in pies and tarts. When you are lucky enough to find good fresh fruit in season, eat it that way. If you think you can't enjoy strawberries without sugar, try this: Wash the strawberries leaving the stems on; add a teaspoon of sea salt to a pint of cold water; leave the strawberries in the cold salt water mixture for a half hour or so. Now taste. We all know what a little salt can do for an apple or a melon. Strawberries and raspberries perk up the same way.

One must look carefully to find canned peaches that aren't prepared with heavily sugared syrup. Unsweetened peaches available at natural food stores, make a spectacular pie. Pour the peaches and their natural juice into a Pyrex saucepan, add a little lemon peel—fresh or dried —and bring them to a simmer. Add arrowroot-water mixture to the peach juice. It will turn cloudy at first; when it bubbles and clears, pour the mixture into the pie shell and bake for a few minutes. If the pie is runny after it cools, add more arrowroot. If you want it sweeter, add chopped raisins or raisin water.

For a special topping on a fruit pie, take leftover pie crust, crumble it into a bowl which has a few tablespoons of wheat germ, roasted rolled oats, a little date sugar or honey, crushed sesame seeds, some coconut, a dribble of sesame oil, and a little water. Blend these ingredients and crumble the mixture on top of the pie filling. Brown under the broiler until the topping is golden brown.

Too many cooks ignore the potential of the root vegetables such as onions, pumpkins, and squash. Fragrant pie fillings from these vegetables are simple. Peel and slice onions into bite-sized slivers. Sauté slowly in sesame oil until soft and golden; add a little water. Simmer gently while you mix a tablespoonful of arrowroot powder with enough cold water to make a paste. When the paste is added to the onion-water mixture, it will turn cloudy. Keep stirring, over a low heat, until it bubbles and becomes clear. Then add a good jolt of tamari soy sauce.

It will take trial and error to find what suits your taste. After the filling is thoroughly mixed and bubbling, pour into the prebaked pie shell. Return to the broiler for a few minutes until the filling bubbles, then remove from the oven. It is delicious at any temperature.

Furikake is a spectacular Japanese sesame condiment made of soybean purée, soy flour, nori (a dried sea vegetable), and bonita (dried fish flakes). Add furikake before you add the arrowroot mixture and soy sauce, or after, or just before baking. If you can't find furikake, dust the top of the pie with roasted sesame seeds before baking.

Turnips or parsnips, sliced and sautéed with onion, make delicious pies. The variations are endless. The important thing to remember is that handling root vegetables this way brings out their natural sweetness. Leeks, scallions, pumpkin, and squash can be used in combination with onions. Some need more sautéeing than others. Experiment.

A crepe, as we all know, is nothing but a delicate pancake. Crepe suzettes are thin pancakes with a filling added. The crepe is simple to make and delicious. I use whole wheat pastry flour. Sometimes I add fine corn meal for texture and variety. Mix the flour in a bowl with a pinch of sea salt. Add two or three tablespoons of sesame oil per cup. Blend thoroughly. Add raw milk, sour milk, sour cream and water, or just plain water. Add an egg if you wish; for a large batch, add two. The milk and the eggs are good on occasion but not crucial. Keep adding liquid until the batter is thin but not runny. The thinner the batter, the thinner the crepe. A heavy batter makes a thick crepe. Suit yourself. The ideal utensil for making crepes is a light, French crepe pan. But any kind of pan or griddle will do. Simply pour your batter onto a hot griddle which has a light coating of sesame or corn oil. Let it cook until the top of the crepe is completely dry. Say a prayer or two before poking the edge of the spatula around the edge of the crepe. When the time comes, flip it over. The French jiggle the pan while the crepe is cooking over the flame then flip it over without the spatula. The huge Brittany buckwheat crepes sold on the Paris streets are too huge to be flipped without an instrument. (Sometimes they measure 18 inches across, the size of an East Indian roti.) When the crepe has cooked through on both sides, flip onto a plate.

For a dessert crepe, the variety of fillings is infinite: Natural, unsweetened apple butter; apple, chestnut, and raisin mixture; thickened raisin water—chopped raisins stewed in water—with arrowroot for a raisin syrup; or stewed apricots, dried currants, and lemon peel blended together. Just spoon your favorite mixture onto the crepe, fold or roll them and serve.

Shelled walnuts lightly dusted with sea salt, freshly roasted over a low heat, and served warm make an incomparable snack or dessert. Most everyone appreciates the difference in taste between roasted and unroasted peanuts, but for some reason the walnut is often presented as a soggy decoration or fresh from the nutcracker. You haven't lived until you've tried walnuts fresh roasted and warm.

Other familiar nuts like the cashew or filbert may be served the same way. Store-bought nuts are usually preroasted in oil, often too much poor quality salt is used; sometimes sugar and chemical preservatives are used to prevent nuts from turning rancid. The trick is to find nuts that have been grown, harvested, and stored without chemicals.

Shelled almonds with their natural membrane lend themselves to a Japanese treatment. Pour almonds into a glass bowl, then dribble tamari soy sauce over them. (The quality of the soy sauce is all-important.) Stir the nuts in the soy sauce until well coated; the membrane will absorb the liquid. Then arrange in a Pyrex dish. I use a slotted spoon, or a fork, so that the excess soy sauce can be saved for future use. Put the almonds under the broiler at a low heat, 200 degrees or less. Watch carefully and turn them over every few minutes. It usually takes ten to twenty minutes until the nuts are crisp enough to serve.

Warm chestnuts, freshly pan-roasted in their slashed

shells, are a familiar seasonal delicacy sold on the streets of Paris and other cosmopolitan cities. Dried chestnuts can be stored and kept indefinitely. Chestnut flour or chestnut meal is fragile and should be used freshly ground. The chestnut has a natural sweetness. It combines beautifully with apples and raisins for tarts, pies, or compotes. Chestnut flour can be used with whole wheat pastry flour in crepes, waffles, chapati, or donuts.

When you blend a little daring, imagination and quality ingredients, the results are delicious, sugarfree, natural foods. Once you decide to make this transition, you'll be trimmer and healthier, more mentally alert, and free of the sugar blues.

Notes

The Mark of Cane

1. Reay Tannahill, *Food in History*.
2. Ibid.
3. *Journals of Leonhard Rauwolff*. A collection of curious travels and voyages in two tomes. The first containing Dr. Leonhard Rauwolf's itinerary into the Eastern countries: Syria, Palestine in the Holy Land, Armenia, Mesopotamia, Assyria, Chaldea, etc. Translated from the High Dutch by Nicholas Staphorst. London, S. Smith and B. Walford, 1693. Edited by John Ray (1627-1705). Second Edition, London, S. Smith and B. Walford, 1705. (The reader will note that the above author's name is spelled with one and with two Fs. This text follows that prevailing in reference works, Rauwolf.)
4. Noel Deerr, *The History of Sugar*.
5. L. A. Strong, *The Story of Sugar*.
6. Mark Twain, *Mark Twain's Autobiography*, vol. 1, pp. 8-9.

How We Got Here From There

1. Bernard Fergusson, *Beyond the Chindwin*, p. 198.

2. E. M. Abrahamson and A. W. Pezet, *Body, Mind, and Sugar*.

3. Ibid., p. 129.

4. Stewart Alsop writes in *Stay of Execution* that Dr. John Glick of the National Institute of Health was skeptical of steroids (cortisone), since they do not get to the root of the trouble and, although one feels full of beans for a while, one pays a high price in side effects. "This disappointed me. Remembering Jack Kennedy, who took steroids for adrenal insufficiency I had envisaged myself filled with uncontrollable energy. . . ." Alsop goes on to note that when he asked one of the President's closest friends about the course of steroids the President received, he said that "Kennedy never talked about it . . . but that [Charlie Bartlett] sensed when Kennedy had had a steroid treatment, 'you could feel him sort of going into high gear.' " In the book by O'Donnell and Powers, *Johnny, We Hardly Knew Ye*, there are horrendous tales of the Kennedy consumption of ice cream, malted milk shakes, and such.

On May 2, 1969, a Canadian Newspaper, *The Toronto Telegram*, carried Sid Adilman's article on Helen Lewis, a CBC editor for 14 years and chief editor for Josef von Sternberg, the director. Among Helen Lewis's recollections of her early days in Hollywood was the experience of being "the only person in Canada who bought John Kennedy ice cream cones." As Helen Lewis puts it, "One of the people I really didn't like at all in Hollywood was Joe Kennedy—cold fish of a man . . . he'd bring his boys to the studio on Saturdays. He'd order me to take 'the little beggars,' Joe who later was killed, and John, both so cute in their sailor suits—to the commissary. I always paid; Joe never gave me any money."

5. John W. Tintera, "What You Should Know About Your Glands," (as told to Delos Smith) reprinted from *Woman's Day*, February 1958.

6. Jules Michelet, *Satanism and Witchcraft*, p. xi.

7. Peter Tompkins and Christopher Bird, *The Secret Life of Plants*, Harper & Row, New York, 1973.

8. T. Szasz, *The Manufacture of Madness*.

9. Ibid.

10. J. Sprenger and H. Kramer, *Malleus Maleficarum,* p. 47.

11. H. Graham, *Surgeons All, A History of Surgery*, foreword by Oliver St. John Gogarty, Rich & Cowan LTD., London, 1939.

12. Quoted in Gregory Zilboorg, *The Medical Man and the Witch During the Renaissance*, p. 140.

13. Szasz, pp. 93-94.

In Sugar We Trust

1. M. Foucault, *Madness and Civilization: A History of Insanity*, translated by R. Howard.

2. L. Pauling, "Orthomolecular Psychiatry," *Science*, April 19, 1968, vol. 160, pp. 265-271.

3. A. Hoffer, "Megavitamin B_3 Therapy for Schizophrenia," *Canadian Psychiat. Ass. J.*, 1971, vol. 16, p. 500.

4. A. Cott, "Orthomolecular Approach to the Treatment of Learning Disabilities," synopsis of reprint article issued by The Huxley Institute for Biosocial Research, New York.

5. T. Szasz, *The Manufacture of Madness*.

6. Benjamin Rush, *Medical Inquiries and Observations upon the Diseases of the Mind* (1812).

7. E. H. Hare, *J. Ment. Sci.*, January 25, 1962, vol. 108, p. 4.

8. A Comfort, *The Anxiety Makers, Some Curious Preoccupations of the Medical Profession*, p. 192.

9. N. Ridenour, *Mental Health in the United States: A Fifty Year History*, Harvard Univ. Press, 1961.

10. Quoted in J. Duffy, "Masturbation and Clitoridectomy," *J.A.M.A.*, October 19, 1963, vol. 186, p. 246.

11. Sigmund Freud, *The Standard Edition of the Complete Psychological Works of Sigmund Freud*, Letter 79, December 22, 1897, vol. 1, p. 272.

12. Ibid. *The Psychopathology of Everyday Life* (1901), vol. VI, pp. 199-200.

13. Quoted in Goffredo Parise, "No Neurotics in China," *Atlas*, February 1967, vol. 13, p. 47.

14. Sakurazawa Nyoiti, *You Are All Sanpaku*, pp. 62 ff.

15. Michio Kushi, *The Teachings of Michio Kushi*.

16. John W. Tintera, *Hypoadrenocorticism*.

Blame It On the Bees

1. Quoted in W. R. Aykroyd, *Sweet Malefactor.*
2. E. M. Abrahamson and A. W. Pezet, *Body, Mind, and Sugar*, p. 22.
3. G. D. Campbell, *Nutrition and Diseases*—1973. Part III—Appendix to Hearings of the United States Senate, Series 73/ND3.
4. G. Schwab, *Dance With the Devil*, p. 86.
5. J. Von Mering and O. Minkowski, *Arch. Exper. Path. Pharm.*, 1889, vol. 26, p. 371.
6. *Strength and Health Magazine*, May-June 1972.
7. Seale Harris, *J.A.M.A.*, 1924, vol. 83, p. 729.
8. F. G. Banting, *Strength and Health*, May-June 1972.
9. Schwab, p. 86.
10. H. P. Himsworth, *Clinical Science*, 1935, vol. 2, p. 117.
11. C. Fredericks and H. Goodman, *Low Blood Sugar and You*, pp. 16-19.
12. Letter from Department of Health, Education and Welfare, M. A. Hight, to M. H. Light; September 10, 1973.

Of Cabbages and Kings

1. I. Stone, *The Healing Factor*, p. 26.
2. Stone, pp. 26-27.
3. E. Voltaire, *Philosophical Dictionary* (1764), translated by Peter Gay, Basic Books, New York, 1962.
4. Stone, p. 27.
5. E. V. McCollum, *A History of Nutrition*, p. 254.
6. W. Price, *Nutrition and Physical Degeneration*, pp. 73-75.
7. *East West Journal*, Boston, letter from Dale Jones of Seattle.

How to Complicate Simplicity

1. Abstract from the *Pageant of Cuba*, Hudson Strode, H. Smith & R. Haas, New York, 1934, pp. 248-279.
2. E. V. McCollum, *A History of Nutrition*, p. 217.
3. Ibid., p. 216.
4. Ibid., p. 254.
5. H. Bailey, *The Vitamin Pioneers*, p. 34.
6. McCollum, pp. 274-276.

7. E. V. McCollum and M. Davis, *J. Biol. Chem.*, 1913, vol. 15.

8. Bailey, pp. 119-120.

9. P. de Kruif, *Hunger Fighters*, pp. 40-44.

10. L. J. Picton, *Nutrition and the Soil*, pp. 243-244.

11. Ibid., p. 248.

12. "Ailment Striking Young in Vietnam," *The New York Times*, July 22, 1973.

Dead Dogs and Englishmen

1. E. V. McCollum, *A History of Nutrition*, p. 87.

2. Ibid., p. 88.

3. *Los Angeles Times* (UPI), September 27, 1973.

4. *East West Journal*, vol. 1, no. 12, p. 1.

5. McCollum, p. 86.

6. W. C. Martin, "When is a Food a Food—and When a Poison?" *Michigan Organic News*, March 1957, p. 3.

7. F. Slare, *Vindication of Sugar Against the Charge of Dr. Willis*.

8. F. J. Stare, *W*, January 11, 1974.

9. G. D. Campbell, *Nutrition and Diseases*.

Codes of Honesty

1. R. Tannahill, *Food in History*, p. 346.

2. H. W. Wiley, *The History of a Crime Against the Food Law*, pp. 57, 376-381.

3. Ibid., pp. 376-381.

4. Ibid.

5. Ibid.

6. W. Longgood, *The Poisons in Your Food*, pp. 200-201.

What the Specialists Say

1. H. M. Shelton, *Food Combining Made Easy*, p. 32.

2. Ibid., p. 34.

3. Richard D. Lyons, *The New York Times*, June 7, 1973.

4. J. Yudkin, *Sweet and Dangerous*.

Reach for a Lucky Instead of a Sweet?

1. *Medical World News*, January 14, 1972, March 16, 1973.

2. "The Chinese Smoke Rings Around Us," *New York Post*, January 2, 1974.

3. H. J. Roberts, "Sugar Unmasked as Highway Killer," *Prevention*, March 1972.

4. H. J. Roberts, *The Causes, Ecology, and Prevention of Traffic Accidents.*

Bibliography

Abrahamson, E. M., and Pezet, A. W. *Body, Mind, and Sugar.* New York: Pyramid, 1971.

Alsop, Stewart. *Stay of Execution, A Sort of Memoir.* Philadelphia: Lippincott, 1973.

Aykroyd, W. R. *The Sweet Malefactor.* London: Heinemann, 1967.

Bailey, Herbert. *Vitamin E.: Your Key to a Healthy Heart.* New York: Arc Books, 1964.

———— *The Vitamin Pioneers.* New York: Pyramid, 1970.

Boffey, Philip. *The Brain Bank of America.* New York: McGraw-Hill, 1975.

Chestnut, Mary Boykin. *A Diary from Dixie.* Boston: Houghton Mifflin, 1949.

Clark, Linda. *Get Well Naturally.* New York: Devin-Adair, 1965.

Cartwright, Frederick F., with Biddiss, Michael D. *Disease and History.* New York: Crowell, 1972.

Chapman, John Jay. *The Selected Writings of John Jay Chap-*

man. Edited by, with Introduction by Jacques Barzun. New York: Farrar, Straus & Giroux, Inc., 1957.

Cheraskin, E., and Ringsdorf, W. M. *Predictive Medicine: A Study in Strategy.* California: Pacific Press Publishing Company, 1973.

Cleave, T. L., et al. *Diabetes, Coronary Thrombosis, and the Saccharine Disease.* Bristol: John Wright & Sons, Ltd., 1969.

Comfort, A. *The Anxiety Makers: Some Curious Preoccupations of the Medical Profession.* London: Nelson, 1967.

Cott, Allan. *Orthomolecular Approach to the Treatment of Learning Disabilities.* New York: Huxley Institute for Biosocial Research.

Dalton, John E. *Sugar: A Case Study of Government Control.* New York: Macmillan, 1937.

de Kruif, Paul. *Hunger Fighters.* New York: Harcourt, Brace and Company, 1928.

Deerr, Noel. *The History of Sugar.* London: Chapman & Hall, 1949.

Donnenfeldt, Karl Henry. *Leonhard Rauwolf, 16th Century Physician, Botanist and Traveler.* Cambridge: Harvard University Press, 1968.

East West Journal. volume I, number 12. Boston, 1971.

Ellis, Ellen D. *An Introduction on to the History of Sugar as a Commodity.* Philadelphia: J. C. Winsten, 1905.

Evans, Isabelle Walsh. *Sugar, Sex and Sanity.* New York: Carlton Press, 1970.

Fay, Paul B. *The Pleasure of His Company.* New York: Harper & Row, 1966.

Fergusson, Bernard. *Beyond the Chindwin.* London: Collins, 1945.

Fiennes, Richard. *Man, Nature and Disease.* New York: The New American Library, 1965.

Flipo, Rene. "The Chinese Smoke Rings Around Us." *New York Post*, January 2, 1974.

Forbes, T. R. *The Midwife and The Witch.* New Haven: Yale University Press, 1966.

Foucault, Michel. *Madness and Civilization: A History of Insanity in the Age of Reason.* Translated by Richard Howard. New York: Pantheon, 1965.

Fredericks, Carlton, and Goodman, Herman. *Low Blood Sugar and You.* New York: Constellation International, 1969.

Freud, Sigmund. *The Standard Edition of the Complete Psychological Works of Sigmund Freud.* London: Hogarth, 1966.

Grimes, John Maurice. *When Minds Go Wrong: The Truth About Our Mentally Ill and Their Care in Mental Hospitals.* New York: Devin-Adair, 1954.

Hawken, Paul. *The Magic of Findhorn.* New York: Harper & Row, 1975.

Hay, William Howard. *A New Health Era.* New York: H. W. Hay, 1933.

Hoffer, Abram. "Megavitamin B_{3R} Therapy for Schizophrenia." *Canadian Psychiatric Association Journal.* vol. 16, 1971.

Hole, Christina. *Witchcraft in England.* New York: Collier Books, 1966.

Hooton, E. A. *Apes, Men, and Morons.* New York: Putnam, 1937.

Jacob, Francois. *The Logic of Life: A History of Heredity.* New York: Pantheon, 1974.

Kallet, Arthur, and Schlink, F. J. *100,000,000 Guinea Pigs.* New York: Vanguard, 1933.

Knaggs, Henry V. *The Truth About Sugar.* London, 1913.

Kushi, Michio. *The Teachings of Michio Kushi.* Boston: East West Foundation, 1972.

LaFollette, Robert. *The Sugar Trust, An Amazing Conspiracy.* Washington, 1925.

Longgood, William. *The Poisons in Your Food.* New York: Simon & Schuster, 1960.

MacDari, Conor. *Irish Wisdom.* Boston: Four Seas Company, 1923.

McCollum, Elmer Verner. *A History of Nutrition—The Sequence of Ideas in Nutritional Investigation.* Boston: Houghton Mifflin Co., 1957.

McQuade, Walter, and Aikman, Ann. *Stress: What It Is; What It Can Do To Your Health; How To Fight Back.* New York: E. P. Dutton, 1974.

Mességué, Maurice. *Of Men and Plants.* New York: Bantam Books, 1974.

Michelet, Jules. *Satanism and Witchcraft: A Study on Medieval Superstition.* Translated by A. R. Allinson. New York: Citadel Press, 1965.

New York Magazine, "Secrets of My Life," by Andy Warhol. March 31, 1975.

O'Donnell, Kenneth P., and Powers, David. *Johnny, We Hardly Knew Ye: Memories of John Fitzgerald Kennedy.* Boston: Little, Brown, 1972.

Osmond, Humphrey. Postscript to *In Search of Sanity*, by Gregory Stefan. New York: University Books, 1965.

Pauling, Linus. "Orthomolecular Psychiatry." *Science Magazine*, Vol. 160. April, 1968.

Picton, Dr. Lionel James. *Nutrition and the Soil: Thoughts on Feeding.* New York: Devin-Adair, 1949.

Philippides, Nikos G. *The Conquest of Disease (My Philosophy of Life and Health).* Athens: Liberty Press International, 1971.

Price, Weston. *Nutrition and Physical Degeneration: A Comparison of Primitive and Modern Diets and Their Effects.* California: The American Academy of Applied Nutrition, 1948.

Quigley, D. T. *The National Malnutrition.* Milwaukee: The Lee Foundation for Nutritional Research, 1943.

Reed, William. *History of Sugar.* London: Longmans Green & Co., 1866.

Robbins, William. *The American Food Scandal.* New York: William Morrow & Co., 1974.

Roberts, H. J. *The Causes, Ecology and Prevention of Traffic Accidents.* Illinois: Charles C. Thomas, 1971.

Sakurazawa, Nyoiti, *You Are All Sanpaku.* English version by William Dufty. New York: Award Books, 1969.

Sakurazawa, Nyoiti, and de Morant, Soulié. *The Yellow Emperor's Classic of Internal Medicine.* Translated and with an Introductory Study by Ilza Veith. Berkeley: University of California Press, 1966.

Schwab, Günther. *Dance With the Devil.* London: Geoffrey Bles, 1963.

Shelton, Herbert M. *Food Combining Made Easy.* Texas: Shelton Health School, 1951.

Sinclair, William J. *Semmelweis, His Life and His Doctrine: A Chapter in the History of Medicine.* Manchester, England: University Press, 1909.

Sprenger, J., and Kramer, H. *Malleus Maleficarum (1486).* Translated with an Introduction, Bibliography, and Notes by Montague Summers. London: Pushkin Press, 1948.

Stone, I. *The Healing Factor*, New York: Grosset & Dunlap, 1972.

Strength and Health Magazine. May-June 1972.

Strong, L. A. G. *The Story of Sugar*. London: George Weidenfeld & Nicolson, 1954.

Szasz, Thomas S. *The Manufacture of Madness: A Comparative Study of the Inquisition and the Mental Health Movement*. New York: Harper & Row, 1970.

Tannahill, Reay. *Food In History*. New York: Stein and Day, 1973.

Tintera, John W. *Hypoadrenocorticism*. Mt. Vernon, New York: Adrenal Metabolic Research Society of the Hypoglycemia Foundation Inc., 1969.

———— "What You Should Know About Your Glands," February, 1958; "What You Should Know About Your Glands and Alcoholism," May 1958; and "What You Should Know About Your Glands and Allergies," February 1959. *Woman's Day*. Edited by Delos Smith.

"Tobacco: Is There a 'Cure' for Cancer?" *Medical World News*, March 16, 1973.

Tompkins, Peter, and Bird, Christopher. *The Secret Life of Plants*. New York: Harper & Row, 1973.

Twain, Mark. *Autobiography*, Volume I. New York: Harper and Bros., 1924.

Watson, George. *Nutrition and Your Mind: The Psychochemical Response*. New York: Harper & Row, 1972.

White, Andrew Dickson. *A History of the Warfare of Science with Theology in Christendom*. Abridged, with Preface and Epilogue by Bruce Mazlish. New York: Free Press, 1965.

Wiley, Harvey W. *The History of a Crime Against the Food Law*. Washington, D.C.: Harvey W. Wiley, Publisher, 1929.

Williams, Roger J. *Nutrition in a Nut Shell*. New York: Doubleday, 1962.

W. Interview with F. Slare, January 1974.

Yudkin, John. *Sweet and Dangerous*. New York: Bantam Books, 1972.

Index